SYNTAX CRITICISM OF JOHANNINE LITERATURE, THE CATHOLIC EPISTLES, AND THE GOSPEL PASSION ACCOUNTS

SYNTAX CRITICISM OF JOHANNINE LITERATURE, THE CATHOLIC EPISTLES, AND THE GOSPEL PASSION ACCOUNTS

Raymond A. Martin

Studies in Bible and Early Christianity
Volume 18
The Edwin Mellen Press
Lewiston/Lampeter/Queenston

Library of Congress Cataloging in Publication Data

This volume has been registered with The Library of Congress.

This is volume 18 in the continuing series
Studies in Bible & Early Christianity
Volume 18 ISBN 0-88946-618-1 *c*
SBEC Series ISBN 0-88946-913-X *C*

6 6 0 3 7 3 1 0 5 4
A CIP catalog record for this book
is available from the British Library.

Copyright 1989 The Edwin Mellen Press.

The Edwin Mellen Press
Box 450
Lewiston, N.Y.
USA 14092

The Edwin Mellen Press
Box 67
Queenston, Ontario
CANADA, LOS 1L0

Edwin Mellen Press, Ltd
Lampeter, Dyfed, Wales,
UNITED KINGDOM SA48 7DY

Printed in the United States of America

To Wartburg Theological Seminary
which for some twenty years has provided a setting
which encouraged and fostered study, teaching,
and research.

and

To the many students who over the years have
assisted in that research.

TABLE OF CONTENTS

PREFACE

This volume completes a trilogy of studies analyzing the Greek of much of the New Testament to determine which parts, if any, have been translated from a Semitic language:

1. Syntactical Evidence of Semitic Sources in Greek Documents (Scholars Press, 1974)
2. Syntax Criticism of the Synoptic Gospels (Edwin Mellen Press, 1987)
3. Syntax Criticism of Johannine Literature, the Catholic Epistles, and the Gospel Passion Accounts (Edwin Mellen Press, 1989)

These studies bring to fruition the investigations begun into this area in the 1950's. For a succinct summary presentation of the methodology the reader is referred to Syntax Criticism of the Synoptic Gospels, Appendix 1, and to Appendix 5 of this present study.

It is with sincere appreciation to Wartburg Theological Seminary and its Board of Directors for making available to me this period of Sabbatical study and research that this volume is dedicated. I wish to express my gratitude also to The Lutheran Brotherhood for the grant they have so generously provided and to Austin Presbyterian Theological Seminary for making it possible for Alice and myself to be in their Seminary community and to share with the faculty and students this period of study, teaching and reflection.

Raymond A. Martin

Wartburg Theological Seminary
Dubuque, Iowa
1989

TABLE OF CHARTS

INTRODUCTION

In an earlier study, <u>Syntax Criticism of the Synoptic Gospels,</u>[1] the Synoptic Passion and Resurrection narratives were not analyzed, nor was the Gospel of John. It is probable that the Fourth Gospel has Palestinian roots and certainly the Passion and Resurrection accounts do. Syntax Criticism, therefore, of these materials is surely appropriate and will comprise the first two chapters of this study.

The Johannine epistles by wide admission have some relationship to the Fourth Gospel and thus it is appropriate to include a study of each of them as well,[2] and these will be analyzed in the third and final chapter.

In that final chapter the rest of the Catholic Epistles[3] are also analyzed since it is possible that one or more of them may have some connection with early Jewish Christianity and, if so, may possibly evidence that relationship in their use of the 17 criteria studied by Syntax Criticism[4].

The analysis of these documents has produced in some cases an unexpected result. Four of them show up

---

[1] Edwin Mellen Press, 1987.

[2] The book of Revelation is not included since so much of its language appears directly related to the language of the Old Testament.

[3] I and II Peter, James and Jude. Hebrews was analyzed in the earlier study, <u>SC Syn G.</u>

[4] As in previous studies the Greek text of the United Bible Societies (3rd edition, 1975) is being used and all matter in bold type (quotations from the Old Testament) is excluded in the count of lines and of the individual criteria.

2

as translation Greek. They are I and II John[5] as well
as probably also the Gospel of John[6] and much of the
Epistle of James.[7]

As can be seen from the analysis of the individual
smaller units of these documents[8] in nearly every case
their net frequencies fall within the pattern of
translated documents from the Old Testament. This
consistency of distribution of these translation Greek
net frequencies throughout these documents is quite
different than the erratic distribution of translation
net frequencies in the book of Acts and in the Synoptic
Gospels studied earlier,[9] where it was seen that such
erratic distribution was to be explained by the use of
the Semitic sources.[10]

In the earlier study[11] the four possible
explanations for Semitisms were pointed out as follows:

> "A very important aspect to be kept in mind
> in the study of this problem concerning the nature
> and origin of Semitisms in the Gospels and Acts is
> the degree of consistency in distribution of the
> Semitisms.
>
> "Some of the above explanations of Semitisms
> require a more or less consistent distribution of
> Semitisms throughout the document, namely, 2.)

---

[5]Cf. Charts XVI and XIX in Chapter III.

[6]Cf. Chart IA in Chapter I and the discussion pp. 6ff.

[7]Cf. Chart XVI in Chapter III and the discussion pp. 100ff.

[8]Cf. Charts III-V for the Gospel and Charts XVIII-XX for I and II John and James.

[9]Cf. Syn Ev and SC Syn G.

[10]SC Syn G, pp. 28-31.

[11]Ibid., p. 4.

translation of an entire Semitic document and 3.)
thinking in Aramaic or Hebrew (due to influence
of the vernacular and/or unconscious familiarity
with the LXX). Other of the explanations listed
above require an <u>inconsistent or erratic</u>
distribution of Semitisms -- namely 1.) use of
<u>some</u> Semitic sources or 4.) conscious imitation
of the LXX."[12]

Thus, in the case of the Gospel of John, I and II
John and James either no.2)translation of an entire
Semitic document is involved or no.3.) thinking in
Aramaic as the author writes in Greek.

While it is not possible at present to demonstrate
conclusively which of these explanations is correct, a
number of observations makes translation of a Semitic
document most probable.

First of all, the 17 criteria of translation Greek
were isolated by observation of the occurrence of these
features in <u>written</u> translation of the Old Testament
and thus there is no doubt that they do reflect the
type of Greek such translation of Hebrew and Aramaic
documents produces.

Second, at least 3 of the original Greek writers
studied as controls (II Maccabees, Philo and Josephus)
are Jews who might be expected to have their natural
Greek style influenced by their Semitic background
and/or use of the Septuagint, but at least as far as
the 17 criteria of Syntax Criticism is concerned they
have clear original Greek net frequencies and do not

---

[12]This listing of possible explanations of Semitisms is similar to that of Brown's
in <u>Epistles</u>, p. 24.

come out with net frequencies which Syntax Criticism designates as translation Greek.[13]

Thus it would seem most probable that basically these four writings are translations of Semitic documents in the main, though in the case of the Fourth Gospel and James the -3 net frequencies for so many lines of text indicate that some of their smaller units may be expected to reflect original Greek composition, which may indicate additions at a later stage in the transmission of these writings.[14]

---

[13]Cf. Chart IA; probably also the author of Hebrews.

[14]This is the case as the analysis of smaller units in the subsequent chapters will reveal.

CHAPTER I
Analysis of the Gospel of John

The origin and composition of John's Gospel has been an enigma for generations of scholars and the suggestions offered in explanation are numerous and varied.[15]

Theories range from those of Torrey and Burney who consider the entire Gospel to have been translated from an Aramaic original;[16] to those who see the Gospel to be made up of various sources and/or to have gone through a number of stages and redaction by one or more persons;[17] to the judgment of C.K. Barrett, who understands the Gospel to have been written in Greek that "shows a genuine unity of language and style, which is no more than the outward expression of an inward unity of thought and purpose," needing "neither displacement theories nor redaction theories to explain the present state of the gospel."[18]

When the Fourth Gospel is analyzed by the 17 criteria of translation Greek isolated in earlier studies,[19] it is found that Burney's judgment, that the

---

[15]Cf. e.g., the surveys in W.F. Howard (rev. by C.K. Barrett), The Fourth Gospel in Recent Criticism (1955); R. Kysar, The Fourth Evangelist and His Gospel (1975) and the detailed bibliographic references throughout Brown, John 1 and 2.

[16]C.C. Torrey, Our Translated Gospels (1936), C.F. Burney, The Aramaic Origin of the Fourth Gospel (1922).

[17]Cf. the surveys e.g., of Kysar, op.cit., "Part One" and Brown, John 1, "Introduction"; Fortna, The Gospel of Signs, pp. 1ff. Haenchen, John 1, pp. 257, 260. He sees the Evangelist using an earlier "written gospel" which he found in his community. p. 283.

[18]John, p. 20.

[19]Cf. Martin, Syn Ev. and SC Syn G.

Gospel is a translation into Greek of a written Aramaic Gospel, receives a greater measure of support, as will be seen in the subsequent pages. This result was not anticipated and is in sharp contrast with the book of Acts and the Synoptic Gospels which do not show up as translations of entire Semitic documents, but rather only give evidence of Aramaic sources lying behind some of their smaller units of tradition.[20]

Before proceeding further with this study, it is good to recall Lindar's comment concerning the importance of this issue. He writes:

"...our assessment of John is bound up with the theory we form about its origins. The effort to get behind the Fourth Gospel is not simply a literary-critical game, but an inescapable task in the process of discovering the real meaning of it in the form in which we know it."[21]

John's gospel has a total of 1756 lines and a net translation Greek frequency according to Syntax Criticism of -3.[22] As will be seen from Charts IA and IB below this net frequency lies just at the edge of the range of translation Greek for documents of more than 50 lines in length (-4 to -14) and is radically

---

[20]Cf. Martin, SC Syn C, pp. 25-36 and pp. 37-46 especially; cf. also charts IA and IB below.

[21]B. Lindars, Behind the Fourth Gospel (1971), p. 22.

[22]The percentages and net frequencies for the Fourth Gospel as a whole are found in Chart X at the end of this chapter. The numerical count on which these percentages are based are found in Appendix 1.

CHART I A [1]
Net Frequencies in Original Greek Documents of More Than 50 Lines in Length

	No. of Lines	Net No. of Frequencies Characteristic of Original Greek																		Net No. of Frequencies Characteristic of Translation Greek														
		17	16	15	14	13	12	11	10	9	8	7	6	5	4	3	2	1	0	-1	-2	-3	-4	-5	-6	-7	-8	-9	-10	-11	-12	-13	-14
Plutarch - Selections	325		X																														
Polybius - Bks I,II	192			X																													
Epictetus - Bks III.IV	138	X																															
Bks I.II	349									X																							
Bks I,II,III,IV	487							X																									
Josephus - Selections	215		X																														
Papyri - Selections	630	X																															
II Maccabees 2:13-6:31	495	X																															
Philo - On Creation I-VIII	251									X																							
Hebrews	535		X																														
Acts 15:36-28:31	1056	X																															
Mark 1-10^2	840												X																				
Acts 1:1 - 15:35^3	1144										X																						
Fourth Gospel	1756																				X												

1. Cf. SC Syn G, p. 16. 2. Ibid., p. 38. 3. Ibid., p. 26.

CHART I B [4]
Net Frequencies in Translated Documents of More Than 50 Lines in Length

	No. of Lines	Net No. of Frequencies Characteristic of Original Greek																		Net No. of Frequencies Characteristic of Translation Greek														
		17	16	15	14	13	12	11	10	9	8	7	6	5	4	3	2	1	0	-1	-2	-3	-4	-5	-6	-7	-8	-9	-10	-11	-12	-13	-14
Genesis 1-4,6,39	382																			X													
1 Samuel 3,4,22	194																								X								
1 Kings 17	58																						X										
2 Kings 13	71																									X							
Dan. - Hebrew - LXX	482																								X								
Hebrew - Theod.	460																									X							
Dan. - Aramaic - LXX	595																									X							
Aramaic - Theod.	634																										X						
Ezra - Hebrew	328																											X					
Aramaic	211																									X							
Jer.-Prose A (Chaps 1,3,7,11,16)	201																							X									
Poetic A (Chaps 2,4,5,6,10)	357																											X					
Jer.-Prose B (Chaps 33-36)	216																						X										
Poetic B (Chaps 30,31,37,38)	171																						X										
Ezek.-Prose A (Chaps 2-5)	200																											X					
Poetic A (Chaps 19,27)	74																								X								
Ezek.-Prose B (Chaps 28,30-32)	203																												X				
Poetic B (Chaps 33-35)	132																								X								
I Maccabees (Chaps 1-5)	732																									X							

4. Ibid., p. 17.

different than the net frequencies of documents known
to have been written originally in Greek (+9 to +17).

This indicates that the Fourth Gospel as a whole
is most likely translated from a Semitic document, but
may have a small number of sub sections which were not,
but were orginally composed in Greek.[23]

Chart II ("Classification of Material in the
Fourth Gospel"), which lists all the sub units[24] of
John's Gospel and their net frequencies, shows that of
the 118 sub units in the Gospel only 10 fall outside
the area of translation Greek units of the same size,
as determined by Syntax Criticism and as is evident
from Charts III-V below.

In Chart III it will be seen that only one passage
of 31-50 lines occurs in John -- John 21:1-14 (33
lines). Its net frequencies of +5 is well removed from
the highest net frequencies of any of the translation
Greek controls studied (the lower half of the chart)and
at the very edge of the lower extremity of the net
frequencies of the original Greek controls (the top
half of the chart).

In Chart IV it will be seen that there are 5
passages of 16-30 lines in length in John whose net
frequencies are those of clearly original Greek,
falling within the area occupied only by units of this
length of the original Greek controls studied (+5 to
+9). These 5 passages are: 3:22-30 (18 lines);
19:1-7 (16 lines); 6:1-15 (29 lines); 20:1-10 (19
lines); 12:1-8 (16 lines).

---

[23]Cf. Syn Ev, pp. 40-43 and SC Syn G, p. 18.

[24]The subdivisions of the United Bible Societies' Greek Text were used.

CHART II
CLASSIFICATION OF MATERIAL IN THE FOURTH GOSPEL

	Locat.	Lines	Net Freq	Clear Orig.					Clear Trans.
The Eternal Word	1:1-5	6	+2				X		
The Witness to the Light	1:6-13	12	+2				X		
The Incarnate Word	1:14-18	10	+3			X			
Testimony of Jn. the Bapt.	1:19-28	17	0					X	
The Lamb of God	1:29-34	13	+1				X		
The First Disciples	1:35-42	17	+1					X	
Calling of Phil. and Nath.	1:43-51	19	-1						X
The Wedding at Cana	2:1-12	24	+3				X		
Cleansing of the Temple	2:13-22	19	-3						X
Jesus Knows all Men	2:23-25	6	0				X		
Jesus and Nicodemus	3:1-15	30	-2						X
The Writer's Witness	3:16-21	14	+7		X				
Jesus and Jn. the Baptist	3:22-30	18	+9	X					
He Who Comes from Heaven	3:31-36	11	-2				X		
Jesus Comes to Jacob's Well	4:1-6	10	+5		X				
Dialogue About Living Water	4:7-15	20	-3						X
Dialogue About the Messiah	4:16-26	21	-3						X
The Return of the Disciples	4:27-30	7	0				X		
Dialogue with the Disciples	4:31-38	15	0				X		
The Samaritans Believe	4:39-42	8	+3			X			
Departure to Galilee	4:43-45	6	+3			X			
Nobleman's Son Healed	4:46-54	19	0				X		
The Healing at the Pool	5:1-9a	14	+1				X		
Dialogues with the Jews	5:9b-18	18	0				X		
The Authority of the Son	5:19-29	25	+1					X	
The Various Witnesses	5:30-40	22	-2						X
The Witnesses Rejected	5:41-47	12	+4		X				
The Feeding of the 5000	6:1-15	29	+6	X					
Walking on the Water	6:16-21	11	+3			X			
The Request for Signs	6:22-23	27	-1						X
The Lifegiving Bread	6:34-40	15	+3			X			
Jesus' Origin	6:41-51	20	+2				X		
Eating Jesus' Flesh	6:52-59	16	0				X		
Many Disciples Leave	6:60-65	13	+3			X			
Peter's Confession	6:66-71	10	+2				X		
Unbelief of Jesus' Brothers	7:1-9	16	+2				X		
Jesus Goes to the Feast	7:10-13	7	+2				X		
Jesus Accuses the Jews	7:14-24	21	+3				X		
Is This the Christ?	7:25-31	14	0					X	
Officers Sent/Arrest Jesus	7:32-36	12	+1				X		
Rivers of Living Water	7:37-39	7	+4		X				
Division Among the People	7:40-44	7	+1				X		
Unbelief of the Authorities	7:45-52	13	+2				X		

	Locat.	Lines	Net Freq	Clear Orig.					Clear Trans.
Jesus - Light of the World	8:12-20	20	+4		X				
Where I Go You Cannot Come	8:21-30	21	-2					X	
The Truth Will Free You	8:31-38	14	+1					X	
Your Father Is the Devil	8:39-47	22	-2					X	
Before Abraham Was, I Am	8:48-59	25	-3						X
[Woman Caught in Adultery]	7:53-8:11	21	+4		X				
The Man Born Blind Healed	9:1-12	23	-2					X	
The Blind Man's Witness	9:13-17	12	+5		X				
The Parents' Witness	9:18-23	14	+1				X		
The Blind Man Cast Out	9:24-34	21	-3					X	
Jesus Finds the Blind Man	9:35-39	9	+1				X		
The Pharisees' Blindness	9:40,41	4	+4			X			
Parable of the Sheepfold	10:1-6	12	+7	X					
Jesus The Good Shepherd	10:7-18	25	0					X	
Is Jesus Demonized?	10:19-21	5	+4			X			
Jesus' Unity With Father	10:22-30	15	-6						X
Jesus Accused of Blasphemy	10:31-39	16	+2				X		
Many Believe	10:40-42	5	+3			X			
The Death of Lazurus	11:1-16	29	-1					X	
Jesus the Resurrection/Life	11:17-27	18	0					X	
Jesus Weeps	11:28-37	20	+4			X			
Lazurus Brought to Life	11:38-44	15	+7	X					
The Plot to Kill Jesus	11:45-53	18	+1					X	
Jesus Hides	11:54-57	10	+4			X			
The Annointing at Bethany	12:1-8	16	+6	X					
The Plot Against Lazurus	12:9-11	6	+4			X			
The Triumphal Entry	12:12-19	14	+3			X			
Some Greeks Seek Jesus	12:20-26	15	+4			X			
Lifting Up of Son of Man	12:27-36a	20	+2				X		
The Unbelief of the Jews	12:36b-43	11	+7	X					
Judgment by Jesus' Words	12:44-50	14	+1				X		
The Foot Washing	13:1-11	24	+1					X	
The Lesson About Serving	13:12-20	16	+1					X	
Jesus Foretells Betrayal	13:21-30	19	+3			X			
The New Commandment	13:31-35	10	-1					X	
Peter's Denial Foretold	13:36-38	7	+3			X			
Jesus The Way to the Father	14:1-14	27	-5						X
The Spirit Promised	14:15-24	21	-2					X	
The Work of the Spirit	14:25-31	15	0				X		
Jesus the True Vine	15:1-10	20	-5						X
Chosen by Jesus	15:11-17	13	-1					X	
The World's Hatred	15:18-25	17	+2			X			
The Witness of the Spirit	15:26,27	4	+3			X			

	Locat.	Lines	Net Freq	Clear Orig.					Clear Trans.
They Will Seek to Kill You	16:1-4	6	+1				X		
The Coming of the Spirit	16:5-11	12	+3			X			
The Spirit's Guidance	16:12-15	8	+4			X.			
Sorrow Turned to Joy	16:16-24	22	0					X	
Jesus Has Overcome World	16:25-33	18	-6						X
Jesus Prays f. Glorification	17:1-5	10	+9	X					
Jesus Prays for Disciples	17:6-19	28	-4						X
Jesus Prays f. All Believers	17:20-26	16	-2					X.	
Betrayal and Arrest	18:1-11	23	+4		X				
Before the High Priest	18:12-14	6	+3			X			
Peter's First Denial	18:15-18	11	+8	X					
Jesus Questioned b. H. Priest	18:19-24	13	+2				X		
Peter Denies Jesus Again	18:25-27	6	-1					X	
Jesus Before Pilate	18:28-38a	28	+4		X				
Barabas Requested	18:38b-40	6	+2				X		
Jesus Mocked and Whipped	19:1-7	16	+6	X					
Pilate Questions Jesus	19:8-12	12	+6		X				
Jesus Condemned to Death	19:13-16a	9	+3			X			
The Crucifixion	19:16b-22	14	+2				X		
Scenes Around the Cross	19:23-27	13	+9	X					
The Death of Jesus	19:28-30	6	+3			X			
Jesus' Side Pierced	19:31-37	14	-1					X	
The Burial	19:38-42	13	0					X	
The Resurrection of Jesus	20:1-10	19	+6	X					
Appearance t. Mary Magdalene	20:11-18	20	+1					X	
Appearance to Disciples	20:19-23	10	+6		X				
Jesus and Thomas	20:24-29	16	-3						X
The Purpose of the Book	20:30,31	5	+2				X		
Appearance to 7 Disciples	21:1-14	33	+5	X					
Jesus and Peter	21:15-19	15	-3					X	
Future of Beloved Disciple	21:20-23	10	+5		X				
The Final Testimony	21:24-25	5	+8	X					

CHART III

Net Original Greek Frequencies Appearing in Each Unit of Text 31 to 50 Lines in Length

Name	No. of Units	17	16	15	14	13	12	11	10	9	8	7	6	5	4	3	2	1	0	-1	-2	-3	-4	-5	-6	-7	-8	-9	-10	-11	-12	-13	-14
Plutarch - Selections	4					3	1																										
Polybius - Books I,II	3						1	1	1																								
Epictetus - Bks III,IV	2					1			1																								
Bks I,II	2										1		1																				
Bks I,II,III,IV	4						1			1	1		1																				
Josephus - Selections	1								1																								
Papyri - Selections	3							1		1		1																					
II Maccabees 2:13-6:31	2			1				1																									
Philo - On Creation I-VIII	4				2						1	1																					
Hebrews	5			1		1	1				1	1																					
Acts 15:36-28:31	2										1	1																					
John	1																		1														

Net Translation Greek Frequencies Appearing in Each Unit of Text 31 to 50 Lines in Length

Name	No. of Units	17	16	15	14	13	12	11	10	9	8	7	6	5	4	3	2	1	0	-1	-2	-3	-4	-5	-6	-7	-8	-9	-10	-11	-12	-13	-14
Genesis 1-4,6,39	4																			1	1		2										
1 Samuel 3,4,22	--																																
1 Kings 17	--																																
2 Kings 13	--																																
Dan. - Hebrew - LXX	1																1																
Hebrew - Theod.	1																							1									
Dan. - Aramaic - LXX	--																																
Aramaic - Theod.	--																																
Ezra - Hebrew	3																								1		1	1					
Aramaic	2																							1			1						
Jer. - Prose A	2																									1							1
Poetic A	1																														1		
Prose B	2																						1						1				
Poetic B	4																		1					1	1		1						
Ezek. - Prose A	1																													1			
Poetic A	--																																
Prose B	--																																
Poetic B	--																																
I Maccabees 1-5	--																																

CHART IV

Net Original Greek Frequencies Appearing in Each Unit of Text of 16 to 30 Lines in Length

Name	No. of Units	17	16	15	14	13	12	11	10	9	8	7	6	5	4	3	2	1	0	-1	-2	-3	-4	-5	-6	-7	-8	-9	-10	-11	-12	-13	-14
Plutarch - Selections	7						1	1		1	1			2		1																	
Polybius - Books I,II	5							1	2	1	1																						
Epictetus - Bks III,IV	5							1		1	1	1	1																				
Bks I,II	10									1	1	2		3	3																		
Bks I,II,III,IV	15							1		2	2	3	1	3	3																		
Josephus - Selections	5							1				3		1																			
Papyri - Selections	12							2	2	3	3	1			1																		
II. Maccabees 2:13-6:31	15				3		5			5	1	1																					
Philo - On Creation 1-VIII	4								1			1	1	1																			
Hebrews	9					1				1	2	2	1	1		1																	
Acts 15:36-28:31	27			1	1	1	2	3	8	2	2	1	3																				
Gospel of John 7:53 - 8:11	**50**									1			4		4	3	5	6	7	3	6	7	1	2	1								
														X																			

Net Translation Greek Frequencies Appearing in Each Unit of Text 16 to 30 Lines in Length

Name	No. of Units	17	16	15	14	13	12	11	10	9	8	7	6	5	4	3	2	1	0	-1	-2	-3	-4	-5	-6	-7	-8	-9	-10	-11	-12	-13	-14
Genesis 1-4,6,39	5																1		2	1		1											
1 Samuel 3,4,22	4																			1	1	2											
1 Kings 17	--																																
2 Kings 13	1																			1													
Dan. - Hebrew - LXX	6																1		2	2	1												
Hebrew - Theod.	4																			2				2									
Dan. - Aramaic - LXX	10													1	1	2			3		1		1			1							
Aramaic - Theod.	13															1			1	2	1	3	2		1	1	1						
Ezra - Hebrew	10																						1	1	1	5			2				
Aramaic	7																		1		1	1	2	2									
Jer. - Prose A	5																			2	1		1	1									
Poetic A	3																				1	1	1										
Jer. - Prose B	1																		1														
Poetic B	1															1																	
Ezek. - Prose A	4																	1	1				1	1									
Poetic A	3																					1					2						
Ezek. - Prose B	6																2		1			1		1		1							
Poetic B	3																								1	1	1						
1 Maccabees 1-5	13															1		2	2	1	2		2	1	1		1						

Units of 4-15 lines in length are presented in
Chart V below. From that chart it will be seen that 4
units with their net frequencies of +8 and +9 fall just
outside the extreme limits of the range of similar
units of the translation Greek controls and fairly deep
into the area occupied by such units of clearly
original Greek texts. These four are:

      17:1-5 (10 lines)
      18:15-18 (11 lines)
      19:23-27 (13 lines)
      21:24,25 (5 lines)

Before studying in more detail the above 10 units
with clear original Greek frequencies, it should be
noted that all the other sub units of the gospel fall
within the net frequency limits which can characterize
translated Greek documents from the Old Testament, as
can be seen from Charts III-V; and, further, the
overall distribution pattern is very similar to the
pattern of translation Greek units of 16-30 lines in
length,[25] and in the case of units 4-15 lines in
length, most similar to the distribution pattern of the
LXX translation of the Aramaic parts of Daniel.[26]

Further, when this distribution of net frequencies
of the Fourth Gospel is compared, on the other hand, to
known original Greek, whether written by Jews or non-
Jews, it will be seen that the pattern is radically
different from the pattern of original Greek units of
31-50 and 16-30 lines; and also quite different from
the pattern of units of 4 to 15 lines in length (cf.
the extremes at either end of the scales in Chart V).

---

[25]Cf. Chart IV above.

[26]Cf. Chart V above.

CHART V

Net Original Greek Frequencies Appearing in Each Unit of Text 4 to 15 Lines in Length

Name	No. of Units	17	16	15	14	13	12	11	10	9	8	7	6	5	4	3	2	1	0	-1	-2	-3	-4	-5	-6	-7	-8	-9	-10	-11	-12	-13	-14
Plutarch - Selection	49							1	5	3	6	12	8	4	6	2	2																
Polybius - Bks I,II	12								1	3	2	1	2	3																			
Epictetus - Bks III,IV	2								1						1																		
Bks I,II	30										3	2	4	5	7	5	2	1	1														
Bks I,II,III,IV	32								1		3	2	4	5	7	6	2	1	1														
Josephus - Selections	22									1	2	3	3	6	6	1																	
Papyri - Selections	75							2	1	2	5	7	16	9	13	12	2	2	3	1													
II Maccabees 2:13-6:31	8					1	1	1	1	3		1																					
Philo - On Creation I-VIII	30											4	4	8	5	3	4		1	1													
Hebrews	46								2	5	1	5	3	6	7	4	6	4	1	2													
Acts 15:36-28:31	36								2	1	2	3	9	7	7	3	2																
John - Gospel	66									2	2	4	3	3	7	14	9	9	6	4	1	1			1								

Net Translation Greek Frequencies Appearing in Each Unit of Text 4 to 15 Lines in Length

Name	No. of Units	17	16	15	14	13	12	11	10	9	8	7	6	5	4	3	2	1	0	-1	-2	-3	-4	-5	-6	-7	-8	-9	-10	-11	-12	-13	-14
Genesis 1-4,6,39	13															2	3			2	3		3										
1 Samuel 3,4,22	12																1	1		5			1	2	2								
1 Kings 17	5																1	1		1	1		1										
2 Kings 13	5																	1			1	1	1	1	1								
Dan. - Hebrew - LXX	35											1				1	3	2	5	7	8	4	3	1									
Hebrew - Theod.	37															2	3	3	2	7	8	10	2										
Dan. - Aramaic - LXX	38										1	1			3	4	3	4	6	3	6	4	2	1									
Aramaic - Theod.	36															2	5	1	4	6	3	6	5	3	1								
Ezra - Hebrew	15																	1		2	3		2	2	2	2	1						
Aramaic	6																		2		1	2		1									
Jer. - Prose A	12																		1	2	2		1	1	5								
Poetic A	28																			3	5	4	1	5	3	4	1	2					
Jer. - Prose B	19											1			1	1	2	1	2	3	1	1	3	2	1								
Poetic B	18																	1	4	2	2	5	1	3									
Ezek.-Prose A	15																	1	4	2	3	1	1	2		1							
Poetic A	2																						1		1								
Ezek. Prose B	12														1	2		2	1		3	1	2										
Poetic B	9																		1	3	2	1	1	1									
1 Maccabees 1-5	45															1	2		7	6	6	7	7	3	4	2							

If, then, the Fourth Gospel was originally written
in a Semitic language, as the above data suggests, and
then later translated into Greek, it remains to be
studied how the above noted 10 original Greek units
came to be a part of that Gospel. The detailed
discussion of that question will need to be carried out
more fully than is possible in connection with the
present study; but a few suggestions, first in general
and, after that, concerning individual units, may be
appropriate at this point.

It is, of course, possible that it was the Greek
translator of the Aramaic gospel who inserted the
original Greek material; or it may be that this
original Greek material was added in one of the later
Greek stages in the transmission/redaction of the
Gospel. Most scholars today posit two or more such
stages.[27]

Now to be considered are the 10 original Greek
units. They are:

1. Jesus and John the Baptist   3:22-30
2. The Feeding of the 5000   6:1-15
3. The Annointing at Bethany   12:1-18
4. Jesus Prays for Glorification   17:1-5
5. Peter's First Denial   18:15-18
6. Jesus Mocked and Whipped   19:1-7
7. Scenes around the Cross   19:23-27
8. The Resurrection of Jesus   20:1-10
9. Appearance to 7 Disciples   21:1-14
10. The Final Testimony   21:24,25

---

[27]Cf. e.g. Brown, John 1, pp. xxxii-xxxix; Barrett, John, pp. 113f.; Kysar, Fourth
Evangelist, pp. 38-54 especially.

Most of these (nos. 3-10) occur in the Passion account (whether unique to John's Gospel or as a parallel to a section of the Synoptic Passion Account) and will be considered in that connection (Chapter II).

The Feeding of the 5000 (no. 2) will be considered below with other passages in John's Gospel that are or may be parallel to Synoptic material.

This leaves no. 1. Jesus and John the Baptist (3:22-30) for consideration at this point. It is generally conceded that these verses do not fit well in their present context. Brown has stated the situation well: "This scene is a difficult one because, externally, its sequence is poor and, internally, the logic of the story is not clear."[28] He sees in these verses "fragments of a larger Johannine tradition about John the Baptist."[29]

Barrett, however, while noting that many scholars consider these verses not to fit very well in their present context, sees no reason to remove them to some other place but is able to see all of chapter 3 as "a unity" as it now stands.[30] Bultmann considers the verses to be "the Evangelist's own composition" based probably on "some kind of tradition."[31]

Because most of the Gospel shows up as translation Greek by the criteria of Syntax Criticism, and since it is generally agreed these verses do not appear integral

---

[28]Brown, John 1, p. 153. Cf. e.g. also Kysar, Fourth Evangelist, p. 45 and John in The Augsburg Commentary on the New Testament (1986), p. 57.

[29]John 1, p. 154.

[30]Cf. John, p. 183.

[31]Cf. John, pp. 167-169. Fortna also considers 3:22-30 to be the work of the Johannine redactor. The Gospel of Signs, pp. 6-8 and p. 169, no. 3.

to their present context, it is not surprising to find
that 3:22-30 has clear original Greek net frequencies
and therefore it is likely that these verses belong to
the later stages of the Gospel's redaction.

The next group of passages to be considered
consists of those that are quite similar to narratives
in the Synoptics, namely:

1:19ff	The Testimony of John the Baptist
4:46-54	The Nobleman's Son Healed
5:1-9a, 9b-18	The Healing of the Paralytic at the Pool
6:1-15	The Feeding of the 5000
6:16-21	Walking on the Water
6:66-71	Peter's Confession
9:1-12	The Man Born Blind Healed

The Feeding, Walking, Confession Accounts
(6:1-15, 16-21, 66-71)

First of all, the 3 narratives in John 6 will be
taken together. Many have noted the similarity of this
material to the stories in Mark 6-8, including the
general sequence of the material.[32] While some have
considered this to be evidence of Johannine dependence
on Mark, the more likely judgment, since John has very
few verbal contacts with the Synoptic accounts, is that
both John and Mark are here drawing independently on an
earlier grouping already in the traditions that lay
before them.[33]

---

[32]Cf. e.g. Haenchen, John 1, pp. 273ff.; Brown, John 1, pp. 236-239; for a survey
and critique of views concerning John's relation to the Synoptics cf. Kysar, Fourth
Evangelist, pp. 54-66.

[33]Cf. Brown, ibid., p. 250; Barrett, John, p. 34; Bultmann, John 1, p. 210;
Haenchen, John 1. p. 274.

It is striking that in the Johannine material only John 6:1-15 (The Feeding of the 5000) has clear original Greek net frequencies whereas the other elements of the grouping, as well as the context on both sides of chapter 6, do not.[34] This suggests that the present form of the Feeding in John belongs to a later and Greek stage of the Gospel. It may be that a later form of the Feeding has been substituted for the form in the earlier editions of the text.[35] This would not be surprising given the popularity of the story and its early association in the Church and its liturgy with the Lord's Supper.[36]

For convenience Chart VI below presents the net frequencies of the parallel John and Synoptic material. It is clear from this chart that the Feeding of the 5000 in John, according to the 17 criteria of translation Greek, is original Greek and much closer to the Synoptic Feeding of the 5000 than to the rest of the Johannine material in this grouping of traditions, and quite different than the clear translation Greek account of the Feeding of the 4000 in Mark.

The Testimony of John the Baptist (1:19-34)

This section has 2 parts: the testimony of John to himself (vv. 19-28) and the testimony of John to Jesus (vv. 29-34). The parts individually and in their

---

[34]Cf. Chart II above.

[35]For the view that John's account here is a late form of the tradition cf. remarks in Barrett, John 1, p. 226; Brown, John 1, p. 236 (though he himself holds it to be early); Bultmann, John, p. 211, note 1.

[36]Cf. Bultmann, ibid.

CHART VI
JOHN 6 AND SYNOPTIC PARALLELS[1]

	Lines	Net Freq	Clear Orig.			Clear Trans.
Feeding of the 5000						
Mark 6:30-44	30	+9	Mk			
Matt. 14:13-21	19	+11	Mt			
Luke 9:10-17	21	+10	Lk			
John 6:1-15	29	+6	Jn			
Feeding of the 4000						
Mark 8:1-10[2]	18	-1				Mk
Matt. 15:32-39	16	+5	Mt			
Walking on the Water						
Mark 6:45-52	16	+2			Mk	
Matt. 14:22-23	22	+8	Mt			
John 6:16-21	11	+3			Jn	
Peter's Declaration About Jesus						
Mark 8:27-30	8	+4			Mk	
Matt. 16:13-20[3]	17	-2				Mt
Luke 9:18-21	8	+6		Lk		
John 6:66-71	10	+2			Jn	

[1] For the John material cf. Chart II above and note 3, p. 6; for the Synoptic material cf. Martin, SC Syn G, p. 44 and note 1, p. 40.

[2] Cf. Martin, ibid., p. 31.

[3] Cf. ibid., p. 68.

combined total are compared on Chart VII below with the Synoptic Gospels' parallels.

From Chart VII it is apparent that the Johannine material is more Semitic than the Synoptic accounts, both 1:19-28 and the total[37] having clear translation Greek net frequencies, whereas this is not the case for any of the Synoptic accounts.

CHART VII
THE TESTIMONY OF JOHN THE BAPTIST

	Lines	Net Freq	Clear Orig.		Clear Trans.
Testimony of Jn. the Baptist[a]					
John 1:19-28	17	0			Jn
John 1:29-34	13	+1		Jn	
John 1:19-34[b]	30	-1			Jn
The Markan Preaching of John[c]					
Mark 1:1-8	13	+1		Mk	
Matt. 3:1-6,11	14	+3	Mt		
Luke 3:1-6,15,16	16	+2		Lk	
The Q Preaching of John[d]					
Luke 3:7-9	8	+4	Lk		
Matt. 3:7-10	9	+3	Mt		

[a]Cf. Chart II above.

[b]The percentages for this total are found on the last page of Chart X at the end of this chapter.

[c]Cf. Martin, SC Syn G, p. 41.

[d]Cf. ibid., p. 91.

[37]The fact that the total has more Semitic net frequencies is not surprising since in the larger section more of the 17 criteria occur and the demarcation between original and translation frequencies becomes sharper.

This situation makes it most probable that the Johannine material is basically independent of the Synoptics[38] and contacts with the Synoptics are probably best understood as redaction at a later stage in the transmission of the Gospel, whether by the Evangelist[39] or by a later editor.[40]

Whatever the conclusion about the Semitic nature of the Gospel as a whole, the "Testimony of John the Baptist" section (1:19-34) is clearly translation Greek and goes back to a Semitic, Palestinian milieu, whether of the writer or of the source used.

The Nobleman's Son Healed (4:46-54)

A similar story is found in Q (Matt. 8:5-13; Luke 7:1-10). As Chart VIII below shows both Matthew and John are clear translation Greek, whereas Luke's account is clearly original Greek.

Most scholars consider the same incident to be behind both the Johannine and Synoptic accounts.[41] In his detailed comparison of the various stories Brown finds more similarities between John and Matthew than between John and Luke;[42] nevertheless there are also

---

[38]So Brown, John 1, pp. 45-54; Fortna, op. cit., pp. 167, 169. But cf. Barrett, John, pp. 142 and 143-149 for the view that John here knew and used the Synoptics.

[39]So Brown, ibid., pp. 67-71, esp. p. 69.

[40]So Bultmann, John, pp. 84f. and 94f.

[41]So Brown, John 1, p. 193; Bultmann, John, p. 204f., Haenchen, John 1, p. 78.

[42]Brown, loc. cit.; cf. Fortna, op. cit., pp. 46f.

CHART VIII
MORE JOHN AND SYNOPTIC COMPARISONS

	Lines	Net Freq	Clear Orig.		Clear Trans.
The Nobleman's Son Healed[1]					
John 4:46-54	19	0			Jn
Luke 7:1-10	23	+6	Lk		
Matt. 8:5-13	15	-2			Mt
The Healing of the Paralytic at the Pool[2]					
John 5:1-9a	14	+1		Jn	
John 5:9b-18	18	0			Jn
John 5:1-18	32	-1			Jn
Mark 2:1-12	24	+1			Mk
Matt. 9:1-8	15	+1		Mt	
Luke 5:17-26	26	0			Lk
The Man Born Blind Healed[3]					
John 9:1-12	23	-2			Jn
Mark 8:22-26	10	+1		Mk	
Mark 10:46-52	15	+2		Mk	
Matt. 20:29-34	10	+5	Mt		
Luke 18:35-43	13	+5	Lk		

[1] The percentages and net frequencies for John are found in charts at the end of this chapter; for the Synoptics cf. SC Syn G, pp. 90,91.

[2] The percentages for John, ibid., above; for Synoptics, ibid., p. 41.

[3] The percentages for John, ibid.; for Synoptics, ibid., pp. 44, 46.

considerable differences[43] between John and the
Synoptics and these make direct dependence of John on
the Synoptics here improbable.[44]

The Healing of the Paralytic at the Pool (5:1-18)

While many commentators have noted the similarity
of this story to Mark 2:1-12 and its parallels, direct
dependence of John on the Synoptics is considered
unlikely, but rather the use of a common earlier
tradition.[45]

Chart VIII shows that the tradition behind the
healing of the paralytic is clear translation Greek in
three of the accounts (John, Mark and Luke). In all
three of these the narrative is mixed in form, having
both miracle story and controversy story features.[46]
By contrast the somewhat less Semitic Matthean account
is a classic example of a pure controversy form.[47]

This interplay between miracle story and
controversy story forms in the various accounts may
suggest the following aspects in the history of the
tradition:

Because of the close association of sin and
sickness it appears that an original healing/for-
giveness incident was handed on in a variety of ways in

---

[43]Cf. Bultmann, ibid., p. 205; Barrett, John, p. 205; Brown, ibid.

[44]So Haenchen, John 1 p. 238; Brown, ibid., Barrett grants this as a possibility,
however, cf. ibid. Cf. also Fortna, ibid., pp. 39, 47.

[45]Fortna, ibid., p. 54; Kysar, John, p. 76; Barrett, ibid., p. 208; Bultmann,
John, p. 242, note 2; Brown, ibid., pp. 208f.

[46]Cf. the commentaries.

[47]With the possible exception of the final verse (taken in part from the Markan
account.)

the early Church. Matthew reflects awareness of its
use as purely a controversy story to demonstrate
the authority of the Church to forgive sins.

John 5:1-9a contains no hint of controversy and
reflects the early Church's use of the story to
demonstrate the power of Jesus to heal.

The addition of the controversy dialogue in
5:9b-18 of John and the controversy insert in Mark
2:5b-10 (Luke 5:20b-24a) reflect awareness of the
controversy aspect of the original tradition, bringing
both elements together again in the collecting and
transmission of the material.

The Man Born Blind (9:1-12)

As Chart VIII shows only John's healing of a blind
man has clear translation Greek net frequencies; and it
is the following verses of John's account (9:13ff)
which uses the miracle story in a controversy setting.

Bultmann is correct in noting: "There is no strict
literary dependence of the healing of the blind man in
Jn. 9 upon the stories in Mk. 8:22-26; 10:46-52..."[48]
The possibly Semitic net frequencies of the Markan
account in chapter 8 and the use of spittle in the
healing (Mark 8:23; John 9:6) may suggest some
commonality in underlying tradition, though both
Bultmann and Brown interpret the latter detail in other
ways.[49]

---

[48]John, p. 330. So also Brown, John 1, p. 378.

[49]Bultmann, ibid.; Brown, ibid., p. 379.

There are 3 other sections in the Fourth Gospel
which warrant comment before taking up the Passion
accounts in the next chapter. They are:

       The Prologue (1:1-18)

       The Writer's Witness (3:16-21)

       Lazurus Brought to Life (11:38-44)

CHART IX
THE PROLOGUE AND THE COMPOSITION OF JOHN 3[1]

	Lines	Net Freq	Clear Orig.		Clear Trans.
The Prologue					
1:1-5	6	+2		X	
1:6-13	12	+2		X	
1:14-18	10	+3		X	
Total 1:1-18	28	+1			PROL.
The Writer's Witness and Related Passages					
3:1-13	27	-3			X
3:31-36	11	-2			X
3:1-13, 31-36	38	-2			X
3:14-21	16	+5	X		
3:22-30	18	+9	X		

[1]The percentages and net frequencies for these units are found at the end of Chart
X at the end of this chapter. The numerical count on which these percentages are based
are at the bottom of the first page of Appendix 1.

THE PROLOGUE

In the continuing debate over the years on how much, if any, of the Fourth Gospel goes back to Semitic sources, concerning the Prologue in particular the claim has been made that it may go back to a Semitic original. Bultmann, for example, writes: "The hypothesis, advocated primarily by Burney, that the Johannine Gospel is a work translated in its entirety from Aramaic into Greek [sic], can only be maintained, in my opinion, in respect of the source underlying the Prologue and the Jesus-discourses in the Gospel."[50]

Chart IX above shows that the Prologue taken in its entirety has net frequencies of +1 for 28 lines, which puts it within the area of clear translation Greek.[51] The net frequencies of the smaller units fall within the range of such smaller units of the translated Greek documents studied as controls; particularly, for example, the LXX translation of the Aramaic parts of Daniel (cf. Chart V "Units of Text 4 to 15 Lines in Length" above).[52]

Given, then, the high probability that the Prologue was written originally in a Semitic language (as the 17 criteria for translation Greek of Syntax Criticism indicate) two passages which are a bit surprising in the Prologue may receive needed

---

[50]John, p. 18. Brown, however, claims "the evidence is not conclusive," John 1, p. 23 and Haenchen, John 1, p. 129 rejects the view.

[51]Cf. Chart IV supra.

[52]Cf. also note 37 above concerning the net frequencies of the total of a number of small sections being a clearer indication of the nature of the Greek of the section than are the net frequencies of the smaller sub units individually. Simply put, the larger the unit of text the sharper the demarcation between original and translation Greek net frequencies--cf. Charts I, III, IV, V above.

28

clarification, if the possible Aramaic underlying them is reconstructed.[53]

The first one to be considered is the strange use of ἦν in the first member of the quoted words of John the Baptist about Jesus in 1:15: John bore witness to him and cried, "This was he of whom I said, 'He who comes after me ranks before me, for he was before me.'" (RSV, italics added).

John the Baptist, however, is presented as speaking of his contemporary, Jesus, and the Greek here should be present tense: "This is he of whom I said, 'He...'". That the present tense is needed here is shown by the repetition of this statement in 1:30 where ἐστιν is used: "This is [italics added] he of whom I said, 'After me comes a man who ranks before me, for he was before me'" (RSV 1:30).

Brown in his English translation of 1:15 correctly uses the present tense: John testified to him by proclaiming: "This is [italics added] he of whom I said, 'The one...'".[54]

Various suggestions have been made for this anomaly, which is particularly striking in light of the correct usage in 1:30 later, as noted above.

Bultmann considers it the result of attraction. He writes: "Instead of ἦν one expects ἐστιν , as in v. 30; the ἦν is probably an attraction to εἶπον

---

[53]As indicated in earlier studies (cf. e.g., Martin, SC Syn G, p. 3) proposed mistranslations of the Aramaic behind a document written in Greek as a way of demonstrating the document was originally written in Aramaic (or Hebrew) is too hypothetical and subjective. If, however, by other methods (namely, Syntax Criticism in this case), a document is seen to have most likely been translated from a Semitic language, then there is a strong basis for proposed mistranslations being more seriously considered.

[54]John 1, p. 4. He does not, however, discuss the incorrect Greek.

and is to be explained psychologically..."[55]

Barrett notes the problem but considers it to be only "superficially difficult," explaining it, apparently, as though the Gospel writer envisions John the Baptist to be currently present and speaking at the time of the written Gospel![56] It is, then, of course, surprising that in v. 30 the writer has the Baptist use the proper Greek construction in the present tense.

More probable, especially in the light of the clear translation Greek net frequencies of the entire Prologue, is to see here a simple misunderstanding of the underlying Aramaic, as Torrey has proposed.[57]

In Aramaic the copula "is" is often expressed by the 3rd person personal pronoun הוא . In the unpointed text this would look exactly like the perfect tense of the verb "to become" הוָא "he was." Without vowels both are written the same הוא ; and it may be that the translator of the Aramaic Prologue vocalized the text as the verb "he was," rather than correctly understanding it as the pronoun being used as a copula "(he) is."

Of more import, perhaps, is the possibility of a mistranslation behind the surprising, but best attested reading in 1:18 μονογενὴς θεός "an only God, who is the bosom of the Father."

That this is indeed a difficult phrase is testified to by the numerous textual variants,[58]

---

[55]John, note 3, p. 75.

[56]John, p. 140. He writes: "John's witness at the time of writing can only be 'This Jesus was the person I spoke of.'

[57]The Four Gospels, p. 316 and Our Translated Gospels, pp. 117f.

[58]Cf. Brown, John 1, p. 17 for a survey of the readings.

witnessing clearly to the problems the text caused for
the copyists, as well as by the variety of English
translations of the phrase. The problem is that here
the adjective "only" modifies "God" in a context where
"Son" is expected and which alone agrees with the
writer's usage of "only" throughout the Gospel.[59] The
lack of an article with the phrase is also strange.[60]

Wikgren's judgment is: "It is doubtful that the
author would have written μονογενής θεός, which may
be a primitive, transcriptional error..."[61] With this
Bultmann agrees.[62]

Burney's suggestion[63] that a misreading of the
unpointed Aramaic text lies behind the Greek offers a
reasonable explanation of all the difficulties
involved--including the strange omission of the
article. He posits that a construct relationship in
the Aramaic (אלהא יחיד) "the only (one) of God" was
misread by the translator as an absolute (אלהא יחיד)
"the only God." In an unpointed text both
constructions appear the same יחיד אלהא !

Since in Semitic languages the construct element
can never have the article, the missing article with

---

[59]Cf. Barrett, <u>John</u>, p. 141; cf. also Burney, <u>op. cit.</u>, pp. 39f.

[60]Cf. B.M. Metzger, <u>A Textual Commentary on the Greek N.T.</u> (1971), p. 198.

[61]<u>Ibid</u>.

[62]<u>John 1</u>, p. 82, note.

[63]Cf. <u>op. cit.</u>, pp. 39f.

θεός is now less surprising.[64]

Black, after a careful study of the various
mistranslations proposed by Burney, rightly calls this
suggestion "one of Burney's most valuable
observations."[65]

In conclusion, while the above proposed
mistranslations cannot determine whether a document was
originally written in a Semitic language, if on other
grounds (Syntax Criticism, for example) an Aramaic or
Hebrew original seems likely, then proposed
mistranslations as solutions to admitted difficulties
in the Greek text would, it appears, warrant more
serious consideration in those instances.

The Writer's Witness (3:16-21)

From Chart II it will be seen that this section is
nearly in the original Greek area. The section
immediately following (Jesus and John the Baptist
3:22-30), which has been discussed earlier, has clear
original Greek net frequencies. The subsequent
section, however, (He Who Comes from Heaven 3:31-36) is
very similar to 3:16-21 and yet is clearly translation
Greek.[66] The solution to this surprising situation may

---

[64]This phrase, understood then as having been original construct relation that should have been translated ὁ μονογενής τοῦ θεοῦ --"the only (Son) of God", is very similar to 1:14 ὡς μονογενοῦς παρὰ πατρός --"as of the only (Son) from the Father"(RSV, parenthesis added)--The construct relation in this case being represented by the preposition in Greek.

[65]An Aramaic Approach to the Gospels and Acts (1946), p. 10.

[66]Cf. Chart IX.

be found in the rearrangement of material, as many commentators have suggested (without, however, attaining much agreement on the rearrangements proposed!).[67]

Both Bultmann and Brown note, without accepting, Gourbillon's proposal that 3:14-30 are later and that originally the text was 3:1-13, 31-36.[68] This view agrees with Macgregor's, as described by Bultmann.[69] While Bultmann prefers 3:1-21, 31-36, he notes that 3:1-16, 31-36 could be a possibility.[70]

The Gourbillon and Macgregor proposal has much to commend it. As was discussed earlier 3:22-30 are probably a later insertion.[71] Verses 14 and 15 interject a new concept for which the reader has not been prepared--the concept of the death of Christ as a lifting up, whereas in 3:1-13 above and below has been the theme. Verses 16-21 deal with believing and not believing; life and judgment--again new elements being introduced. Verses 31-36, as noted by many commentators, returns to the above and below contrast of 3:1-13. Thus by placing 3:31-36 after 3:13 a unity of thought is achieved.

It is interesting to note that making this rearrangement of material (namely 3:1-13, 31-36; and 3:14-21, 22-30), the clear translation Greek and the

---

[67]For surveys of suggested rearrangements cf. Brown, John 1, p. 159 and espec. Bultmann, John, p. 131, note 5.

[68]Ibid.

[69]Bultmann, ibid.

[70]Ibid.

[71]Cf. pp. 17f supra.

clear original Greek units of chapter 3 are brought
together, as Chart IX shows.[72]

It therefore appears most likely that originally
the Semitic form of the Gospel contained 3:1-13, 31-36
and that later the Greek translator or editor(s)
supplemented this by the insertion of 3:14-21; 22-30.[73]

Lazarus Brought to Life (11:38-44)

As can be seen from Chart II the net frequencies
of this section of the Gospel nearly fall into the area
of clear original Greek. From that chart it can also
be seen that the net frequencies of 2 other sections
(11:28-37 and 11:54-57) are fairly close to the area of
clear original Greek net frequencies, while the rest of
the Lazarus story are clearly translation Greek. This
suggests that there has been editorial work on the
story, particularly in connection with the narration of
the miracle itself.

Brown notes, and favors to some extent, the view
of Wilkens which "finds beneath the Johannine account a
brief narrative of the raising of Lazarus..."[74], so
that Brown speaks of a "skeleton of the story" in early
tradition,[75] which was circulating independently and

---

[72]Brown considers vv. 31-36 at one time to have been "an isolated discourse of
Jesus" and only later attached to Chap. 3, (John 1, p. 160), having noted earlier
Dodd's observation: "even if vvs. 31-36 are placed after 1-21, the connection between
21 and 31 remains awkward; the theme of 31-36 is closer to that of 11-15 than to that
of 21." Ibid., p. 159.

[73]It may be noted that under this rearrangement vv. 35 and 36 lead nicely over to
the themes of vv. 14-21.

[74]John 1, p. 429.

[75]Ibid.

"has been used in one of the later stages in Johannine
editing...in the evangelist's second edition of
redaction."[76]

Conclusion

The fact that so much of the Fourth Gospel has
clear translation Greek net frequencies does not in
itself require that the material goes back to Jesus or
to one of his early disciples, for Aramaic was the
language of the Church in Palestine (and in parts of
Syria) throughout the first Christian century. These
results of Syntax Criticism of the Fourth Gospel,
however, confirm in a striking manner that this
Gospel's earliest milieu is to be sought in Palestine
(or Southern Syria)[77] and, further, that in the case at
least of those sections that have clear translation
Greek net frequencies it is legitimate to give closer
attention to mistranslation as a possible solution to
some of the difficulties presently noted by scholarship
in the Greek text[78] and finally to see in those
sections that have clear original Greek net frequencies
a means of isolating some of the later redactional
activity that has gone on in the Greek stages of the
Gospel's transmission.

---

[76]Ibid., p. 430; cf. also p. xxxvii.

[77]Cf. also D.M. Smith "John, Gospel of" in Supplement to IDB (1976), p. 486.

[78]Cf. again the comments above on 1:15 and 18.

CHART X

Frequencies of the 17 Criteria in the Gospel of John

Translation Frequencies	No. of lines of Greek text	No. of occur. of en	die W. gen.	die W. all cases	eis	W. accus.	kata W. all	Peri W. all cases	Pros W. dative	Hupo W. genitive	No. of occ. of kai for each occ. of de	Percent, of separ. articles	No. of dep. gen. post ea. prec. dep. gen.	No. of lines ea. dep. gen. pers. pronoun	Lines ea. gen. dep. pron. pers. on anarth. subst.	No. of prec. attr. adj. for each attr. adj. post position	No. of lines ea. attrib. adjec.	No. of lines each adverb. participle	No. of dat. not used w. en for ea. occur. of en	Tot. no. of transl. Grk. frequencies	Tot. no. of orig. Grk frequencies	No. of inst. where occ. of criter. are too few to be indic.	Net original Grk. frequencies	Net translat. Grk. frequencies
			.06-.01	.18-.01	.49-.01	.18-.01	.19-.01	.27-.01	.024-.01	.07-.01	2.1+	.05-	22+	9-	77-	.35-	10.1+	6+	2-	17			17	17
1:1-5	6	4	.25	.25	–	–	–	–	–	–	6	–	1	12.0	–	–	6	6	–	2	4	11	+2	
6-13	12	1	2.0	2.0	4.0	–	–	2.0	–	–	3.0	.10	4	5.0	–	–	12.0	12	1.0	4	6	7	+2	
14-18	10	1	2.0	2.0	1.0	–	–	1.0	–	–	4	.06	5	17	–	–	10	10.0	.00	4	7	6	+3	–1
19-28	17	2	–	–	–	–	–	.50	–	–	10	–	2.0	13	–	–	17	17.0	.50	4	4	9		
29-34	13	3	–	.33	–	–	–	–	–	–	7	.05	3	17.0	–	–	13.0	2.2	.67	3	4	10	+1	
35-42	17	1	–	–	.50	–	–	.50	–	–	2.5	.05	4	19	–	–	17	2.1	1.6	5	4	8	+1	
43-51	19	2	.38	.46	.46	–	–	.38	–	–	8.0	.04	25.0	23.5	94	–	19	6.3	1.5	6	6			–1
Total 1	94	13									10.8						47.0	4.9	1.0					
2:1-12	24	2	–	–	1.5	.50	.50	–	–	–	2.6	.08	14	3.0	–	3.0	8.0	8.0	2.0	4	7	6	+3	3
13-22	19	3	–	–	.33	–	–	.33	–	–	12.0	.07	8.0	4.8	–	–	19	9.5	1.0	6	3	8		
23-25	6	4	–	.25	.25	–	–	.25	–	–	.00	.13	1.0	6.0	–	–	6	6.0	.25	5	5	7		
Total 2	49	9		.11	.56	.11	.11	.22	–	–	3.1	.08	11.5	3.8	–	3.0	16.3	8.2	.89	9	4	4	+	–5
3:1-15	30	3	1.0	–	1.5	–	–	–	–	–	13.0	.03	10	10.0	–	–	30.0	30.0	.50	5	3	9		–2
16-21	14	1	1.0	1.0	5.0	–	–	1.0	–	–	.33	.13	1.5	14.0	–	.50	4.7	14	.00	2	9	6		
22-30	18	1	–	1.0	2.0	–	–	1.0	–	–	2.0	.10	4	18.0	–	1.0	9.0	18.0	3.0	1	10	6		–2
31-36	11	1	.20	.40	1.0	–	–	–	–	–	3.0	.13	7.0	5.5	–	–	11.0	11	1.0	5	3	9	+7	2
Total 3	73	5	.20	.27	2.2	–	–	.20	.018	–	2.9	.09	7.0	10.4	–	.40	10.4	73.0	1.0	5	7	5	+9	3
John Entire	1756	221	.06	.27	.82	.03	.04	.30	.018	.01	2.4	.06	7.0	7.0	195.1	.65	12.9	9.0	1.0	10	7	–		

CHART X

Frequencies of the 17 Criteria in the Gospel of John

Translation Frequencies	No. of lines of Greek text	No. of occur. of en	dia W. gen .06-.01	dia W. all cases .18-.01	eis .49-.01	W. accus. .18-.01	kata W. all .19-.01	Peri W. all cases .27-.01	Pros W. dative en .024-.01	Hupo W. genitive .07-.01	No. of occ. of kai for each occ. of de 2.1+	Percent of separ. articles .05-	No. of dep. gen. post ea. prec. dep. gen. 22+	No. of lines/ea. dep. gen. pers. pronoun 9-	Lines ea. gen. dep. pers. pron. dep. on anarth. subst. 77-	No. of prec. attr. adj. for each attr. adj. post position .35-	No. of lines/ea. attrib. adjec. 10.1+	No. of lines/each adverb. participle 6+	No. of dat. not used w. en for ea. occur. of en 2-	Tot. no. of trans. Grk. frequencies 17	Tot. no. of orig. Grk. frequencies	No. of inst. where occ. of criter. are too few to be indic	Net original Grk. frequencies	Net translat. Grk. frequencies 17
4:1-6	10	-	1	1	2	-	-	-	-	-	.50	.07	4	5.0	-	-	10	10.0	1.0	2	7	8	+5	3
7-15	20	1	-	-	3.0	-	-	-	-	-	5.0	.04	6	5.0	-	.00	6.7	6.7	1.0	6	3	8		3
16-26	21	6	-	-	-	-	-	-	-	-	6	.05	2.0	10.5	-	1.0	21.0	21	-	6	3	8	+3	-1
27-30	7	-	-	-	1.0	-	-	-	-	-	5	-	3.0	3.5	-	-	7	7	.50	3	3	11	+3	-1
31-38	15	2	-	3	1.0	-	-	-	-	-	4.0	-	4	7.5	-	1.0	7.5	15.0	-	4	4	9		
39-42	8	-	-	-	1.0	-	-	-	-	-	3.0	.20	-	8.0	-	1.0	8.0	8.0	.00	3	6	8		
43-45	6	3	-	-	.75	-	-	-	-	-	.00	.29	8	-	-	1.0	6.0	6.0	.50	2	5	10		
46-54	19	4	-	-	-	-	-	-	-	-	2.0	.00	-	3.2	-	-	19	4.8	.88	4	4	9		
Total 4	106	16	.06	.25	.94	-	-	-	-	-	3.5	.05	9.3	5.6	106	1.0	13.3	9.6	.75	7	5	5	+1	0
5:1-9a	14	4	-	-	.50	-	-	-	-	-	1.7	-	8	4.7	-	-	14	4.7	.75	3	4	10	+1	2
9b-18	18	4	-	.50	-	-	-	-	-	-	1.8	.12	3	6.0	-	-	18.0	9.0	1.5	4	4	9		
19-29	25	4	-	-	1.0	-	-	2.0	-	-	4.0	.11	7	12.5	-	1.0	12.5	25.0	.75	4	5	8		
30-40	22	3	-	-	-	-	-	.33	-	-	2.3	.08	6	4.4	11.0	.00	7.3	22.0	.67	6	4	7	+1	-2
41-47	12	3	-	-	.33	-	-	-	-	-	2.0	.23	3.0	12.0	-	2.0	4.0	12.0	1.3	3	7	7		
Total 5	91	18	-	.11	.39	-	-	.39	-	-	2.1	.11	27.0	6.5	45.5	.50	10.1	11.4	1.0	9	3	5	+4	0
6:1-15	29	1	-	-	4.0	-	-	-	-	-	.50	.09	7.0	9.7	-	-	14.5	4.8	3.0	1	7	9	+6	7
16-21	11	-	-	-	4	-	-	-	-	-	2.5	.08	1	11.0	-	-	11.0	2.2	4.0	2	5	10	+3	
22-33	27	1	-	-	5.0	-	-	-	-	-	4	.02	9	5.4	-	.33	6.8	9.0	.00	5	4	8		
34-40	15	2	-	-	1.0	-	-	-	-	-	3.0	.10	4	15.0	-	1.0	3.8	15	.00	3	6	8		
41-51	20	3	-	-	.33	-	-	.33	-	-	4.0	.11	4.0	10.0	-	1.0	10.0	20	.20	4	6	7	+2	-1
52-59	16	5	-	.40	.20	-	-	-	-	-	4	.15	1.0	5.3	-	3.0	4.0	8.0		5	5	7		

CHART X

Frequencies of the 17 Criteria in the Gospel of John

Translation Frequencies	No. of lines of Greek text	No. of occur. of en	dia W. gen. .06-/.01	dia W. all cases .18-/.01	eis .49-/.01	kata W. accus. .18-/.01	kata W. all .19-/.01	Peri W. all cases .27-/.01	Pros W. dative .024-/.01	Hupo W. genitive .07-/.01	No. of occ. of kai for each occ. of de 2.1+	Percent. of separ. articles .05-	No. of dep. gen. post ea. prec. dep. gen. 22+	No. of lines ea. pers. gen. dep. pronoun 9-	Lines ea. gen. dep. pers. pron. on anarth. subst. 77-	No. of prec. attr. adj. for ea. attr. adj. post position .35-	No. of lines ea. attrib. adjec. 10.1+	No. of lines/each adverb. participle 6+	No. of dat. not used w. en for ea. occur. of en 2-	Tot. no. of transl. Grk. frequencies 17	Tot. no. of orig. Grk. frequencies	No. of inst. where occ. of criter. are too few to be indic.	Net original Grk. frequencies	Net translat. Grk. frequencies 17
6:60-65	13	1	-	1.0	-	-	-	1.0	-	-	1.0/3.0	-	3	6.5/10.0	-	-	13/10.0	4.3/10.0	.00	3	5	9	3+	
66-71	10	-	-	.23	1.4	-	-	.15	-	-	3.0	-	5	10.0	-	-	10.0	10.0	-	2	4	11	2+	
Total 6	141	13	-	1.0	-	-	-	1.0	-	-	2.3	.07	5.4	7.8	141	.64	7.8	7.1	.77	5	7	5	2+	
7:1-9	16	5	-	-	.80	-	-	.20	-	-	.75	.08	5.0	4.0	-	.50	5.3	16.0	.20	4	6	7	2+	
10-13	7	3	-	.33	.33	.25	-	.67	-	-	1.0	.11	2	7.0	-	-	7	7	.33	4	6	7	2+	
14-24	21	4	-	.25	.25	-	-	.25	-	-	3.0	.17	3	21.0	-	-	14	7.0	.50	5	8	4	3+	
25-31	14	1	-	-	1.0	-	-	1.0	-	-	4.0	.09	1	14.0	-	2.0	12.0	7.0	1.0	4	4	9		
32-36	12	-	-	-	-	-	-	-	-	-	.6	-	3	12	-	-	3.5	12.0	.00	3	7	10	1+	
37-39	7	1	-	1.0	2.0	-	-	1.0	-	-	1.0	.11	-	7.0	-	1.0	7	7.0	.00	3	3	7	4+	
40-44	7	-	-	-	-	-	-	-	-	-	.00	-	1	-	-	-	13	13	-	2	4	12	1+	
45-52	13	-	-	1.5	2	-	-	.50	-	-	-	-	-	-	-	-	13/10.8	10.8	.40	2	7	11	2+	
Total 7	97	15	-	.27	.73	.07	.07	.40	-	-	2.0	.08	16.0	13.0	97	.80	10.8	13	.40	5	9	3	4+	
8:12-20	20	4	-	-	-	.25	.25	1.0	-	-	1.3	.08	8.0	3.3	-	-	10.0	10.0	.25	3	7	7		2-
21-30	21	3	-	-	.67	-	-	1.0	-	-	.5	-	4	7.0	14.0	-	21	21.0	.33	5	3	9	4+	
31-38	14	3	-	-	.67	-	-	.33	-	-	4.0	.10	4	14.0	22.0	-	7.0	14	1.3	4	5	8		2-
39-47	22	2	-	1.5	-	-	-	.50	-	-	1.0	.00	10	4.4	25.0	1.0	11.0	22	1.0	6	4	7	1+	3-
48-59	25	1	-	-	2	-	-	-	-	-	3.3	.05	8	2.8	34.0	1.0	12.5	25	-	6	6	8		
Total 8	102	12	-	.25	.50	.08	.08	.50	-	-	2.8	.04	32.0	4.3	34.0	.14	12.8	34.0	.75	11	6	3		8-
7:53-8:11	21	3	-	-	1.7	.33	.33	-	-	-	.82	.05	3	10.5	-	-	21	1.9	1.3	3	7	7	4+	

CHART X

Frequencies of the 17 Criteria in the Gospel of John

Translation Frequencies	No. of lines of Greek text	No. of occur. of en	dia w. gen. (.06-/.01)	dia w. all cases (.18-/.01)	eis (.49-/.01)	kata w. accus. (.18-/.01)	kata w. all (.19-/.01)	Peri w. all cases (.27-/.01)	Pros w. dative (.024/-.01)	Hupo w. genitive (.07-/.01)	No. of occ. of de for each occ. of kai (2.1+)	Percent of separ. articles (.05-)	No. of dep. gen. post ea. prec. dep. gen. (22+)	No. of lines ea. dep. gen. pers. pronoun (9-)	Lines ea. gen. pers. pron. dep. on anarth. subst. (77-)	No. of prec. attr. adj. for each attr. adj. post position (.35-)	No. of lines/ea. attrib. adjec. (10.1+)	No. of lines each adverb. participle (6+)	No. of dat. not used w. en for ea. occur. of en (2-)	Tot. no. of transl. Grk. frequencies (17)	Tot. no. of orig. Grk. frequencies	No. of inst. where occ. of criter. are too few to be indic.	Net original Grk. frequencies	Net translat. Grk. frequencies (17)
9:1-12	23	2	–	–	1.0	–	–	–	–	–	.9	.04	2.3	7.7	–	1.0	23 / 6.0	3.3	.50 / .00	5	3	9	+5 +1	2
13-17	12	2	–	–	–	–	–	.50	–	–	.75	.07	.00	12	–	–	14 / 21	12 / 14	–	2	7	8	+1	–
18-23	14	–	–	1	–	–	–	2	–	–	2.0	–	6.0	2.3	–	–	21	21.0 / 14	1.0	3	4	10	+1	3
24-34	21	2	–	1	4	–	–	–	–	–	4.0	–	.75	21.0	–	–	9	9.0	–	5	2	10	+4	–
35-39	9	–	–	–	–	–	–	–	–	–	6.0	.25	1	–	–	–	4	4	–	2	3	12	+4	–
40,41	4	–	–	–	–	–	–	–	–	–	1.0	.04	1	4.0	–	–	–	–	.67	1	5	11	+4	–
Total 9	83	6	–	.17	1.0	–	–	.50	–	–	3.1	.04	1.5	7.5	83	1.0	41.5 / 12.0	8.3	.67	7	10	5	+7	– 6
10:1-6	12	–	2	2	1	1	1	–	–	–	1.3	.12	4.0	6.0	–	1.0	12 / 12.0	12	3	3	10	4	+7 0	–
7-18	25	–	1	2	–	–	–	1	–	–	12	.00	6	5.0	–	.00	8.3	25.0	–	5	5	7	+4	–
19-21	5	1	–	1.0	–	–	–	–	–	–	1.0	.00	1.0	–	–	–	5	5	.00	1	5	11	+2	–
22-30	15	4	–	.33	.25	–	–	.25	–	–	9	–	8	3.0	–	.00	5.0 / 5.3	15 / 16.0	.75	8	2	7	+3	6
31-39	16	3	–	–	.33	–	–	.67	–	–	2.0	.00	6.0	5.3	–	2.0	5.3	5	2.0	4	6	7	+3	–
40-42	5	–	–	1.0	2	–	–	1	–	–	5.0	–	–	–	–	–	5	–	5.0	1	4	12	+3	1
Total 10	78	8	.38	.75	.63	.13	.13	.63	–	–	5.5	.02	8.3	5.2	78	.43	7.8	39.0	1.6	7	8	2	+7	–
11:1-16	29	4	.25	.50	.25	–	–	.50	–	–	.43	.00	12	4.8	–	–	29 / 18.0	14.5	.75	6	5	6	+4	–
17-27	18	4	–	–	1.0	–	–	.25	–	–	.33	.10	3	9.0	–	1.0	18.0	18.0	.25	5	5	7	+7	1
28-37	20	2	–	–	1.0	–	–	–	–	–	2.0	.14	1.0	20.0	–	–	20 / 15.0	2.5	2.0	2	6	9	+1	–
38-44	15	1	–	1.0	1.0	–	–	–	–	–	1.3	.06	3	15.0	–	–	15.0	5.0	5.0	1	8	8	+4	–
45-53	18	–	–	–	3	–	–	–	–	–	1.7	.00	1	18	–	–	18	18.0	–	3	4	10	+1	–
54-57	10	2	–	–	2.0	–	–	–	–	–	1.5	.07	1	10	–	–	10	10.0	1.2	2	6	9	+4	–
Total 11	110	13	.08	.23	1.2	–	–	.23	–	–	1.0	.06	7.3	11.0	110	1.0	55.0	6.9	1.2	4	9	4	+5	–

CHART X

Frequencies of the 17 Criteria in the Gospel of John

Translation Frequencies	No. of lines of Greek text	No. of occur. of en	die W. gen. (.06/.01)	die W. all cases (.18/.01)	eis (.49/.01)	W. accus. (.18/.01)	kata W. all (.19/.01)	Peri W. all cases (.27/.01)	Pros W. dative en (.024/.01)	Hupo W. genitive (.07/.01)	No. of occ. of kai for each occ. of de (2.1+)	Percent of separ. articles (.05-)	No. of dep. gen. post ea. prec. gen. (22+)	No. of lines ea. dep. gen. pers. pronoun (9.)	Lines ea. gen. dep. on anarth. subst. pers. pron. (77.)	No. of prec. attr. adj. for each attr. adj. post position (.35-)	No. of lines ea. attrib. adjec. (10.1+)	No. of lines/each adverb. participle (6+)	No. of dat. not used w. en ea. occur. of en (2-)	Tot. no. of trans. frequencies (17)	Tot. no. of orig. Grk. frequencies	No. of inst. where occ. of criter. are too few to be indic.	Net original Grk frequencies	Net translat. Grk. frequencies (17)
12:1-8	16	-	-	1	2	-	-	1	-	-	.60	.17	10	4.0	-	-	8.0	8.0	4	2	8	7	+6	
9-11	6	-	-	2	1	-	-	-	-	-	1.0	-	1	-	-	-	6	6	-	1	5	11	+4	
12-19	14	-	-	1	3	-	-	-	-	-	2.0	.05	2.0	14	-	-	14	14	5	3	6	8	+3	
20-26	15	2	-	-	1.0	-	-	-	-	-	1.6	.04	5	7.5	-	2.0	7.5	5.0	2.5	2	6	9	+4	
27-36a	20	2	-	1.5	1.5	-	-	-	-	-	5.0	.04	6.0	20.0	-	-	10.0	20.0	1.0	4	6	7	+2	
36b-43	11	-	-	2	2	-	-	1	-	-	2.0	-	4	11.0	-	1.0	11.0	5.5	.00	4	8	8	+7	
44-50	14	2	-	1.5	2.5	-	-	-	-	-	4.0	.11	4.0	7.0	-	1.0	7.0	14	.00	4	5	8	+1	
Total 12	96	6	-	1.5	3.0	-	-	.33	-	-	1.7	.07	10.0	9.6	96	.80	10.7	9.6	2.7	2	10	5	+8	0
13:1-11	24	1	-	1.0	5.0	-	-	-	-	-	3.0	.00	1.3	24.0	-	-	24	4.0	1.0	4	5	8	+1	-1
12-20	16	-	-	-	-	-	-	-	-	-	3.0	.07	1.5	5.3	-	-	16	16	1.0	3	4	10	+1	
21-30	19	1	-	-	3.0	-	-	2.0	-	-	1.5	.00	5	19.0	-	-	19	3.8	2.0	4	6	10	+3	
31-35	10	1	-	-	-	-	-	-	-	-	.4	-	1	10	-	-	10.0	10	.20	2	3	10		
36-38	7	5	-	1	-	-	-	.43	-	-	.00	-	2	3.5	-	-	7	7	3	5	5	7		
Total 13	76	-	.11	.29	1.1	-	-	-	-	.20	2.3	.01	3.0	10.9	-	-	76.0	6.9	1.1	5	5	7	0	0
14:1-14	27	r.	-	.22	.33	-	-	-	-	-	3.0	.03	6	5.4	-	1.0	27.0	27.0	1.1	8	3	6		-5
15-24	21	5	-	-	.20	-	-	-	-	.20	5.0	.09	7	3.5	-	1.0	10.5	21	.78	6	4	7		-2
25-31	15	5	-	-	-	-	-	-	-	-	.4	.13	.50	15.0	-	-	7.5	15.0	1.0	4	4	9		
Total 14	63	16	.06	.13	.25	-	-	-	-	.06	3.8	.07	4.7	5.3	-	.67	12.6	31.5	.94	9	3	5	+6	

CHART X

Frequencies of the 17 Criteria in the Gospel of John

Translation Frequencies	Net translat. Grk. frequencies (17)	Net original Grk. frequencies	No. of inst. where occ. of criter. are too few to be indic.	Tot. no. of orig. Grk. frequencies	Tot. no. of transl. Grk. frequencies (17)	No. of dat. not used w. en for ea. occur. of en (2-)	No. of lines/ea. adverb. participle (6+)	No. of lines/ea. attrib. adjec. (10.1)	No. of prec. attr. adj. for each attr. adj. post position (.35-)	Lines ea. dep. pers. pron. subst. on anarth. subst. (77-)	No. of lines ea. dep. gen. pers. pronoun (9-)	No. of dep. gen. post ea. prec. gen. (22+)	Percent. of separ. articles (.05-)	No. of occ. of kai for each occ. of de (2.1+)	Hupo w. genitive (.07-.01)	Pros w. dative (.024-.01)	Peri w. all cases (.27-.01)	kata w. all (.19-.01)	w. accus. (.18-.01)	eis (.49-.01)	dia w. all cases (.18-.01)	dia w. gen. (.06-.01)	No. of occur. of en	No. of lines of Greek text
15:1-10	5		8	2	7	.14	10.0	10.0	-	-	3.3	7	.00	7	-	-	-	-	-	.07	.07	-	14	20
11-17	-1	+2	8	4	5	1.5	13	4.3	.50	13.0	2.5	7.0	-	1.0	-	-	.50	-	-	-	-	-	2	13
18-25		+3	7	6	4	.00	17	17/4	-	-	2.4	7	.10	.00	-	-	.25	-	-	.50	1.0	-	2	17
26,27			12	4	1	-			-	-	-	-	-	.00	-	-	-	-	-	-	-	-	-	4
Total 15	8	0	5	2	10	.28	27.0	10.8	.25	54.0	2.7	22.0	.03	1.6	-	-	.11	-	-	.11	.17	-	18	54
16:1-4		+1	12	3	2	-	6.0	6	-	-	6.0	1	-	1	-	-	-	-	-	-	-	-	-	6
5-11		+3	10	5	2	-	12.0	12	-	-	12	1.0	-	.40	-	-	6	-	-	1	1.0	-	-	12
12-15	6	+4	11	5	1	3.0	8	8	-	-	-	1	.06	1.0	-	-	-	-	-	.67	.33	-	1	8
16-24	6		7	5	5	.00	22	22	-	-	3.1	7.0	-	3.0	-	-	.33	-	-	.25	-	-	3	22
25-33			9	1	7	.38	18	18	-	-	9.0	-	-	6	-	-	.25	-	-	.42	.17	-	8	18
Total 16	4		7	2	8	.67	33.0	66	-	-	6.6	6.0	.02	2.1	-	-	.75	-	-	-	-	-	12	66
17:1-5	-2	+9	8	9	0	3	5.0	2.5	3.0	-	10.0	2.0	.25	2.0	-	-	-	-	-	-	-	-	-	10
6-19	2		7	3	7	.33	28	9.3	.00	-	7.0	5.0	.00	16.0	-	-	.33	-	-	.22	.14	.14	9	28
20-26			7	4	6	.14	16	8.0	-	-	8.0	3	-	2.5	-	-	.29	-	-	.29	.06	.06	7	16
Total 17	2		5	5	7	.44	27.0	6.0	.50	-	7.7	5.0	.06	5.8	-	-	.31	-	-	.31	-	-	16	54

41

CHART X

Frequencies of the 17 Criteria in the Gospel of John

Translation Frequencies	Net transl. Grk. frequencies (17)	Net original Grk. frequencies	No. of inst. where occ. of criter. are too few to be indic.	Tot. no. of orig. Grk. frequencies	Tot. no. of transl. Grk. frequencies (17)	No. of dat. not used w. en for ea. occur. of en (2-)	adverb. participle No. of lines each (6+)	attrib. adjec. No. of lines ea. (10.1+)	adj. post position for each prec. attr. No. of attr. (.35-)	pers. pron. dep. on anarth. subst. Lines ea. gen. (77-)	pers. pronoun dep. gen. No. of lines ea. (9-)	dep. gen. post gen. No. of dep. gen. prec. (22+)	Percent. of separ. articles (.05-)	No. of occ. of kai for each occ. of de (2.1+)	Hupo w. genitive (.07-/.01)	Pros w. dative (.024/-.01)	Peri w. all cases (.27-/.01)	kata w. all cases (.19-/.01)	w. accus. (.18-/.01)	eis (.49-/.01)	dia w. all cases (.18-/.01)	dia w. gen. (.06-/.01)	No. of occur. of en	No. of lines of Greek text
18:1-11		+4	9	6	2	3	5.8	23.0	-	-	7.7	2.0	.07	1.0	-	-	-	-	-	3	-	-	-	23
12-14		+3	12	4	1	1	6	6	-	-	-	2	.10	2.0	-	-	-	-	-	1	-	-	-	6
15-18		+8	7	9	1	4	11.0	3.7	.50	-	11	-	.09	.80	-	1	-	-	-	1	-	-	3	11
19-24		+2	9	5	3	1.3	4.3	13	-	-	6.5	3	.07	.50	-	-	1.0	-	-	-	-	-	1	13
25-27			10	3	4	.00	6	6	-	-	6.0	2	-	-	-	-	-	-	-	6	-	-	-	6
28-38a		+4	5	8	4	3	28.0	4.7	.20	-	28.0	3.0	.00	2.0	-	-	1	2	1	6	-	-	2	28
38b-40		+2	11	4	2	1.5	3.0	6	-	-	-	1	-	2.5	-	-	-	-	-	-	-	-	-	6
Total 18	-1	+4	3	9	5	3.0	8.5	9.3	.25	96	13.3	6.0	.05	1.2	-	.17	.67	.33	.17	1.7	.67	-	5	93
19:1-7		+6	7	8	2	1.5	5.3	5.3	2.0	-	16	2.0	.13	8	-	-	-	.50	.50	1	-	-	2	16
8-12		+6	7	8	2	1	12.0	12.0	1.0	-	12	1	.23	1.0	-	-	-	1	-	1	-	-	-	12
13-16a		+3	10	5	2	5	9.0	9	-	-	4.5	3	.11	1.0	-	-	-	-	-	1	-	-	-	9
16b-22		+2	9	5	3	1	14.0	14	-	-	14	5.0	.00	1.0	-	-	-	-	-	1	-	-	-	14
23-27		+9	6	10	1	-	4.3	6.5	1.0	-	2.6	8	.08	1.0	-	-	-	-	-	-	1	1	-	13
28-30		+3	14	3	0	2.0	2.0	6	-	-	14	.50	-	-	-	-	-	-	-	-	-	-	-	6
31-37			8	4	5	.67	14.0	14.0	1.0	-	13.0	.60	.10	6.0	-	-	-	-	-	-	-	-	1	14
38-42			9	4	4	3.2	6.5	13.0	-	-	-	7	.00	1.0	-	-	-	-	-	-	-	-	3	13
Total 19	1 / 0	+7	2	11	4	3.2	6.5	12.1	1.7	97	12.1	3.3	.07	2.0	-	-	.17	.33	.17	.67	.67	.17	6	97

CHART X

Frequencies of the 17 Criteria in the Gospel of John

Translation Frequencies	No. of lines of Greek text	No. of occur. of ēn	dia W. gen. (.06-.01)	dia W. all cases (.18-.01)	eis (.49-.01)	kata W. accus. (.18-.01)	kata W. all cases (.19-.01)	Peri w. all cases (.27-.01)	Pros w. dative (.024-.01)	Hupo w. genitive (.07-.01)	No. of occ. of kai for each occ. of de (2.1+)	Percent of separ. articles (.05-)	No. of dep. gen. post ea. prec. gen. (22+)	No. of lines/ea. dep. gen. pers. pronoun (9-)	Lines/ea. gen. dep. pers. pron. on anarth. subst. (77-)	No. of prec. attr. adj. for each attr. adj. post position (.35-)	No. of lines/ea. attrib. adjec. (10.1-)	No. of lines each adverb. participle (6+)	No. of dat. not used w. en for ea. occur. of (2-)	Tot. no. of transl. Grk. frequencies (17)	Tot. no. of orig. Grk. frequencies	No. of inst. where occ. of criter. are too few to be indic.	Net original Grk. frequencies	Net translat. Grk. frequencies (17)
20:1-10	19	1	–	–	6 / 2.0	–	–	–	3.0	–	6.0	.18	2	19.0	–	4.0	3.8 / 20.0	2.4	–	1	7	9	+6	
11-18	20	1	–	–	1	–	–	–	–	–	3.5	–	7	3.3	6.7	–	20.0 / 10.0	2.9	5.0	4	5	8	+1	
19-23	10	–	–	1	4.0	–	–	–	–	–	5	.04	7	10	–	1.0	10.0 / 16.0	2.0	.5 / 1.0	1	7	9	+6	
24-29	16	1	–	–	–	1	1	1	–	–	4.0	–	12.0	2.5	–	1.0	16.0 / 5.0	16.0	.00	6	3	8	+2	
30,31	5	2	–	–	3.3	–	–	–	–	–	.00	.07	3	3.7	23.3	2.0	5.0 / 7.8	5.0	3.3	3	5	5		
Total 20	70	4	–	.25	3.3	–	–	.50	.75	–	4.6	.07	26.0	3.7	23.3	2.0	7.8	3.2	3.3	4	8		+4	-3
21:1-14	33	1	–	–	6.0	–	–	–	–	–	1.8	.04	8	33.0	–	2.0	11.0	4.1	5.0	2	7	8	+5	
15-19	15	–	–	–	–	–	–	–	–	–	2.5	–	7	3.8	–	–	15	7.5	–	4	1	12		
20-23	10	1	–	–	1.0	–	–	–	–	–	.50	.17	1	10.0	–	–	10	3.3	1.0	1	6	10	+5	
24-25	5	–	–	–	–	1	1	1	–	–	1.0	–	.00	–	–	–	5	5	–	0	8	9	+8	
Total 21	63	2	–	–	3.5	.50	.50	.50	.50	–	1.6	.04	16.0	10.5	–	2.0	21.0	4.8	4.0	2	10	5	+8	-3
The Prologue 1:1-18	28	6	.83	.83	.83	.50	.50	.50	.50	–	13.0	.03	9	9.3	–	–	28.0	28.0	.17	5	6	6	+	1
The Writer's Witness 3:1-13,31-36	28	1	–	–	4.0	–	–	–	–	–	2.5	.08	13.0	5.6	–	–	28.0	28.0	2.0	5	3	9	+	
3:14-21	16	3	.33	.33	1.7	–	–	–	–	–	.67	.11	2	16.0	–	.33	4.0	16	.00	3	8	6	+5	-2

CHAPTER II
The Gospel Passion and Resurrection Accounts

The Passion traditions of the Gospels are
generally considered to be the oldest materials to have
been collected and shaped into a consecutive narrative
by the Church,[79] reflecting the Church's earliest
period; and these materials have, at the same time, the
most complex history of transmission,[80] with
considerable scholarly disagreement over their
relationship to the Primitive Passion account and to
one another.[81]

Thus it may be hoped that Syntax Criticism will
help in unravelling the earliest strands and isolating
that material which most clearly still reflects its
early Palestinian milieu.

For the purposes of this study the Passion and
Resurrection accounts will be taken as consisting of
Mark 11:1-16:8 (starting from the Triumphal Entry into
Jerusalem)[82] and its parallels (Matt. 21:1-28:20;
Luke 19:28-24:53; John 12:1-21:25).

If the net frequencies of these large blocks are
compared to one another, as is done in Chart XI below,
it will be seen that the net frequencies of Mark 11:1-
16:8 (447 lines, +4) are nearly identical with those of
the first part of Mark (Chaps. 1-10--840 lines, +3).

---

[79]Cf. e.g. Brown, John 2, 787. Haenchen, John 1, p. 78.

[80]Cf. Martin SC Syn G, p. 37, note 2.

[81]Cf. Brown, ibid., pp. 787-791; J.A. Fitzmyer, Luke 2, pp. 1359-1366; Bultmann,
John, pp. 6, 632-635.

[82]This continues where the earlier study (SC Syn G) left off.

CHART XI

Net Frequencies in Original Greek Documents of More Than 50 Lines in Length

	No. of Lines	17	16	15	14	13	12	11	10	9	8	7	6	5	4	3	2	1	0	-1	-2	-3	-4	-5	-6	-7	-8	-9	-10	-11	-12	-13	-14
				Net No. of Frequencies Characteristic of Original Greek																Net No. of Frequencies Characteristic of Translation Greek													
Plutarch - Selections	325		X																														
Polybius - Bks I,II	192			X																													
Epictetus - Bks III,IV	138	X																															
Bks I.II	349										X																						
Bks I,II,III,IV	487								X																								
Josephus - Selections	215		X																														
Papyri - Selections	630	X																															
II Maccabees 2:13-6:31	495	X																															
Philo - On Creation I-VIII	251									X																							
Hebrews	535		X																														
Acts 15:36-28:31	1056		X																														
Mark 1-10[1]	840													X																			
Mark 11:1-16:8	447												X																				
Matt. 21:1-28:20	718																						X										
Luke 19:28-24:53	524																								X								
John 12-21	732																					X											
John 12, 13, 18-21	495												X																				
John 14-17	237																											X					

1. The percentages and net frequencies for Mark 1-10 are taken from SC Syn G, Chart XII, p. 87. The percentages and net frequencies of the other Gospel materials and the data on which these percentages are based are found in Appendix 3 "Various Re-groupings of Gospel Material" (No. 1).

Net Frequencies in Translated Documents of More Than 50 Lines in Length

	No. of Lines	17	16	15	14	13	12	11	10	9	8	7	6	5	4	3	2	1	0	-1	-2	-3	-4	-5	-6	-7	-8	-9	-10	-11	-12	-13	-14
				Net No. of Frequencies Characteristic of Original Greek																Net No. of Frequencies Characteristic of Translation Greek													
Genesis 1-4,6,39	382																		X														
1 Samuel 3,4,22	194																													X			
1 Kings 17	58																							X									
2 Kings 13	71																														X		
Dan. - Hebrew - LXX	482																										X						
Hebrew - Theod.	460																														X		
Dan. - Aramaic - LXX	595																														X		
Aramaic - Theod.	634																															X	
Ezra - Hebrew	326																																X
Aramaic	211																														X		
Jer.-Prose A (Chaps 1,3,7,11,16)	201																									X							
Poetic A (Chaps 2,4,5,6,10)	357																																X
Jer.-Prose B (Chaps 33-36)	216																							X									
Poetic B (Chaps 30,31,37,38)	171																							X									
Ezek.-Prose A (Chaps 2-5)	200																																X
Poetic A (Chaps 19,27)	74																													X			
Ezek.-Prose B (Chaps 28,30-32)	203																															X	
Poetic B (Chaps 33-35)	132																													X			
I Maccabees (Chaps 1-5)	732																														X		

However, somewhat surprising is the fact that the net
frequencies of both Matthew's and Luke's accounts are
much more Semitic, falling into the clearly translation
Greek area! This leads to the surmise that in some sub
units both Matthew and Luke will have net frequencies
which are clearly translation Greek more often than
does Mark. That this is the case will be seen as each
account is analyzed in more detail below.

From Chart XI it can be seen that the Passion and
Resurrection account of John's Gospel (chaps. 12-21)
has net frequencies of -3 which is at the border of the
clear translation Greek area. It is interesting to
note at this point already, that the Final Discourse
(chaps. 14-17) falls deep into the clear translation
Greek area (237 lines, -8); whereas the rest of this
part of John (12, 13, 18-21--495 lines, +4) is in the
middle between the clear original Greek and clear
translation Greek areas and the same as the parallel
section in Mark (11:1-16:8).

For the detailed analysis of this complex and
diverse material the accounts will be considered under
the following headings:

A. Material from the Triumphal Entry to the
    Apocalyptic Discourse: Mark 11:1-13:37 and
    parallels (Matt. 21:1-25:46; Luke 19:28-21:38;
    John 12:1-50).

B. Material from The Plot to Kill Jesus to His
    Burial: Mark 14:1-15:47 and parallels
    (Matt. 26:1-27:66; Luke 22:1-23:56; John 13:1-
    19:42).

C. The Resurrection Accounts: Mark 16:1-8
    (Matt. 28; Luke 24; John 20, 21).

D. Blocks of Johannine Material from Chapters
    12 to 17 Not Paralleled in the Synoptics.

A.   Triumphal Entry to the Apocalyptic Discourse

In this section, as will be seen from Chart XII "Classification of Material in Gospel Passion and Resurrection Accounts,"[83] only a very few of the sections of any of the Gospels fall into the areas of either clearly original or clearly translation Greek. It is these instances which will be looked at in more detail at this point.   They are:

Section Number	Where Found	Clear Orig.	Clear Trans.
1. The Triumphal Entry	(all 4)	Matt.	Mark
2. Crying Stones	(Luke)		Luke
9. Parable of the Banquet	(Q)		Luke
11. Question about the Resurrection	(All Syn)		(All Syn)
14. Denouncing the Scribes	(All Syn)		Matt.
15. Various Sins	(Matt.)		Matt.
21. Great Tribulation	(All Syn)		Matt., Luke
24. Coming of the Son of Man	(All Syn)		Matt., Luke
26. The Unknown Hour	(Matt.,Mk.)		Matt.
28. The Faithful or Unfaithful Servant	(Q)		Luke
30. The Parable of the Talents	(Q)	Matt.	Luke
31. Judgment of Nations	(Matt.)		Matt.

---

[83]The percentages and net frequencies are found in Chart XV at the end of this chapter and the data on which these percentages are based are found in Appendix 2.

From this listing, and from Chart XII which
follows, it can be seen that only Matthew has any
sections that clearly fall into the original Greek area
(nos. 1, 30). Most of the clear translation Greek
sections are in Matthew's or Luke's unique material
(nos. 2, 15, 31), or in Q sections (nos. 8, 28, 30), or
in sections where both Matthew and Luke have clear
translation Greek net frequencies and Mark does not
(nos. 21, 24), which may indicate Q material being used
there. Mark has clearly translation Greek net
frequencies only in nos. 1 and 11 and Matthew alone has
them in no. 14--a passage which is found in all three
Synoptic Gospels. John has parallel material only to
nos. 1 and 4, in neither instance being clear
translation.[84] Now to a few remarks on each of the
above sections.

1. The Triumphal Entry (no. 1)
This is found in all 4 gospels and scholars are
not agreed whether all are using only Mark[85] or whether
Luke[86] or John[87] also have independent traditions.
Only Mark is clearly translation Greek here. The
verbal contacts of John with Mark or any of the
Synoptics are so slight that it is most probable as
Knox says, "...the Fourth Evangelist seems to have been

---

[84]See, however, earlier comments pp. 14,27.

[85]Cf. Brown, John 1, p. 459; cf. also Barrett, John, p. 346; Fitzmyer, Luke 2, p. 1242; J.N. Sanders, "John, Gospel of", IDB, Vol. 2, p. 937.

[86]Cf. Fitzmyer, ibid.; Beare, Records pp. 204 and 205; W.L. Knox, The Sources of the Synoptic Gospels (1953), Vol. 1, p. 78.

[87]Cf. Brown, ibid., p. 461; Knox, ibid.; Bultmann, John, p. 417.

CHART XII

Classification of Material in Gospel Passion and Resurrection Accounts

Section Title	Location	Lines	Net Freq.	Original	Original/Translation	Translation
1. The Triumphal Entry	Mk 11:1-11	21	0			Mk
	Mt 21:1-11	19	+7	Mt		
	Lk 19:28-38	19	+3		Lk	
	Jn 12:12-19	14	+3		Jn	
2. Crying Stones	Lk 19:39-44	11	-4			Lk
3. Cursing of the Fig Tree	Mk 11:12-14	6	+2		Mk	
	Mt 21:18,19	4	+1		Mt	
4. Cleansing of the Temple	Mk 11:15-19	11	+1		Mk	
	Mt 21:12-17	13	0		Mt	
	Lk 19:45-48	6	+7		Lk	
	Jn 2:13-17	10	+2		Jn	
5. Lesson from Withered Fig Tree	Mk 11:20-26	12	+1		Mk	
	Mt 21:20-22	7	+4		Mt	
6. Authority of Jesus Questioned	Mk 11:27-33	15	+1		Mk	
	Mt 21:23-27	13	+2		Mt	
	Lk 20:1-8	14	+3		Lk	
7. Parable of Two Sons	Mt 21:28-32	12	+6		Mt	
8. Parable of Vineyard and Tenants	Mk 12:1-12	19	+2		Mk	
	Mt 21:33-46	26	+3		Mt	
	Lk 20:9-19	24	+3		Lk	
9. Parable of the Banquet	Mt 22:1-14	26	+3		Mt	
	Lk 14:15-24	22	-1			Lk
10. Paying Taxes to Caesar	Mk 12:13-17	12	+5		Mk	
	Mt 22:15-22	14	+2		Mt	
	Lk 20:20-26	13	+3		Lk	

Classification of Material in Gospel Passion and Resurrection Accounts

Section Title	Location	Lines	Net Freq.	Original	Original/Translation	Translation
11. Question about the Resurrection	Mk 12:18-27	16	0			Mk
	Mt 22:23-33	15	-1			Mt
	Lk 20:27-40	22	+1			Lk
12. The Great Commandment	Mk 12:28-34	10	+4		Mk	
	Mt 22:34-40	7	+3		Mt	
13. Question about David's Son	Mk 12:35-37	5	+1		Mk	
	Mt 22:41-45	5	+2		Mt	
	Lk 20:41-44	(3)	(+2)		(Lk)	
14. The Denouncing of the Scribes	Mk 12:38-40	6	0			Mk
	Mt 23:1-10	18	+1			Mt
	Lk 20:45-47	7	0			Lk
15. Various Sins	Mt 23:11-36	53	-4			Mt
16. Lament over Jerusalem	Mt 23:37-39	5	+3		Mt	
	Lk 13:34,35	5	+4		Lk	
17. Widow's Offering	Mk 12:41-44	9	+2		Mk	
	Lk 21:1-4	7	+4		Lk	
18. Destruction of the Temple Foretold	Mk 13:1,2	5	+6		Mk	
	Mt 24:1,2	5	+3		Mt	
	Lk 21:5,6	(3)	(+5)		(Lk)	
19. Beginning of Woes (A)	Mk 13:3-8	11	+7	Mk		
	Mt 24:3-8	11	+7	Mt		
	Lk 21:7-11	11	+7	Lk		
20. Beginning of Woes (B)	Mk 13:9-13	12	+2		Mk	
	Mt 24:9-14	10	+2		Mt	
	Lk 21:12-19	12	+1		Lk	

Classification of Material in Gospel Passion and Resurrection Accounts

Section Title	Location	Lines	Net Freq.	Original	Original/Translation	Translation
21. Great Tribulation (A)	Mk 13:14-20	11	+1		Mk	
	Mt 24:15-22	11	-1			Mt
	Lk 21:20-24	11	-2			Lk
22. Great Tribulation (B)	Mk 13:21-23	5	+3		Mk	
	Mt 24:23-25	6	+1		Mt	
23. Great Tribulation (C)	Mt 24:26-28	5	+1		Mt	
	Lk 17:23-24	4	+3		Lk	
24. The Coming the Son of Man	Mk 13:24-27	5	0		Mk	
	Mt 24:29-31	7	-3			Mt
	Lk 21:25-28	7	-1			Lk
25. Lesson of the Fig Tree	Mk 13:28-31	7	+2		Mk	
	Mt 24:32-35	7	+2		Mt	
	Lk 21:29-33	8	+4		Lk	
26. The Unknown Day and Hour	Mk 13:32-37	10	+3		Mk	
	Mt 24:36-44	16	-4			Mt
27. Exhortation to Watch	Lk 21:34-36	7	0		Lk	
28. The Faithful or the Unfaithful Servant	Mt 24:45-51	12	+1		Mt	
	Lk 12:42-46	12	-3			Lk
29. Parable of the Ten Virgins	Mt 25:1-13	21	+4		Mt	
30. Parable of the Talents	Mt 25:14-30	34	+7	Mt		
	Lk 19:11-27	33	+1			Lk
31. Judgment of the Nations	Mt 25:31-40	20	-3			Mt
	41-46	13	+5		Mt	
32. Jesus Lodges on Mt. Olive	Lk 21:37,38	(3)	(+4)		(Lk)	

Classification of Material in Gospel Passion and Resurrection Accounts

Section Title	Location	Lines	Net Freq.	Original	Original/Translation	Translation
33. The Plot to Kill Jesus	Mk 14:1,2	4	+2		Mk	
	Mt 26:1-5	8	0		Mt	
	Lk 22:1,2	(3)	(+5)		(Lk)	
	Jn 11:45-53	18	+1			Jn
34. Annointing at Bethany	Mk 14:3-9	15	+2		Mk	
	Mt 26:6-13	13	+3		Mt	
	Jn 12:1-8	16	+6		Jn	
35. Judas' Agreement to Betray	Mk 14:10,11	4	+2		Mk	
	Mt 26:14-16	4	+5		Mt	
	Lk 22:3-6	6	+2		Lk	
36. Preparation for Passover	Mk 14:12-16	12	+2		Mk	
	Mt 26:17-19	7	+4		Mt	
	Lk 22:7-13	12	+5		Lk	
37. Betrayal Foretold	Mk 14:17-21	9	+10	Mk		
	Mt 26:20-25	11	+6		Mt	
	Lk 22:14, 21-23	6	+6		Lk	
	Jn 13:21-30	19	+3		Jn	
38. Institution of the Lord's Supper	Mk 14:22-26	9	+1		Mk	
	Mt 26:26-30	10	+5		Mt	
	Lk 22:15-20	13	+3		Lk	
	1 Cor. 11:23-25	8	+6		Cor	
39. Dispute about Greatness	Lk 22:24-30	13	-5			Lk
40. Peter's Denial Foretold	Mk 14:27-31	8	+3		Mk	
	Mt 26:31-35	9	-1			Mt
	Lk 22:31-34	7	+3		Lk	
	Jn 13:36-38	7	+3		Jn	

Classification of Material in Gospel Passion and Resurrection Accounts

Section Title	Location	Lines	Net Freq.	Original	Original/Translation	Translation
41. Purse, Bag and Sword	Lk 22:35-38	9	+1		Lk	
42. Prayer in Gethsemane	Mk 14:32-42	22	+3		Mk	
	Mt 26:36-46	24	0			Mt
	Lk 22:39-46	11	+4		Lk	
43. Betrayal and Arrest of Jesus	Mk 14:43-50	15	+2		Mk	
	Mt 26:47-56	22	0			Mt
	Lk 22:47-53	15	+6		Lk	
	Jn 18:1-11	23	+4		Jn	
44. Young Man Who Fled	Mk 14:51,52	(3)	(+3)		(Mk)	
45. Jesus Before the Council (A)	Mk 14:53-61a	16	+4		Mk	
	Mt 26:57-63a	12	+7	Mt		
	Lk 22:54,55	4	+3		Lk	
	Jn 18:13,14	4	+4		Jn	
46. Jesus Before the Council (B)	Mk 14:61b-65	9	+3		Mk	
	Mt 26:63b-68	10	+5		Mt	
	Lk 22:63-71	13	+2		Lk	
	Jn 18:19-24	13	+2		Jn	
47. Peter's Denial of Jesus	Mk 14:66-72	15	0		Mk	
	Mt 26:69-75	13	+4		Mt	
	Lk 22:56-62	13	+5		Lk	
	Jn 18:15-18, 25-27	17	+8	Jn		
48. Jesus Brought Before Pilate	Mk 15:1-5	9	+5		Mk	
	Mt 27:1, 2, 11-14	11	+5		Mt	
	Lk 23:1-5	11	+2		Lk	
	Jn 18:28-38a	28	+4		Jn	

Classification of Material in Gospel Passion and Resurrection Accounts

Section Title	Location	Lines	Net Freq.	Original	Original/Translation	Translation
49. Death of Judas	Mt 27:3-10	11	+8	Mt		
50. Jesus Before Herod	Lk 23:6-12	15	+7	Lk		
51. Jesus Sentenced to Die (A)	Lk 23:13-17	7	+3		Lk	
52. Jesus Sentenced to Die (B)	Mk 15:6-15	16	+8	Mk		
	Mt 27:15-26	23	+6	Mt		
	Lk 23:18-25	13	+1		Lk	
	Jn 18:38b-40; 19:4-16a	38	+6	Jn		
53. Soldiers Mock Jesus	Mk 15:16-20	9	+5		Mk	
	Mt 27:27-31	11	+1		Mt	
	Jn 19:1-3	5	+2		Jn	
54. Crucifixion of Jesus (A)	Mk 15:21-26	8	+1		Mk	
	Mt 27:32-37	8	+4		Mt	
	Lk 23:26, 32-38	14	+5		Lk	
	Jn 19:16b-24	21	+8	Jn		
55. Women Weeping	Lk 23:27-31	8	+1		Lk	
56. Crucifixion of Jesus (B)	Mk 15:27-32	10	-2			Mk
	Mt 27:38-44	11	+2		Mt	
	Lk 23:39-43	8	+2		Lk	
57. Death of Jesus	Mk 15:33-41	16	+6	Mk		
	Mt 27:45-51, 54-56	18	+9	Mt		
	Lk 23:44-49	11	+5		Lk	
	Jn 19:25-30	12	+2		Jn	
58. Earthquake	Mt 27:51b-53	4	+4		Mt	

Classification of Material in Gospel Passion and Resurrection Accounts

Section Title	Location	Lines	Net Freq.	Original	Original/Translation	Translation
59. Burial of Jesus	Mk 15:42-47	13	+1			Mk
	Mt 27:57-61	9	+4		Mt	
	Lk 23:50-56	12	0			Lk
	Jn 19:31-42	27	+1			Jn
60. Guard at the Tomb	Mt 27:62-66	11	+5		Mt	
61. Women Visit the Tomb	Mk 16:1-8	17	0			Mk
	Mt 28:1-8	16	+6	Mt		
	Lk 24:1-7	14	+7	Lk		
	Jn 20:1,2	6	+5		Jn	
62. Mark's Longer Addition	Mk 16:9-20	24	+9	Mk		
63. Mark's Shorter Addition		4	+9	Mk		
64. Matt. Resurrect Events (A)	Mt 28:9,10	5	+3		Mt	
65. Matt. Resurrect Events (B)	Mt 28:11-15	10	+8	Mt		
66. Matt. Resurrect Events (C)	Mt 28:16-20	10	+7		Mt	
67. Luke Resurrect Events (A)	Lk 24:8-12	9	+4		Lk	
68. Luke Resurrect Events (B)	Lk 24:13-27	32	0			Lk
69. Luke Resurrect Events (C)	Lk 24:28-35	16	-4			Lk
70. Luke Resurrect Events (D)	Lk 24:36-43	12	0			Lk
71. Luke Resurrect Events (E)	Lk 24:44-49	12	+3		Lk	
72. Luke Resurrect Events (F)	Lk 24:50-53	6	+3		Lk	
73. John Resurrect Events (A)	Jn 20:3-10	13	-6	Jn		
74. John Resurrect Events (B)	Jn 20:11-18	20	+1			Jn
75. John Resurrect Events (C)	Jn 20:19-23	10	+6	Jn		
76. John Resurrect Events (D)	Jn 20:24-29	16	-3			Jn
77. John Resurrect Events (E)	Jn 20:30,31	5	+2		Jn	
78. John Resurrect Events (F)	Jn 21:1-14	33	+5	Jn		

Classification of Material in Gospel Passion and Resurrection Accounts

Section Title	Location	Lines	Net Freq.	Original	Original/Translation	Translation
79. John Resurrect Events (G)	Jn 21:15-19	15	-3			Jn
80. John Resurrect Events (H)	Jn 21:20-23	10	+5		Jn	
81. John Resurrect Events (I)	Jn 21:24,25	5	+8	Jn		

following a different source for his story."[88]

Matthew's original Greek net frequencies have resulted from features of the added material in verses 4-6[89] and 10, and his stylistic improvements of Mark's Greek (re kai/de, use of personal pronouns and use of attributive adjectives).

2. Crying Stones (no. 2)

This is clearly a piece of Semitic tradition whose net frequencies fall deep into the clear translation Greek area. Verses 38 and 39 are somewhat parallel to Matt. 21:15f but fit better in the Lukan setting than the Matthean.[90]

While this contact between Matthew and Luke may suggest a Q context for the material, Fitzmyer prefers to assign it to "L"[91] as an "inherited piece of tradition, which he [Luke] has only slightly redacted."[92] Beare suggests vv. 39 and 40 together with v. 37 "may be an independent version of the approach of Jesus to Jerusalem which Luke has conflated with the Marcan story."[93]

---

[88]Ibid.; so also Brown's conclusion, ibid., and Bultman's, ibid. Further John's net frequencies here should probably be understood as indicating an Aramaic Vorlage (cf. the reference in note 84, supra).

[89]The quoted material from the O.T. has been left out of the calculation as noted earlier.

[90]So Beare, Matthew, p. 418 and Records, p. 205.

[91]Fitzmyer, Luke 2, p. 1253; cf. Vol. 1, pp. 82-85 for his discussion and description of this "source".

[92]Ibid, Vol. 2, p. 1253.

[93]Beare, Records, p. 205. Similarly Knox sees 39-44 as possibly having "come to Luke from the same source as the version of the entry which he has combined with Mark's.". Op. cit., Vol. I, p. 79.

3. Parable of the Banquet (no. 9)

The Matthean and Lukan parables are clearly
versions of the same story, as is also the Gospel of
Thomas (Logion 64). The relationship between these,
however, is unclear. The similarities between Matthew
and Luke are not as great as in much of their Q
material, so that while many scholars consider this
parable to be from Q,[94] others grant that, as Beare
states, it may have "come to them through independent
channels of transmission."[95] Luke's version is clearly
translation Greek and this confirms the judgment of
most scholars that the Lukan form is "closer to the
original" than Matthew's.[96] The Gospel of Thomas
version seems independent of the Canonical accounts,
and may be "more primitive."[97]

4. Question about the Resurrection (no. 11)

This is found in all three Synoptics and is clear
translation Greek in all of them, with Matthew and Luke
improving Mark's Greek somewhat.[98] While Matthew
follows Mark very closely,[99] Luke may be using another
source also.[100] Taylor considers that Mark here

---

[94]So Fitzmyer, Luke 2, p. 1052.

[95]Matthew, p. 434.

[96]Beare, Records, p. 210; cf. also Bultmann, History, pp. 175, 195.

[97]Fitzmyer, Luke 2, pp. 1050f; cf. also Beare, Records, p. 210f., but cf. his
later judgment in Matthew, p. 434.

[98]Fitzmyer, ibid., p. 1299.

[99]Beare, Records, p. 212.

[100]Ibid., p. 213; Fitzmyer disagrees, ibid.

"preserves genuine tradition of the most primitive
kind."[101]

5. Denouncing the Scribes (no. 14)

This is found in all 3 Synoptics. Matthew alone
is clearly translation Greek, and Luke and Mark nearly
so. While Luke follows Mark "almost word for word,"[102]
Matthew is considerably longer with much additional
material, some of which is Q and some Special
Matthew.[103] The additional material is Palestinian[104]
and, according to Bultmann, may go back even to
Jesus![105]

6. Various Sins (no. 15)

This continues the additional material from Q and
Special Matthew of the previous section (no. 14) and,
like these, Matthew is clearly translation Greek.[106]

7. Subsections from the Synoptic Apocalypses
(nos. 18-31)

The Synoptic apocalypses (Mark 13; Matt. 24,25;
Luke 21:5-38 and some material elsewhere in his Gospel)
are seen by all to be extremely complex compositions of
a variety of materials,[107] which go back to earlier

---

[101]The Gospel According to St. Mark (1966), p. 480.

[102]Beare, Records, p. 214.

[103]Ibid., p. 215.

[104]Ibid.

[105]Bultmann, History, p. 144.

[106]Some of this material is in Q. Cf. the analysis in SC Syn G p. 92, no. 22.

[107]Cf. Beare, Records, pp. 216f.

apocalyptic collections both Jewish and Christian[108] and, in some cases, also back to Jesus himself.[109] This "tangled skein," as Taylor calls it,[110] is indeed, in Fitzmyer's words "...one of the most difficult parts of the Gospel traditions"[111] to unravel and interpret.

While it is readily apparent and generally conceded that Mark's apocalypse is the basis of that of both Matthew and Luke,[112] they have redacted Mark considerably and added materials taken both from Q and other sources of tradition.[113]

When the various segments of these Synoptic accounts are analyzed by Syntax Criticism, it will be seen that a) only in one instance, Matthew's version of the Parable of the Talents (no. 30), do clear original Greek net frequencies occur; but in this Q section,[114] Luke's version, placed earlier in his Gospel, is clearly translation Greek.

While the Markan material never falls into the clearly translation Greek area, surprisingly in many cases either Matthew or Luke (or both) are a bit more Semitic by the criteria of Syntax Criticism; and in a number of instances one or both of them are translation

---

[108]So Bultmann, History, p. 122, as well as others.

[109]E.g. Fitzmyer, Luke 2 , pp. 1324f. Even Bultmann, ibid, p. 122.

[110]Mark, p. 499.

[111]Ibid., p. 1323. Cf. his detailed survey of studies pp. 1324-26, 1332f.

[112]Cf. e.g. Beare, Records, pp. 216f.

[113]Ibid.

[114]This is the most common view, but other relationships between the Matthean and Lukan forms have also been suggested. Cf. Fitzmyer, Luke 2, pp. 1229-1232, for a survey of various proposals.

60

Greek (cf. nos. 21, 24, 26, 28, 30, 31), reflecting
most probably in these sections either Q or material
taken from other Palestinian traditions, which were
used by them.

B. Material from the Plot to Kill Jesus to His Burial
     These events make up the core of the Passion
narrative which, as is generally agreed, took fixed
shape very early. Beare reflects the overwhelming view
of scholarship when he writes:

> "The Passion Narrative has been transmitted to
> us, apparently from the beginning, not as a number
> of self-contained incidents, but as a coherent
> whole...The basic framework of the story thus
> became fixed in the form of its transmission
> relatively early."[115]

It is, further, agreed that Mark's structure of
the Passion account has basically reproduced the fixed
form of this primitive pre-Markan tradition,[116] and
that Matthew and Luke preserve Mark's order here even
closer than elsewhere.[117] So also does John, though,
as Grant indicates, he "no doubt adheres to it, not
because it is Mark's but because it is the traditional
passion narrative."[118]

---

[115]Records, p. 219. Cf. also e.g. F.C. Grant, The Earliest Gospel (1943), p. 175;
Bultmann, History, p. 275; Brown, John 2, p. 787. Beare concludes, further, "In this
we are in close touch with the earliest traditions of the Church." Ibid., p. 220.

[116]Cf. Beare, ibid., p. 220.

[117]Cf. Grant, Earliest Gospel, p. 175; so also Taylor, Formation of the Gospel
Tradition (1964), p. 45.

[118]Ibid., note 1. Beare gives a succinct summary of the contents of that
primitive account (Records, p. 220) and this is very similar to the proposal of Grant,
which he indicates is "as it is reconstructed by various modern scholars, more or less
(Footnote Continued)

Taylor points out, however, that "it cannot be assumed that Mark merely reproduces the earliest narrative; on the contrary, it is probable that he has modified it and has incorporated additional material into it."[119]

Matthew, as Beare indicates, "follows Mark even more closely in the Passion narrative than in the account of the public ministry."[120]

The case is different, however, with Luke where many scholars see evidence of another tradition being used in addition to Mark.[121]

The relation of John to the primitive pre-Markan Passion tradition, as well as to each of the Synoptics is more complex. Fortna summarizes the current situation among scholars quite well:

> ..."all are agreed that the evangelist was dependent on some earlier literary narrative. There is considerable evidence for supposing that this represents a tradition parallel to but essentially distinct from that underlying

---

(Footnote Continued)
in agreement--notably by Martin Dibelius, Rudolf Bultmann, Hans Lietzmann and others."
Earliest Gospel, pp. 176-179.

[119]Mark, p. 524. He separates the Markan account into 2 types of material--a continuous non-Semitic narrative (A) found by Mark in Rome and a number of inserted sections (B) characterized by "a strong Semitic flavor" (which go back to Peter). Ibid., pp. 564-568. Knox (Sources, Vol. 1, pp. 115ff) also sees two sources behind Mark's account, which agree with Taylor's grouping quite closely in the first half of chapter 14, less so in the rest of Mark's account. Cf. also Brown's detailed study of Taylor's suggestion in John 2, pp. 787-790.

[120]Matthew, p. 499.

[121]So Bultmann, History, p. 279 (which he feels was older than Mark--ibid., p. 280). Taylor holds that "fundamentally the Lukan account of the Passion is Non-Markan, but that Luke added extracts from Mark..." Formation, p. 51. Cf. also Brown, John 2, p. 790. Fitzmyer writes about the Lukan account: "A Palestinian background for some of the material cannot be ruled out." Luke 1, p. 116.

the synoptic passion narratives--even some who elsewhere find direct Johannine dependence on one or more of the earlier gospels here argue for an independent source."[122]

Buse[123] has noted close contacts with Taylor's B stratum of Mark's account, and Brown[124] with both A and B, but concludes that John was "independent of them."

Concerning John's relation to Matthew Brown notes that the investigation is "complicated by the failure of Synoptic criticism to reach a consensus on whether Matthew drew on an independent pre-Gospel tradition for the passion or simply modified Mark."[125] He leaves open the possibility that in some instances there may be contact between John and the Matthean traditions.[126]

As noted earlier many scholars posit an additional Passion source for Luke, and Brown feels the parallels between Luke and John (more than 40, some "too precise to be accidental") are best "explained in terms of John's dependence on an earlier tradition that in many instances was close to the special tradition used by Luke."[127] Taylor agrees with this possibility[128] and remarks: "However impossible it may be to distinguish

---

[122]Gospel of Signs, p. 113. Cf. also Lindars, Behind the Fourth Gospel (1971), p. 19; Kysar, John, p. 265. Bultmann, History, p. 275; John, p. 635; Taylor Formation, p. 53.

[123]Igor Buse, "St. John and the Marcan Passion Narrative" in New Testament Studies, Vol. 4 (1957-58), pp. 215-219.

[124]John 2, p. 790.

[125]Ibid.

[126]Ibid.

[127]Ibid., p. 791.

[128]Formation, p. 53.

between the tradition and its form in the gospel, the
evidence suggests that Ephesus had a passion story of
its own."[129]

Thus, as Taylor suggests, it does seem likely that
there is evidence "of three Passion stories in the
gospels"--Mark's, John's, and Luke's, along with other
traditional material as well.[130]

The complex interweaving of passion traditions
suggested by the survey above is witnessed to by Syntax
Criticism of the Gospel accounts. As Chart XII shows
Mark has clear translation net frequencies only once
(no. 56) and clear original Greek net frequencies three
times (nos. 37, 52, 57) which would seem to reflect
that what he is using is a later stage of the Primitive
Passion Narrative. Matthew has clear translation net
frequencies three times (nos. 49, 52, 57). Luke once
has clear net translation frequencies (no. 39). John
has such two times (nos. 33 and 59) and clear original
net frequencies three times (nos. 47, 52, 54).

No clear pattern emerges in the above materials,
but some of the sections warrant comment.

32. The Plot to Kill Jesus

Matthew is more Semitic than Mark here and John
has clear translation Greek net frequencies. It is
noteworthy that Matthew and John agree in two details
not found in Mark (or Luke)--the mention of Caiaphas
and a meeting of the Sanhedrin;[131] and Matthew (26:4)
adds sunebouleusanto which parallels the simple form of

---

[129]Ibid., p. 54.

[130]Ibid., pp. 55f.

[131]Brown has pointed this out. Cf. John 1, p. 441.

the verb in John 11:53 in sentences that are surprisingly similar. These details (in Matthew's considerable added material) agreeing with John, along with their Semitic net frequencies, suggest that Matthew and John may be using traditional material[132] here, not found in Mark.

34. The Annointing at Bethany

The relation of this story to Luke's Annointing by a Sinful Woman (7:36-50) is uncertain. While neither Mark nor the parallels here are clear translation Greek, Luke's account is (33 lines +1).[133] Beare concludes that Luke's account "may be quite independent in origin."[134] Brown, following Benoit, feels that two separate events occurred, one in Galilee (Luke) and the other in Judea (Mark).[135] Matthew reproduces Mark closely,[136] whereas there seems to be "crisscrossing" of traditions between the Lukan and Johannine forms.[137] Luke's account clearly goes back to a Palestinian Semitic tradition, which may also be reflected in the Johannine similarities to it.

37. Betrayal Foretold

---

[132]Beare disagrees, Records, p. 221; see also Taylor, Mark, p. 529.

[133]Cf. SC Syn G, p. 107, no. 25.

[134]Records, p. 222.

[135]John 1, p. 450 where he has a useful harmony in parallel columns of the Mark, John, and Luke accounts.

[136]Brown, ibid., p. 449. Cf. also Taylor, Mark, p. 530.

[137]Brown, ibid., p. 452. So also, Fitzmyer, Luke 1, p. 685.

There are 3 forms of this tradition reflected here: The Markan account, whose clear original Greek net frequencies would seem to indicate Mark's redaction of his tradition;[138] Luke's, which is quite different and acknowledged by many to evidence a non-Markan tradition;[139] and John's account, generally conceded to be independent of the Synoptics.[140] The Matthean account "follows the Marcan closely."[141]

40. Peter's Denial Foretold

Luke here is quite different than Mark and a number of scholars see evidence of another tradition behind Luke, which agrees to some extent with that found in John[142] whom they consider to be following a tradition independent of Mark also.[143]

Matthew's clear translation Greek net frequencies are surprising. Upon examination they are seen to be the result of his addition of 4 occurences of the preposition en, twice with the passive of

---

[138]Cf. Bultmann, History, p. 276.

[139]So Bultmann, ibid., p. 264, which he calls "a clearly more original form"; Taylor, Mark, p. 540 and Passion, p. 61. Fitzmyer disagrees, considering Luke only to be redacting Mark. Luke, p. 1408. It is significant that the next section in Luke (vv. 24-30) are unique to his gospel and fall deep into the translation Greek area.

[140]Cf. Brown, John 2, p. 576; Bultmann, John, pp. 479-481

[141]Cf. Beare, Records, p. 224; Taylor, Mark, p. 542. Matthew's falling outside the clear original area results partly at least from his redactional additions which have added a few more lines of text.

[142]Fitzmyer, Luke 2, p. 1421. Cf. also Taylor, Passion, p. 65.

[143]Ibid. Cf. also Brown, John 2, p. 615ff and the detailed comparison of the accounts there.

skandalidzo[144] and twice in the phrase "in this
night;"[145] otherwise Matthew follows Mark very
closely.[146]

42. Prayer in Gethsemane

Both Matthew and Luke require comments here.
Matthew has clear translation net frequencies and is a
bit longer than Mark. His more Semitic net frequencies
result from additional personal pronouns which he has
(2 in v. 39 and 2 in v. 42). In addition Matthew has a
number of details not found in Mark[147] and some
agreements with Luke against Mark (cf. Mark 14:35, 36,
37). This suggests Matthew may reflect the use of an
additional tradition here.

The situation posed by the Lukan account is
complex. It is much shorter than Mark (omitting Mark's
verses 33, 34, 35a, 37b, 38b, 39-42), and makes little
use of Mark in the parallel material. Further, vv. 43
and 44 of Luke are textually very uncertain.[148] As
Fitzmyer has noted it is "a matter of no little debate
whether Luke here presents a redacted form of 'Mk' or
has made use of an independent non-Marcan source,"[149]
and concludes, finally, that Luke's form represents

---

[144]There are 2 other occurrences of this in Matthew (11:6 = Q) and 13:57 (taken
over from Mark.)

[145]These are the only occurrences of this phrase in Matthew. Luke has it in 12:20
(his special material) and in 17:34 (in the midst of Q material). It is thus not clear
whether this is Matthew's style or not.

[146]Cf. Beare, Records, p. 229.

[147]Cf. ibid., pp. 229f.

[148]In the calculations for Chart XII these verses were not counted.

[149]Luke, p. 1437.

Lukan redactional activity.[150] Taylor[151] and others[152]
see here a non-Markan, independent source.

Whether verses 43 and 44 were part of Luke's text
originally cannot be decided with certainty. Their
absence from "ancient and widely diversified witnesses"
(such as P75,B) and "their transferral to Matthew's
gospel (after 26:39) by family 13 and several
lectionaries...strongly suggests that they are no part
of the original text of Luke."[153] After a detailed
study Fitzmyer agreed.[154] Metzger concludes that
addition to the Lukan text from "an early source, oral
or written," is more likely than that they were omitted
because of their portrayal of the human weakness which
these verses ascribe to Jesus.[155]

When verses 43-45a are analyzed by Syntax
Criticism, they are seen to fall into the area of
clearly translation Greek (4 lines, -1).[156] This fact
along with Luke's little use of Mark and the agreements
with Matthew in the rest of the account support the

---

[150]Ibid., p. 1438.

[151]Cf. the detailed study in Passion, pp. 69-71. Beare fluctuates, supporting
Lucan redaction in Records (p. 230); but in Matthew (p. 512) he says about Luke's
account: "the scene as a whole appears to be drawn from an independent source."

[152]Cf. e.g. Fitzmyer, Luke 2, p. 1438 for a survey.

[153]Metzger, Textual Commentary, p. 177.

[154]Luke 2, pp. 1443f.

[155]Ibid. So also Fitzmyer, ibid., p. 1443. Beare, Records, p. 230; but he grants
the possibility of omission and Taylor prefers that possibility. Passion, p. 72.

[156]Cf. Appendix 3, no. 2.

view that Luke here, like Matthew had available a
Semitic source in addition to Mark for this account.[157]

43. Betrayal and Arrest of Jesus

Here again Matthew alone falls into the area of
clearly translation Greek and fairly deeply so. This
is due to the addition of the saying in vv. 52-54. If
these verses are removed and analyzed separately, it
will be seen that the logion is close to clear
translation Greek (6 lines, +1) and the rest of the
account (26:47-51, 55, 56) is no longer in the area of
clearly translation Greek but has the same net
frequencies as Mark (16 lines, +3).[158] Beare, on other
grounds, has suggested that at least the saying in v.
52 "may be an independent logion."[159]

47. Peter's Denial of Jesus

John has separated the second and third denials
from the first by means of the questioning by Annas.
If the two scenes of the denial are calculated
separately, 18:15-18 (11 lines, +8) is in the clear
original Greek area, but the last two denials
(18:25-27) are clearly translation Greek (6 lines,
-1).[160]

48-52. Trial Before Pilate

---

[157]It is intriguing to speculate whether the agreements of Matthew and Luke here
against Mark would indicate the presence of this tradition in Q.

[158]Cf. Appendix 3, no. 3.

[159]Records, p. 231.

[160]Cf. Chart X at the end of Chapter I.

Luke in these sections has more net translation
frequencies than any of the other accounts. Taylor
considers Luke to be using a second source here in
addition to Mark.[161] If these are taken together as a
unit, they show up as clear translation Greek (46
lines, +1).[162] This would clarify the character of the
smaller individual units, which are well within the
translation Greek frequencies for units of 4 to 15
lines in length in known translation Greek, (cf. Chart
V in Chapter I).

53. Soldiers Mock Jesus

Matthew is more Semitic than Mark here and, as
Beare notes, "contrary to his custom, he adds details
to the picture."[163] Some of Matthew's more Semitic
criteria result from this added material[164] and some
are due to Matthew's changing Mark's feature to a more
Semitic form.[165] All of this may suggest that Matthew
is using an additional tradition here concerning the
mocking of Jesus.[166]

---

[161]Cf. Passion, pp. 84-89. Fitzmyer agrees with this only concerning 23:6-12 (no.
50 Jesus before Herod). Luke 2, p. 1479. Beare sees only Lukan redaction of Mark.
Records, p. 233-235.

[162]Cf. Appendix 3, no. 4.

[163]Records, p. 236.

[164]E.g. the addition of genitive personal pronouns (v. 29).

[165]Cf. the change to an unseparated article (v. 27), of an attrib. adj. to a prep.
phrase (v. 29) and a genitive personal pronoun from a pre to a post position (v. 30).

[166]It is interesting to note that John 19:2 agrees verbally with Matthew 27:29,
which is Matthew's added material containing many of the more Semitic features noted
above. This agreement may reflect a non-Markan tradition in both cases. Cf. Brown,
John 2, p. 886.

54-56. <u>The Crucifixion of Jesus</u>

This section of the Passion accounts is made up of various kinds of material. Luke has 2 sections which are not paralleled in the other Synoptics (55, 56). Neither of these are clear translation Greek. In parallel material both Matthew and Luke improve Mark's Greek with respect to the 17 criteria of Syntax Criticism. John is in the clearly original Greek area.

Mark for part of the material (56) is clearly translation Greek. If the crucifixion accounts A and B (nos. 54 and 56) are combined in each of the Synoptics, it will be seen that Matthew's and Luke's net frequencies do not change much: Matthew becomes 19 lines with +4 net frequencies and Luke becomes 22 lines with +4 net frequencies; but Mark falls still deeper into the clear translation Greek area (18 lines with -4 net frequencies).[167] This is not surprising since here Mark is dealing with one of the very earliest segments of the primitive Passion account.[168]

C. <u>The Resurrection Accounts</u>

There is no concensus as to whether or not the primitive Passion account included a Resurrection account (whether of the empty tomb or of appearances of the risen Christ);[169] however, Brown is probably

---

[167]Cf. Appendix 3, no. 5.

[168]Taylor has attempted to recover the "primitive narrative" behind Mark's account. He considers it to be Mk. 15:21-4, 26, 29f, 34-7, 39 (<u>Mark</u>, p. 651). If these verses are grouped together and analyzed by the criteria of Syntax Criticism, they are found to have 22 lines and net frequencies of +2 which is just outside the clear translation Greek area (cf. Chart IV in Chapter I). For the percentages and count on these verses cf. Appendix 3, No. 5.

[169]Cf. Brown, <u>John 2</u>, p. 977f.

correct when he notes "it is hard to conceive of a basic Christian narrative that ended with the death and burial "without an explicit assurance of Jesus' victory over death."[170]

As Taylor notes, from earliest times "there was no demand for a continuous story" of the resurrection appearances as there was for a Passion Narrative[171] since single stories is what would be required in early Christian witnessing and proclamation.[172] This would clarify the existence of appearance accounts in both Jerusalem and Galilee,[173] and the impossibility now of arranging the various accounts in any sort of chronological sequence.[174]

Of the various accounts only Mark (61), Luke (68, 69) and John (74, 76, 79) have sections which fall into the clear translation Greek area. In the comments that follow The Visit of the Women to the Empty Tomb (61) will be discussed first, then some of the appearance stories of the various Gospels.

The Visit of Women to the Empty Tomb (61)

The contrast between Mark's account here which is deep into the clear translation Greek area and the other Gospels' accounts of the Empty Tomb is

---

[170]Ibid., p. 978.

[171]Formation, p. 59.

[172]Ibid.

[173]Ibid., pp. 59f.

[174]It helps to clarify also the fact, as Beare notes, that "the form of its telling was not so firmly fixed.... In fact there is no part of the Gospel story that shows less fixity than the accounts of the appearances of the risen Jesus..." Records, p. 220.

striking--Matthew being in the clear original Greek
area and the parallel's in Luke and John nearly so.[175]
In the light of this data Beare's judgment that "what
we have here is a legend of relatively late
growth..."[176] needs modification.

Syntax Criticism of the resurrection accounts
clearly indicates both the empty tomb tradition (61)
and the appearances traditions (68f, 74, 76) have their
roots in the early Palestinian, Aramaic-speaking
Church.

It is customary to consider Paul's use of earlier
tradition of the resurrection appearances in 1 Cor.
15:3b-7 as the earliest witness available;[177] but in
this connection it is good to recall Wilken's caution
against assuming "as though this text [sic][of Paul],
which is the oldest we possess, represented the
earliest stage of the tradition..."[178]

When I. Cor. 15:3b-7 is analyzed by Syntax
Criticism it is found to fall into the area between
clear translation and clear original Greek (6 lines, +3
net frequencies).[179]

The Walk to Emmaus (68, 69)

---

[175]If Luke 24:1-7 and 8-12 are taken together as a single account, it then falls
into the clear original Greek area (23 lines, +10 net frequencies); and John nearly so,
if 20:1-18 is taken as a unit (39 lines, +5 net frequencies). Cf. Appendix 3, no. 6.

[176]Records, p. 241.

[177]So Haenchen, for example, when he says that Paul in I Cor. 15 is quoting "the
earliest tradition we possess on the subject..." John 2, p. 213.

[178]"The Tradition-history of the Resurrection of Jesus" in The Significance of the
Message of the Resurrection for Faith in Jesus Christ. (Studies in Biblical Theology,
2nd Series, No. 8, 1968), p. 57. Cf. also Brown, John 2, pp. 975, 978.

[179]Cf. Appendix 3, no. 6.

Luke here is clearly following a Semitic source since this account falls deeply into the clear translation Greek area.[180]

Jesus Appears to the Ten in Jerusalem (70, 71)

If these 2 sections are counted together, it will be seen that then they also fall into the area of clear translation Greek (24 lines, -1 net frequencies.)[181]

John's Resurrection Appearances

In Chapter 20 there are two units (nos. 74 and 76) that have clear translation Greek frequencies[182] and in John 21 there is one small section (vv. 15-19, no. 79) which does also (15 lines, -3 net translation Greek frequencies).[183] This would indicate that, in contrast to the rest of the material in chapters 20 and 21,

---

[180]This is in contrast to the writer's usual style as can be seen in the second half of Acts (Syn Ev, pp. 87-92).

[181]Cf. Appendix 3, no. 7. Since this combining results in a unit of more lines, the demarcation of original and translation Greek is sharper. For example, if Matt. 28:9-20 is taken as a unit (nos. 64-66), the entire section then falls clearly into the original Greek area (25 lines, +9 net frequencies). Cf. Appendix 3, no. 7.

If in such larger units the net frequencies do not come out clearly as original or translation Greek, this is usually an indication that some of the smaller sub-sections fall clearly into one area or the other; see, for example, the material of John 20: The entire chapter has 70 lines of text and +4 net frequencies (cf. Chart X in Chap. I), which puts it in the middle between clear original and clear translation Greek (cf. Charts IA and IB in Chap. I). Thus it is not surprising when studying the smaller sub units of John 20 to find that 2 of them (nos. 74 and 76) fall into the clear translation Greek area (cf. Chart XII).

[182]Cf. previous note.

[183]If this is taken together with the following related unit (vv. 20-23), the combined section has 25 lines, +2 net frequencies. (Cf. Appendix 3, no. 8). This is in the area occupied only by such subsections of the translation Greek documents studied--cf. Chart IV in Chapter I. This is in sharp contrast to the nearly clear original Greek net frequencies of John 21 as a whole (63 lines, +8 net frequencies)--cf. Chart X and Chart IA in Chapter I.

these sections, at least, clearly reflect a Semitic
Palestinian milieu.

D. Blocks of Johannine Material from Chapters 12-17
    Not Paralleled in the Synoptics

In Chapters 12 to 17 there are larger blocks of
material which do not have any parallel in the Synoptic
Gospels. They are:

12:9-11   The Plot Against Lazarus
12:20-50   The Coming of the Greeks and Subsequent
            Dialogue
13:1-20   The Foot Washing and Subsequent
            Dialogue
13:31-35   The New Commandment
14-17   The Last Discourse

From Chart XIII which follows it will be seen that
the net frequencies for John 12-21 as a whole do not
quite fall into the area of clear translation Greek.
This suggests that these chapters are basically
translation Greek and that when analyzed there will be
some sections that are not.[184]

As was seen earlier when John's parallels to
Synoptic material were analyzed, there were some
sections that were clear original Greek (nos. 47, 52,
54, 81). In addition to that it will be seen further
from Chart XIII that Chaps. 12, 13, and 17 have less
Semitic net frequencies than do chapters 14, 15, and
16, which have clear translation Greek net frequencies.
This suggests that in Chaps. 12, 13, and 17 some of
their small units also will not have clear translation
Greek net

---

[184]Cf. note 181 supra.

CHART XIII

Net Frequencies in John 12-17 Compared to Those of Greek Documents of More Than 50 Lines in Length

	No. of Lines	17	16	15	14	13	12	11	10	9	8	7	6	5	4	3	2	1	0	-1	-2	-3	-4	-5	-6	-7	-8	-9	-10	-11	-12	-13	-14
		Net No. of Frequencies Characteristic of Original Greek																		Net No. of Frequencies Characteristic of Translation Greek													
Plutarch - Selections	325		X																														
Polybius - Bks I,II	192			X																													
Epictetus - Bks III,IV	138	X																															
Bks I,II	349										X																						
Bks I,II,III,IV	487							X																									
Josephus - Selections	215		X																														
Papyri - Selections	630	X																															
II Maccabees 2:13-6:31	495	X																															
Philo - On Creation I-VIII	251							X																									
Hebrews	535		X																														
Acts 15:36-28:31	1056		X																														
John entire	1756																					X											
John 1-11	1024														X																		
John 12-21	732																					X											
Chap 12	96									X																							
Chap 13	76																			X													
Chap 14	63																									X							
Chap 15	54																											X					
Chap 16	66																									X							
Chap 17	54																						X										
John 14-17	237																											X					

	No. of Lines	17	16	15	14	13	12	11	10	9	8	7	6	5	4	3	2	1	0	-1	-2	-3	-4	-5	-6	-7	-8	-9	-10	-11	-12	-13	-14
		Net No. of Frequencies Characteristic of Original Greek																		Net No. of Frequencies Characteristic of Translation Greek													
Genesis 1-4,6,39	382																		X														
1 Samuel 3,4,22	194																								X								
1 Kings 17	58																				X												
2 Kings 13	71																											X					
Dan. - Hebrew - LXX	482																						X										
Hebrew - Theod.	460																											X					
Dan. - Aramaic - LXX	595																						X										
Aramaic - Theod.	634																													X			
Ezra - Hebrew	328																																X
Aramaic	211																											X					
Jer.-Prose A (Chaps 1,3,7,11,16)	201																										X						
Poetic A (Chaps 2,4,5,6,10)	357																																X
Jer.-Prose B (Chaps 33-36)	216																						X										
Poetic B (Chaps 30,31,37,38)	171																						X										
Ezek.-Prose A (Chaps 2-5)	200																																X
Poetic A (Chaps 19,27)	74																										X						
Ezek.-Prose B (Chaps 28,30-32)	203																													X			
Poetic B (Chaps 33-35)	132																											X					
I Maccabees (Chaps 1-5)	732																												X				

frequencies, as will be seen to be the case in the listing in Chart XIV below. Some comments now on items from that listing:

1. The Plot Against Lazarus (12:9-11)

Brown notes that this is transitional and editorial and a bit awkwardly joined in the entry story.[185] As Chart V in Chapter I shows, however, with +4 net frequencies for 6 lines of text, it is still within the pattern of translation Greek texts of the Old Testament and of other such units in the Fourth Gospel.

2-7. The Coming of the Greeks and Subsequent Dialogue (12:2-50)

The individual subsections of this block of material are not consistent with each other in their net frequencies.[186] The material may be grouped as to content into 2 sub groups: 12:20-36a (no. 4) and 12:36b-50 (no. 7).[187] As Chart XIV indicates when the net frequencies for these larger units are calculated, they become nearly clear translation Greek.[188]

8-10 The Footwashing and Subsequent Dialogue (13:1-20)

---

[185]"The result is not entirely a happy one." John 1, p. 459. For percentages see Chart X. Haenchen posits that this story was "already being circulated prior to the Evangelist." John 2, p. 91.

[186]Cf. Chart X.

[187]So Barrett, John, p. vi, for example. Brown (ibid., p. XII) and Bultmann (somewhat! cf. John, pp. ixf) have basically 3 groups 12:20-36; 37-43; 44-50.

[188]For percentages and count see Appendix 3, no. 9. Recall comments earlier in this connection--note 37 supra.

77

CHART XIV
JOHN MATERIAL IN 12-17 NOT PARALLELED IN THE SYNOPTICS

	Locat.	Lines	Net Freq	Clear Orig.						Clear Trans.
1. Plot Against Lazarus	12:9-11	6	+4		X					
2. Coming of the Greeks	12:20-26	15	+4	X						
3. Jesus' Prayer	12:27-36a	20	+2				X			
4. Combined (2,3)	12:20-36a	35	+2				X			
5. The Cause of Unbelief	12:36b-43	11	+7	X						
6. Summary of Jesus' Claims	12:44-50	14	+1				X			
7. Combined (5,6)	12:36b-50	25	+2				X			
8. The Foot Washing	13:1-11	24	+1							X
9. Servants Like Master	13:12-20	16	+1							X
10. Combined (8,9)	13:1-20	40	0						X	
11. The New Commandment	13:31-35	10	-1							X
The Last Discourse (Chaps. 14-17)										
12. The Way, Truth, Life	14:1-14	27	-5							X
13. Promise of Holy Spirit	14:15-24	21	-2						X	
14. The Prepared Place	14:25-31	15	0					X		
15. Combined (12-14)	14:1-31	63	-6							X
16. The True Vine	15:1-10	20	-5							X
17. The Commandment to Love	15:11-17	13	-1					X		
18. The World's Hatred	15:18-25	17	+2					X		
19. Witnesses to Christ	15:26,27	4	+3			X				
20. Combined (16-19)	15:1-27	54	-8							X
21. The Coming Persecution	16:1-4	6	+1					X		
22. Jesus' Departure	16:5-11	12	+3			X				
23. The Spirit's Guidance	16:12-15	8	+4		X					
24. The Disciples' Sorrow	16:16-24	22	0					X		
25. Jesus Comes From God	16:25-33	18	-6							X
26. Combined (21-25)	16:1-33	66	-6							X
27. Combined (18-23)	15:18-16:15	47	0					X		
28. Prayer to Be Glorified	17:1-5	10	+9	X						
29. Prayer for the Disciples	17:6-19	28	-4							X
30. Prayer for the Church	17:20-26	16	-2						X	
31. Combined (28-30)	17:1-26	54	-2				X			
32. Combined (29-30)	17:6-26	44	-6							X

Both the individual sub units as well as their combined total have clear translation Greek net frequencies.[189]

12-32. The Final Discourse (Chapters 14-17)

As Chart XIII indicates these chapters as a whole are among the most Semitic of the entire Gospel, falling deep into the area of clear translation Greek.

When the chapters are considered individually, it will be seen that chapters 14, 15 and 16 individually also fall deep into the clear translation Greek area.[190] Chapter 17, however, does not quite do so.[191] This suggests that in Chapter 17 one or more subsections would perhaps be clear original Greek-- which is the case with 17:1-5 (no. 28).

In Chapter 14 one of the smaller sections (no. 14) is not clear translation Greek, but this falls well within the area of the pattern for units of this size of translated documents from the Old Testament.[192]

An interesting pattern occurs in chapters 15 and 16. Four smaller units (18, 19, 22 and 23), while being in the range of the pattern of translated documents of the Old Testament,[193] are quite different as to their net frequencies than the rest of the units of these two chapters.

---

[189]Cf. Chart X and Appendix 3, no. 10.

[190]Cf. Chart XIII and nos. 15, 20, 26 of Chart XIV. For percentages cf. Chart X.

[191]Cf. Chart XIII; no. 31 of Chart XIV. For percentages see Chart X.

[192]Cf. Chart V and Chart X.

[193]Cf. Chart IV for no. 18 and Chart V for nos. 19, 22, and 23. Cf. Chart X for their percentages.

If the material of 15:18 to 16:15 is grouped
together, for these sections do seem to form a natural
unit,[194] their combined net frequencies fall into the
clear translation Greek area (no. 27).[195]

As noted above chapter 17 as a whole (Chart XIV,
no. 31) does not quite fall into the translation Greek
area. The cause for this is the small unit 17:1-5 (no.
28), which has clear original Greek net frequencies.[196]
If the remaining verses of chapter 17 are analyzed
separately (Chart XIV, no. 32), it will be seen to fall
deeply into the clear translated Greek area.[197]

The section 17:1-5 does seem to be a
self-contained unit,[198] which may be an introductory
expansion of the brief reference to Christ's
pre-existent glory in 17:22.

Conclusion

Once again it is clear, as it was in the case of

---

[194]Cf. Bultmann (John, p. xi) who takes 15:18-16:11 as a unit. Brown (John 2, p.
IX) takes chaps. 15 and 16 together, and 15:18-16:4a as a sub unit under that (ibid.);
Barrett (John, p. vi) makes it 2 units--15:18-27 and 16:1-15.

[195]Cf. note 37 supra. For the percentages and numerical count see Appendix 3, no.
11.

[196]Cf. Chart X for percentages.

[197]For percentages see Appendix 3, no. 12.

[198]Brown notes this possibility but sees vv. 6-8 as being closely connected with
them (John 2, p. 750). In his comment (ibid., p. 751), however, he treats vv. 1-5 as a
unit and says "it is not impossible that [in vv. 1-2 and 4-5] we are dealing with
originally independent sayings." (ibid.). Bultmann treats vv. 1-5 as a separate unit
and says "the real intercession starts with v. 9." He sees vv. 6-8 as the introduction
to the intercession portion. John, p. 497.

John 1-11, that in the Passion section wherever the
Fourth Gospel goes most clearly its own way, there it
is very Semitic by the criteria of Syntax Criticism.
Thus also in the Passion narrative half of the Gospel
the Aramaic-speaking, Palestinian milieu is very
apparent. As has been seen in the foregoing studies so
much of the Fourth Gospel falls into the area of
translation Greek that Burney's conclusion seems
inescapable--that John in its present form goes back to
a written Aramaic gospel.[199]

---

[199]Cf. op. cit., pp. 126f.

CHART XV

Frequency of the 17 Criteria in the Gospel Passion and Resurrection Accounts

Translation Frequencies	No. of lines of Greek text	No. of occur. of en	dia W. gen. (.06-.01)	dia W. all cases (.18-.01)	eis (.49-.01)	kata W. accus. (.18-.01)	kata W. all cases (.19-.01)	Peri w. all cases (.27-.01)	Pros w. dative (.024-.01)	Hupo w. genitive (.07-.01)	No. of occ. of kai for each occ. of de (2.1+)	Percent. of separ. articles (.05-)	No. of dep. gen. post ea. prec. dep. gen. (22+)	No. of lines ea. dep. gen. pers. pronoun (9-)	Lines ea. dep. pers. pron. on anarth. subst. (77-)	No. of prec. attr. adj. for each attr. adj. post position (.35-)	No. of lines ea. attrib. adjec. (10.1+)	No. of lines/each adverb. participle (6+)	No. of dat. not used w. en for ea. occur. (2-)	Tot. no. of transl. Grk. frequencies (17)	Tot. no. of orig. Grk. frequencies	No. of inst. where occ. of criter. are too few to be indic.	Net original Grk. frequencies	Net translat. Grk. frequencies (17)
1. The Triumphal Entry																								
Mk 11:1-11	21	1	-	.33	8.0	-	-	-	-	-	8.5	.08	6	5.3	-	-	21	3.0	1.0	4	4	9		17
Mt 21:1-11	19	3	.33	.33	1.7	-	-	-	-	-	1.1	.11	3.0	19.0	-	1.0	19.0	2.1	1.0	2	9	6	+7	
Lk 19:28-38	19	4	-	.25	.75	-	-	.25	.25	-	1.0	.04	6.0	9.5	-	-	19.0	1.6	.50	4	7	6	+3	
Jn 12:12-19	14	-	-	1	3	-	-	-	-	-	2.0	.05	2.0	14	-	-	14	14	5	3	6	8	+3	
2. Crying Stones																								
Lk 19:39-44	11	2	-	-	-	-	-	-	-	-	8.0	-	7	2.2	11.0	-	11	3.7	1.0	6	2	9		- 4
3. Cursing of the Fig Tree																								
Mk 11:12-14	6	1	-	-	1.0	-	-	-	-	-	.5	.25	2	6.0	-	-	6	1.5	1.0	3	5	9	+2	
Mt 21:18, 19	4	1	-	-	2.0	-	-	-	-	-	4.0	-	-	-	-	-	4	2.0	1.0	2	3	12	+1	
4. Cleansing of the Temple																								
Mk 11:15-19	11	1	1.0	1.0	2.0	-	-	-	-	-	7.0	-	3	11.0	-	-	11	11.0	1.0	4	5	8	+1	
Mt 21:12-17	13	3	-	-	.67	-	-	-	-	-	2.7	.06	2	13	-	-	13	6.5	.67	4	4	9	0	
Lk 19:45-48	6	1	-	-	1.0	1.0	-	-	-	-	1.5	.10	1	-	-	-	6	2.0	.00	1	8	8	+7	
Jn 2:13-17	10	1	-	-	1.0	-	1.0	-	-	-	7	.12	5.0	5.0	-	-	10	5.0	.00	3	5	9	+2	
5. Lesson from the Withered Fig Tree																								
Mk 11:20-26	12	2	-	.50	.50	-	-	-	-	-	5	-	4	4.0	-	-	12	2.4	2.0	4	5	8	+1	
Mt 21:20-22	7	1	-	-	1.0	.50	-	-	-	-	2.0	-	1	-	-	-	7	1.4	.00	1	5	11	+4	

CHART XV

Frequency of the 17 Criteria in the Gospel Passion and Resurrection Accounts

Translation Frequencies	No. of lines of Greek text	No. of occur. of en	dia W. gen. (.06/.01)	dia W. all (.18/.01)	eis (.49-/.01)	kata W. accus. (.18-/.01)	kata W. all (.19-/.01)	Peri w. all cases (.27-/.01)	Pros w. dative (.024/-.01)	Hupo w. genitive (.07/.01)	No. of occ. of kai for each occ. of de (2.1+)	Percent. of separ. articles (.05-)	No. of dep. gen. post ea. prec. dep. gen. (22+)	No. of lines ea. dep. gen. pers. pronoun (9-)	Lines ea. gen. pers. pron. dep. on anarth. subst. (77-)	No. of prec. attr. adj. for each attr. adj. post position (.35-)	No. of lines ea. attrib. adjec. (10.1+)	No. of lines each adverb. participle (6+)	No. of dat. not used w. en for ea. occur. of en (2-)	Tot. no. of transl. Grk. frequencies (17)	Tot. no. of orig. Grk. frequencies	No. of inst. where occ. of criter. are too few to be indic.	Net original Grk. frequencies	Net translat. Grk. frequencies (17)
6. Authority of Jesus Questioned																								
Mk 11:27-33	15	4	-	.25	.25	-	-	-	-	-	8.0	.08	1	15	-	-	15/6.3	5.0	1.3	4	5	8	+1	
Mt 21:23-27	13	4	-	.25	.25	-	-	-	-	-	1.0	-	2	13	-	-	13/8.7	2.2	.75	3	5	9	+2	
Lk 20:1-8	14	4	-	.25	-	-	-	-	-	-	2.0	-	2	14	-	-	14/8.0	2.3	.50	2	5	10	+3	
7. Parable of Two Sons																								
Mt 21:28-32	12	2	-	-	.50	-	-	-	-	-	.43	.06	3	12	-	-	12	2.0	2.5	1	7	9	+6	
8. Parable of Vineyard and Tenants																								
Mk 12:1-12	19	1	-	-	-	-	-	-	-	-	8.0	-	3	19.0	-	.50	13.0	3.2	1.0	3	5	9	+2	
Mt 21:33-46	26	3	-	.33	.33	-	-	.33	-	-	2.0	.03	12	2.9	-	3.0	22.0	4.3	.67	4	7	6	+3	
Lk 20:9-19	24	1	-	-	-	-	-	-	-	-	1.0	.03	4	24.0	-	.50	8.0	2.7	2.0	3	6	8	+3	
9. Parable of the Banquet																								
Mt 22:1-14	26	1	-	-	6.0	-	-	1	-	-	1.3	.15	14.0	2.9	-	2.0	13.0	2.4	2.0	3	6	8	+3	
Lk 14:15-24	22	1	-	1.0	2.0	-	-	.50	-	-	6.5	.00	4.5	7.3	-	-	22.0	3.7	2.0	5	4	8		
10. Paying Taxes to Caesar																								
Mk 12:13-17	12	2	-	-	-	-	-	-	-	-	1.0	.07	6.0	12	-	-	12/6.0	6.0	.4	2	7	8	+5	
Mt 22:15-22	14	2	-	-	.50	-	-	-	-	-	2.5	-	7	7.0	-	-	14	2.8	2.5	3	5	9	+2	
Lk 20:20-26	13	-	-	-	-	-	-	-	-	-	1.3	-	1.7	13.0	-	-	13	3.3	-	1	4	12	+3	

CHART XV

Frequencies of the 17 Criteria in the Gospel Passion and Resurrection Accounts

	No. of lines of Greek text	No. of occur. of en	dia W. gen. (.06-.01)	dia W. all cases (.18-.01)	eis (.49-.01)	kata W. accus. (.18-.01)	kata W. all cases (.19-.01)	Peri W. all cases (.27-.01)	Pros W. dative (.024-.01)	Hupo W. genitive (.07-.01)	No. of occ. of de for each occ. of kai (2.1+)	Percent. of separ. articles (.05-)	No. of dep. gen. post ea. prec. gen. (22+)	No. of lines ea. dep. gen. pers. pronoun (9-)	Lines ea. dep. pers. pron. on anarth. subst. (77-)	No. of prec. attr. adj. for each attr. adj. post position (.35-)	No. of lines ea. attrib. adjec. (10.1+)	No. of lines adverb. participle (6+)	No. of dat. not used w. en for ea. occur. of en (2-)	Tot. no. of transl. Grk. frequencies (17)	Tot. no. of orig. Grk. frequencies	No. of inst. where occ. of criter. are too few to be indic.	Net original Grk. frequencies	Net translat. Grk. frequencies (17)
Translation Frequencies																								
11. Question About the Resurrection																								
Mk 12:18-27	16	3		.33				.33			6.0	.06	7	8.0	8.0		16	3.2	.33	5	5	7	+1	0
Mt 22:23-33	15	4						.25			1.0	.00	9	5.0			15	2.1	1.0	5	4	8		-1
Lk 20:27-40	22	1									.67	.08	4.5	7.3	22.0		22	4.4	3.0	4	5	8		
12. The Great Commandment																								
Mk 12:28-34	10	2						1.0			4		3	10.0		1.0	10.0	2.0		1	5	11	+4	
Mt 22:34-40	7	3									.33	.30	1	7.0		1.0	7.0	3.5		3	6	8	+3	
13. Question About David's Son																								
Mk 12:35-37	5	2				.33					3	.14	1.0				5.0	2.5	.20	3	4	10	+1	
Mt 22:41-45	5	1									.00		1	5.0	5.0		5	1.7	1.0	3	5	9	+2	
Lk 20:41-44	(3)	1									1.0		.50				3	3	.00	2	4	11	(+2)	
14. The Denouncing of the Scribes																								
Mk 12:38-40	6	5									1		2	6.0	18.0	1.0	6.0	.6	.20	4	4	9	+1	
Mt 23:1-10	18	3				.33	.33			.33	.57	.04	2.3	3.0			9.0	18.0	1.0	5	6	6		
Lk 20:45-47	7	4									.00		2	7.0		1.0	7.0	7.0	.25	4	4	9		
15. Various Sins																								
Mt 23:11-36	53	16		.06	.06						.90	.04	12.5	4.0		.00	3.2	16	.56	7	3	7		-4

CHART XV

Frequencies of the 17 Criteria in the Gospel Passion and Resurrection Accounts

Translation Frequencies	Lines of Greek text	No. of occur. of en	dia W. gen. (.06-/.01)	dia W. all (.18-/.01)	eis (.49-/.01)	W. accus. (.18-/.01)	kata W. all (.19-/.01)	Peri w. all (.27-/.01)	Pros w. dative en (.024/-.01)	Hupo w. gen. (.07-/.01)	kai/de (2.1+)	% separ. art. (.05-)	No. dep. post (22+)	pers. pron. dep. gen. (9-)	anarth. subst. (77-)	prec. attr. adj. (.35-)	lines attr. adj. (10.1+)	lines adverb. part. (6+)	dat. not used w. en (2-)	Tot. transl. (17)	Tot. orig.	too few to indic.	Net orig.	Net transl. (17)
16. Lament Over Jerusalem																								17
Mt 23:37-39	5	-	-	-	-	-	-	-	-	-	1	-	2	2.5	-	-	5	5	-	1	4	12	+3	
Lk 13:34,35	5	-	-	-	-	-	-	-	-	-	1.0	.17	1.0	5.0	-	-	5	5	-	1	5	11	+4	
17. Widow's Offering																								
Mk 12:41-44	9	-	-	-	2	-	-	-	-	-	4.0	-	3	3.0	-	-	4.5	3.0	-	2	4	11	+2	
Lk 21:1-4	7	-	-	-	2	-	-	1.0	-	-	.33	.11	2	3.5	-	.50	2.3	7.0	-	2	6	9	+4	
18. Destruction of the Temple Foretold																								
Mk 13:1, 2	5	-	-	-	-	-	-	-	-	-	2	.25	1	-	-	3.0	1.7	5.0	-	-	6	11	+6	
Mt 24:1, 2	5	-	-	-	-	-	2	-	-	-	2.0	-	2	5.0	-	-	5	2.5	-	1	4	12	+3	
Lk 21:5, 6	(3) 1	-	-	-	-	-	2	1.0	-	-	1	-	-	-	-	-	3.0	3.0	3.0	-	5	12	(+5)	
19. Beginning of Woes (A)																								
Mk 13:3-8	11	-	-	-	1	2	-	-	-	-	1.0	.14	4	11.0	-	-	11	5.5	-	1	8	8	+7	
Mt 24:3-8	11	-	-	-	-	2	2	-	-	-	1.0	.10	6	11.0	-	1.0	11.0	2.7	-	1	8	8	+7	
Lk 21:7-11	11	-	-	-	-	1	1	-	-	-	.00	-	1	11.0	-	-	5.5	5.5	-	-	7	10	+7	
20. Beginning of Woes (B)																								
Mk 13:9-13	12	-	1.0	1.0	6.0	-	-	-	-	1.0	4.0	.13	1	12.0	-	-	12.0	12.0	1.0	4	6	7	+2	
Mt 24:9-14	10	-	2.0	2.0	3.0	-	-	-	-	1.0	10.0	.08	3	5.0	-	-	10	10	1.0	4	6	7	+2	
Lk 21:12-19	12	-	.50	1.0	1.0	-	-	-	-	1.0	2.0	-	7	1.7	-	-	12	6.0	1.5	4	5	8	+1	

CHART XV

Frequencies of the 17 Criteria in the Gospel Passion and Resurrection Accounts

Translation Frequencies	No. of lines of Greek text	No. of occur. of en	W. gen. .06- .01	W. all cases (dia) .18- .01	eis .49- .01	W. accus. (kata) .18- .01	W. all cases .19- .01	Peri w. all cases .27- .01	Pros w. dative .024- -.01	Hupo w. genitive .07- .01	No. of occ. of kai for each occ. of de 2.1+	Percent of separ. articles .05-	No. of dep. gen. post ea. prec. gen. 22+	No. of lines ea. dep. gen. pers. pronoun 9.	Lines ea. gen. pers. pron. dep. on anarth. subst. 77-	No. of prec. attr. adj. for each attr. adj. post position .35-	No. of lines ea. attrib. adjec. 10.1+	No. of lines each adverb. participle 6+	No. of dat. not used w. en for ea. occur. of ea. 2-	Tot. no. of transl. Grk frequencies 17	Tot. no. of orig. Grk. frequencies	No. of inst. where occ. of criter. are too few to be indic.	Net original Grk. frequencies	Net translat. Grk. frequencies 17
21. Great Tribulation (A)																								
Mk 13:14-20	11	3	-	.33	1.0	-	-	-	-	-	.75	.10	2	5.5	-	-	11	11.0	.67	4	5	8	+1	1
Mt 24:15-22	11	5	-	.40	.20	-	-	-	-	.40	.67	.00	5	3.7	-	-	5.5	11	.60	5	4	8		2
Lk 21:20-24	11	5	-	-	.60	-	-	-	-	-	5.0	.07	5	5.5	11.0	-	11.0	11.0	.80	6	4	7		
22. Great Tribulation (B)																								
Mk 13:21-23	5	-	-	-	-	-	-	-	-	-	2.0	-	-	-	-	-	5	5	-	-	3	14	+3	
Mt 24:23-25	6	-	-	-	-	-	-	-	-	-	1	-	-	-	-	-	6.0	6	-	1	2	14	+1	3
23. Great Tribulation (C)																								
Mt 24:26-28	5	2	-	-	1.0	-	-	-	-	-	2	-	2	4.0	-	-	5	5	.00	2	3	12	+1	
Lk 17:23, 24	4	1	-	-	-	-	-	-	-	-	-	-	2	-	-	-	4	4	.00	2	5	10	+3	1
24. The Coming of the Son of Man																								
Mk 13:24-27	5	1	-	-	-	-	-	-	-	-	3	.17	3	5.0	-	-	5	5	.00	4	4	9	+2	
Mt 24:29-31	7	1	-	-	-	-	-	-	-	-	5.0	.11	7	2.3	7.0	-	7.0	3.5	.00	6	3	8	+2	3
Lk 21:25-28	7	2	-	-	-	-	-	-	-	-	3.0	-	7	3.5	-	-	7	4.0	1.5	4	3	10	+4	1
25. Lesson of the Fig Tree																								
Mk 13:28-31	7	-	-	-	-	-	-	-	-	-	.00	.11	2	3.5	-	-	7	7.0	-	2	4	11	+2	
Mt 24:32-35	7	-	-	-	-	-	-	-	-	-	.00	.11	2	3.5	-	-	7	7	-	2	4	11	+2	
Lk 21:29-33	8	-	-	-	-	-	-	-	-	-	1.0	.11	2	8.0	-	-	8	4.0	-	1	5	11	+4	

CHART XV

Frequencies of the 17 Criteria in the Gospel Passion and Resurrection Accounts

Translation Frequencies	No. of lines of Greek text	No. of occur. of en	dia W. gen. (.06-.01)	dia W. all cases (.18-.01)	eis (.49-.01)	kata W. accus. (.18-.01)	kata W. all (.19-.01)	Peri w. all (.27-.01)	Pros w. dative (.024-.01)	Hupo w. genitive (.07-.01)	No. of occ. of kai for each occ. of de (2.1⁻)	Percent of separ. articles (.05-)	No. of dep. gen. post ea. prec. (22⁺)	No. of lines ea. dep. gen. pers. pronoun (9.)	Lines ea. gen. dep. pers. pron. on anarth. subst. (77-)	No. of prec. attr. adj. for each attr. adj. post position (.35-)	No. of lines ea. attrib. adjec. (10.1+)	No. of lines each adverb. participle (6+)	No. of dat. not used w. en ea. occur. of en (2-)	Tot. no. of transl. Grk. frequencies (17)	Tot. no. of orig. Grk. frequencies	No. of inst. where occ. of criter. are too few to be indic.	Net original Grk. frequencies	Net translat. Grk. frequencies (17)
26. The Unknown Day and Hour																								
Mk 13:32-37	10	1	-	-	-	-	-	1.0	-	-	.50	-	4	3.3	-	-	10	2.5	1.0	2	5	10	+3	-4
Mt 24:36-44	16	3	-	.33	.33	-	-	.33	-	-	1.3	.00	9	8.0	-	-	16	16.0	.33	7	3	7		
27. Exhortation to Watch																								
Lk 21:34-36	7	2	-	-	-	-	-	-	-	-	.50	-	2.0	-	-	-	7.0	7.0	1.5	3	3	11	0	-3
28. The Faithful or the Unfaithful Servant																								
Mt 24:45-51	12	4	-	-	-	-	-	-	-	-	1.0	.10	8.0	2.0	-	2.0	4.0	6.0	.75	4	5	8	+1	+3
Lk 12:42-46	12	4	-	-	-	-	.50	-	-	-	4.0	.05	7	2.0	-	1.0	6.0	6.0	.50	6	3	8		
29. Parable of the Ten Virgins																								
Mt 25:1-13	21	1	-	-	3.0	-	-	-	-	-	.44	.15	10	3.0	21.0	1.0	21.0	3.0	5.0	3	7	7	+4	+3
30. Parable of the Talents																								
Mt 25:14-30	34	2	-	-	1.5	.50	.50	-	-	-	1.5	.35	14	3.8	-	.83	3.1	2.6	1.0	2	9	6	+7	
Lk 19:11-27	33	4	-	.50	.25	-	-	-	-	-	2.2	.17	8.0	4.7	33.0	.50	5.5	2.4	.75	5	6	6	+1	
31. The Judgment of the Nations																								
Mt 25:31-40	20	3	-	-	-	-	-	-	-	-	3.8	.16	11	3.3	6.7	-	20.0	4.0	1.3	6	3	8	+5	-3
41-46	13	2	-	-	1.5	-	-	-	-	-	7.0	.11	2	13.0	-	.00	4.3	3.3	2.5	2	7	8		

CHART XV

Frequencies of the 17 Criteria in the Gospel Passion and Resurrection Accounts

Translation Frequencies	No. of lines of Greek text	No. of occur. of en	dia W. gen.	dia W. all cases	eis	dia W. accus.	kata W. all cases	Peri W. all cases	Pros W. dative	Hupo W. genitive	No. of occ. of kai for each occ. of de	Percent. of separ. articles	No. of dep. gen. post ea. prec.	No. of lines ea. dep. gen.	Lines ea. gen. pers. pron. dep. on anarth. subst.	No. of prec. attr. adj. for each attr. adj. post position	No. of lines ea. attrib. adjec.	No. of lines each adverb. participle	No. of dat. not used w. en for ea. occur. of en	Tot. no. of transl. Grk. frequencies	Tot. no. of orig. Grk. frequencies	Grk. frequencies No. of inst. where occ. of criter. are too few to be indic.	Net original Grk. frequencies	Net transl. Grk. frequencies
		.06- .01	.18- .01	.49- .01	.18- .01	.19- .01	.27- .01	.024- .01	.07- .01	2.1+	.05-	22+	9-	77-	.35-	10.1+	6+	2-	17				17
32. Jesus Lodges on the Mount of Olives																								
Lk 21:37, 38	(3)	2	-	.50							.50	.29	-			-	3	3.0	.00	1	5	11	(+ 4)	17
33. The Plot to Kill Jesus																								
Mk 14:1, 2	4	2	-	1.0							1.0	-	1	-	-	-	4	4.0	.00	2	4	11	+ 2	
Mt 26:1-5	8	2	-	-							3.0	.06	4	8.0	-	-	8	8	.50	4	4	9	0	
Lk 22:1,2	(3)	-	-	-							1.0	.14	1	-	-	-	3	3	-	1	5	12	(+ 5)	
Jn 11:45-53	18	-	-	3							1.7	.00	1.0	18	-	-	18	18.0	-	3	4	10	+ 1	
34. Annointing at Bethany																								
Mk 14:3-9	15	3	-	1.3							.75	.07	5.0	7.5	15.0	.33	3.8	5.0	1.0	4	6	7	+ 2	
Mt 26:6-13	13	3	-	1.0							.25	.08	5	4.3	13.0	-	6.5	2.2	.67	3	6	8	+ 3	
Jn 12:1-8	16	1	1	2			1				1.4	.16	10	4.0	-	-	8.0	8.0	4	2	8	7	+ 6	
35. Judas' Agreement to Betray																								
Mk 14:10, 11	4	-	-	-							3.0	-	1	-	-	-	4	4.0	-	1	3	13	+ 2	
Mt 26:14-16	4	-	-	1							2	.33	1	-	-	-	4	4.0	-	-	5	12	+ 5	
Lk 22:3-6	6	-	-	-							5.0	.17	1	-	-	-	6	6.0	-	2	4	11	+ 2	
36. Preparations for Passover																								
Mk 14:12-16	12	-	-	2							11	.07	7	3.0	-	-	6.0	6.0	5	3	5	9	+ 2	
Mt 26:17-19	7	-	-	1							1.5	.07	3	3.5	-	-	7	7.0	4.0	2	6	9	+ 4	
Lk 22:7-13	12	1	-	3.0							1.0	-	4	12.0	-	-	12.0	2.4	4.0	1	6	10	+ 5	

CHART XV

Frequencies of the 17 Criteria in the Gospel Passion and Resurrection Accounts

Translation Frequencies	No. of lines of Greek text	No. of occur. of en	dia W. gen. (.06-.01)	dia W. all cases (.18-.01)	eis (.49-.01)	W. accus. (.18-.01)	kata W. all (.19-.01)	Peri w. all cases (.27-.01)	Pros w. dative (.024-.01)	Hupo w. genitive (.07-.01)	No. of occ. of kai for each occ. of de (2.1+)	Percent of separ. articles (.05-)	No. of dep. gen. post ea. prec. (22+)	pers. pronoun dep. gen. No. of lines/ea. (9-)	on anarth. subst. pers. pron. dep. Lines ea. gen. (77-)	adj. post position adj. for each attr. No. of prec. attr. (.35-)	attrib. adjec. No. of lines/ea. (10.1+)	adverb. participle No. of lines/each (6+)	ea. occur. of en used w. en for No. of dat. not (2-)	Tot. no. of transl. Grk. frequencies (17)	Tot. no. of orig. Grk. frequencies	No. of inst. where occ. of criter. are too few to be indic.	Net original Grk. frequencies	Net translat. Grk. frequencies (17)
37. Betrayal Foretold																								
Mk 14:17-21	9	-	1.0	1.0	1	-	1	1.0	-	-	1.0	.08	2	-	-	-	9	3.0	-	-	10	7	+10	
Mt 26:20-25	11	1	1.0	1.0	1	1	1	1.0	-	-	.50	.08	2	11	-	-	11.0	2.2	2.0	2	8	7	+6	
Lk 22:14,21-23	6	1	1	1	-	1	-	-	-	-	.2	.09	2	6.0	-	-	6	.6	-	2	8	7	+6	
Jn 13:21-30	19	1	-	-	3.0	-	-	2.0	-	-	1.5	.00	5	19.0	-	-	19	3.8	2.0	3	6	8	+3	
38. Institution of the Lord's Supper																								
Mk 14:22-26	9	1	-	-	1.0	-	-	-	-	-	.6	-	6	4.5	-	-	9	1.5	-	-	4	10	+1	
Mt 26:26-30	10	1	-	-	2.0	-	-	-	-	-	-	.08	8	3.3	-	-	10	1.3	-	-	7	8	+5	
Lk 22:15-20	13	2	-	-	1.0	-	-	-	-	-	-	.28	5	6.5	-	2.0	6.5	2.2	.50	-	6	8	+3	
I Cor 11:23-26	8	2	-	-	1.0	-	-	-	-	-	1	.33	.00	-	-	4.0	2.0	4.0	.00	-	7	9	+6	
39. Dispute About Greatness																								
Lk 22:24-30	13	5	-	-	-	-	-	-	-	-	.60	.05	8	2.2	6.5	-	13	13.0	.40	7	2	8	-	5
40. Peter's Denial Foretold																								
Mk 14:27-31	8	-	-	1	1	-	-	-	-	-	.67	.14	-	-	-	-	8	8.0	-	1	4	12	+3	
Mt 26:31-35	9	4	-	-	.25	-	-	-	-	-	.00	-	-	-	-	-	9	9.0	.25	3	2	12	-	
Lk 22:31-34	7	-	-	1	2	-	-	1	-	-	.33	-	2	3.5	-	-	7	7.0	-	2	5	10	+3	
Jn 13:36-38	7	-	-	1	-	-	-	1	-	-	.00	-	2	3.5	-	-	7	.7	3	2	5	10	+3	1
41. Purse, Bag and Sword																								
Lk 22:35-38	9	1	-	-	-	-	-	1.0	-	-	.75	-	1	9.0	-	-	9	9	.00	3	4	10	+1	

CHART XV

Frequencies of the 17 Criteria in the Gospel Passion and Resurrection Accounts

Translation Frequencies	No. of lines of Greek text
42. Prayer in Gethsemane	
Mk 14:32-42	22
Mt 26:36-46	24
Lk 22:39-46	11
43. Betrayal and Arrest of Jesus	
Mk 14:43-50	15
Mt 26:47-56	22
Lk 22:47-53	15
Jn 18:1-11	23
44. Young Man Who Fled	
Mk 14:51,52 (3)	
45. Jesus Before the Council (A)	
Mk 14:53-61a	16
Mt 26:57-63a	12
Lk 22:54,55	4
Jn 18:13, 14	4

CHART XV

Frequencies of the 17 Criteria in the Gospel Passion and Resurrection Accounts

Translation Frequencies	No. of lines of Greek text	No. of occur. of en	dia w. gen.	dia w. all cases	eis	kata w. accus.	kata w. all cases	Peri w. all cases	Pros w. dative	Hupo w. genitive	No. of occ. of kai for each occ. of de	Percent. of separ. articles	No. of dep. gen. post ea. prec. gen.	No. of lines ea. dep. pers. pronoun gen.	Lines ea. pers. pron. dep. on anarth. subst.	No. of prec. attr. adj. for each adj. post position	No. of lines ea. attrib. adjec.	No. of lines each adverb. participle	No. of dat. not used w. en for ea. occur. of en	Tot. no. of transl. Grk. frequencies	Tot. no. of orig. Grk. frequencies	No. of inst. where occ. of criter. are too few to be indic.	Net original Grk. frequencies	Net translat. Grk. frequencies
			.06-/.01	.18-/.01	.49-/.01	.18-/.01	.19-/.01	.27-/.01	.024/-.01	.07-/.01	2.1+	.05-	22+	9.	77-	.35-	10.1+	6+	2.	17				17
46. Jesus Before the Council (B)																								
Mk 14:61b-65	9	-	-	-	-	-	-	-	-	-	1.0	.27	2.0	9.0	-	-	9	9.0	3	2	5	10	+3	17
Mt 26:63b-68	10	-	-	-	1	-	1	-	-	-	1.0	-	3	5.0	-	-	10	3.3	-	1	6	10	+5	
Lk 22:63-71	13	-	-	-	2	-	-	-	-	-	.83	-	4	6.5	-	-	13	2.6	-	2	4	11	+2	
Jn 18:19-24	13	3	-	-	-	-	-	1.0	-	-	.50	.07	3	6.5	-	-	13	4.3	1.3	3	5	9	+2	
47. Peter's Denial of Jesus																								
Mk 14:66-72	15	1	-	-	1.0	-	-	-	-	-	3.0	.00	2	15	-	-	15	2.1	1.0	4	4	9	0	
Mt 26:69-75	13	1	-	-	1.0	-	-	-	-	-	1.5	.07	2	13.0	-	-	13	2.6	1.0	2	6	9	+4	
Lk 22:56-62	13	1	-	-	-	-	-	-	-	-	1.5	.11	1	13	-	-	13	1.3	3	1	6	10	+5	
Jn 18:15-18, 25-27	17	1	-	-	1.0	-	1	-	1.0	-	1.0	.07	5	17.0	-	.50	5.7	17.0	4.0	1	9	7	+8	
48. Jesus Brought Before Pilate																								
Mk 15:1-5	9	1	-	-	-	1.0	1.0	-	-	-	1.3	.17	1	-	-	-	9	2.3	-	1	5	12	+5	
Mt 27:1,2,11-14	11	1	-	-	-	1.0	1.0	-	-	1.0	1.7	.13	2	11	-	-	11	3.7	1.0	2	7	8	+5	
Lk 23:1-5	11	-	-	-	-	2	-	1	-	-	.20	.13	3	5.5	-	-	11	1.1	.00	3	5	9	+2	
Jn 18:28-38a	28	-	-	-	6	-	-	-	-	1.0	2.5	.00	3.0	28.0	-	.20	4.7	28.0	3	4	8	5	+4	
49. Death of Judas																								
Mt 27:3-10	11	-	-	1	3	-	-	-	-	-	.67	.13	3	11	-	-	11.0	1.2	3	1	9	7	+8	

CHART XV

Frequencies of the 17 Criteria in the Gospel Passion and Resurrection Accounts

Translation Frequencies	No. of lines of Greek text	No. of occur. of en	dia W. gen. .06-.01	dia W. all cases .18-.01	eis .49-.01	kata W. accus. .18-.01	kata W. all .19-.01	Peri w. all .27-.01	Pros w. dative .024-.01	Hupo w. genitive .07-.01	No. of occ. of kai for each occ. of de 2.1+	Percent. of separ. articles .05-	No. of dep. gen. post. ea. prec. dep. gen. 22+	No. of lines ea. dep. gen. pers. pronoun 9.-	Lines ea. gen. pers. pron. dep. on anarth. subst. 77-	No. of prec. attr. adj. for each attr. adj. post position .35-	No. of lines/ea. attrib. adjec. 10.1+	No. of lines each adverb. participle 6+	No. of dat. not used w. en for ea. occur. of en 2-	Tot. no. of transl. Grk. frequencies 17	Tot. no. of orig. Grk. frequencies —	No. of inst. where occ. of criter. are too few to be indic.	Net original Grk. frequencies	Net translat. Grk. frequencies 17
50. Jesus Before Herod																								
Lk 23:6-12	15	5	-	.20	-	-	-	.20	-	.20	.80	.13	2	15.0	-	.50	5.0	1.7	.60	2	9	6	+7	
51. Jesus Sentenced to Die (A)																								
Lk 23:13-17	7	1	-	-	-	-	1.0	-	-	-	2.0	-	-	-	-	-	7	2.3	2.0	1	4	12	+3	
52. Jesus Sentenced to Die (B)																								
Mk 15:6-15	16	1	-	1.0	-	1.0	1.0	-	-	-	.22	.27	2	16	-	-	16	2.7	6.0	1	9	7	+8	
Mt 27:15-26	23	-	-	2	-	2	2	-	-	-	.09	.17	3	7.7	-	-	23.0	2.3	6	2	8	7	+6	
Lk 23:18-25	13	3	-	.67	.33	-	.50	-	-	-	.25	.15	4	4.3	-	-	13.0	2.6	1.3	4	5	8	+1	
Jn 18:38b-40; 19:4-16a	38	4	-	.25	.50	.25	.50	-	-	-	1.7	.16	6	19.0	-	3.0	12.7	6.3	2.0	3	9	5	+6	
53. Soldiers Mock Jesus																								
Mk 15:16-20	9	1	-	-	-	-	-	-	-	-	10.0	.14	1.0	-	-	1.0	9.0	4.5	5	1	6	10	+5	
Mt 27:27-31	11	1	-	-	4.0	-	-	-	-	-	8.0	-	1.0	2.8	-	-	11.0	1.8	3.0	3	4	10	+1	
Jn 19:1-3	5	-	-	-	-	-	-	1	-	-	4	-	1.0	-	-	-	5.0	5.0	-	1	3	13	+2	
54. Crucifixion of Jesus (A)																								
Mk 15:21-26	8	-	-	-	1	-	-	-	-	-	3.5	.14	7.0	2.7	-	1.0	8.0	8.0	-	3	4	10	+1	
Mt 27:32-37	8	-	-	-	1	-	-	-	-	-	2.0	-	5.0	2.0	-	-	8	1.3	-	1	5	11	+4	
Lk 23:26,32-38	14	-	-	1	1	-	-	-	-	-	.43	.13	2.0	14	-	-	14.0	3.5	6	1	6	10	+5	
Jn 19:16b-24	21	-	-	1	1	-	-	1	-	-	1.0	.07	6.0	21.0	-	1.0	21.0	10.5	6	2	10	5	+8	

CHART XV

Frequencies of the 17 Criteria in the Gospel Passion and Resurrection Accounts

Translation Frequencies	No. of lines of Greek text	No. of occur. of en	dia W. gen.	dia W. all cases	eis	kata W. accus.	kata W. all cases	Peri W. all cases	Pros W. dative	Hupo W. genitive	No. of occ. of kai for each occ. of de	Percent. of separ. articles	No. of dep. gen.	No. of lines ea. post ea. prec. dap. gen.	No. of lines ea. pers. pronoun dap. gen.	Lines ea. gen. pers. pron. dep. on anarth. subst.	No. of prec. attr. adj. for each attr. adj. post position	No. of lines ea. attrib. adjec.	No. of lines each adverb. participle	No. of dat. not used w. en for ea. occur. of en	Tot. no. of transl. Grk. frequencies	Tot. no. of orig. Grk. frequencies	No. of inst. where occ. of criter. are too few to be indic.	Net original Grk. frequencies	Net translat. Grk. frequencies
			.06-.01	.18-.01	.49.01	.18-.01	.19-.01	.27-.01	.024-.01	.07-.01	2.11-	.05-	22+	9-	77-	.35-	10.1+	6+	2-	17				17
55. Women Weeping																								
Lk 23:27-31	8	3	-	-	-	-	-	-	-	-	.00	.14	3	8.0	-	1.0	8.0	8.0	.33	4	5	8	+2	+1
56. Crucifixion of Jesus (B)																								
Mk 15:27-32	10	1	-	-	-	-	-	-	-	-	.3 1.0	-	2	5.0 11	10.0	-	10	2.5	2.0	5	3	9	+6	
Mt 27:38-44	11	1	-	-	1.0	-	-	1.0	-	-	1.0	.18	2 1.0	-	-	-	11	5.5	2.0	3	5	9	+9	-1
Lk 23:39-43	8	3	-	-	1.0	-	-	-	-	-	.67	.29	2	8.0	-	-	3	2.7	.33	3	5	9	+5	2
57. Death of Jesus																								
Mk 15:33-41	16	2	-	-	1	-	-	-	-	-	1.5	.20	2.0	16.0	16.0	.00	5.3	1.6	3.0	2	8	7	+5	
Mt 27:45-51;56	18	1	-	-	-	-	-	-	-	-	.29	.33	1.3	18	-	-	9.0	1.5	5.0	1	9	8	+8	
Lk 23:44-49	11	-	-	-	-	-	-	-	-	-	1.0	.06	1	11	-	-	11.0	1.6	3	1	6	10	+5	
Jn 19:25-30	12	-	-	-	-	-	-	-	-	-	2.0	.00	4.0	3.0	-	-	12.0	2.4	3	3	5	9	+2	
58. Earthquake																								
Mt 27:51b-53	4	-	-	-	1	-	-	-	-	-	6	.29	2	4.0	-	1.0	4.0	4.0	-	2	6	9	+4	
59. Burial of Jesus																								
Mk 15:42-47	13	1	-	-	-	-	-	-	-	-	3.5	.18	4	13	-	1.0	3.0	1.9	2.0	4	5	8	+1	
Mt 27:57-61	9	3	-	-	-	-	-	-	-	-	1.5	.13	1.0	-	-	.67	1.8	2.3	1.0	2	6	9	+4	
Lk 23:50-56	12	1	.50	-	-	-	-	-	-	-	2.5	-	6	6.0	-	.00	4.0	3.0	5.0	4	4	9	+4	
Jn 19:31-42	27	4	-	-	-	-	-	-	-	-	2.0	.05	2.0	27.0	-	1.0	13.5	9.0	1.0	4	5	8	+1	0

CHART XV

Frequencies of the 17 Criteria in the Gospel Passion and Resurrection Accounts

Translation Frequencies	No. of lines of Greek text	No. of occur. of en	dia W. gen. (.06-.01)	dia W. all (.18-.01)	eis (.49-.01)	kata W. accus. (.18-.01)	kata W. all (.19-.01)	Peri W. all (.27-.01)	Pros W. dative (.024-.01)	Hupo W. genitive (.07-.01)	No. of occ. of kai for each occ. of de (2.1+)	Percent. of separ. articles (.05-)	No. of dep. gen. post ea. prec. gen. (22+)	No. of lines/ea. dep. gen. pers. pronoun (9-)	Lines ea. gen. pers. pron. dep. on anarth. subst. (77-)	No. of prec. attr. adj. for each attr. adj. post position (.35-)	No. of lines/ea. attrib. adjec. (10.1+)	No. of lines each adverb. participle (6+)	No. of dat. not for en w. pasn ea. occur. of en (2-)	Tot. no. of transl. Grk. freq. (17)	Tot. no. of orig. Grk. freq.	No. of inst. where occ. of criter. are too few to be indic.	Net original Grk. freq.	Net translat. Grk. freq. (17)
60. Guard at the Tomb																								
Mt 27:62-66	11	-	-	-	-	-	-	-	-	-	.50	.22	1	11.0	-	1.0	11.0	2.8	-	1	6	10	+5	17
61. Women Visit the Empty Tomb																								
Mk 16:1-8	17	1	-	-	2.0	-	-	-	-	-	8.0	.00	4	17.0	-	-	17.0	2.4	2.0	4	4	9	+6	
Mt 28:1-8	16	1	-	-	2	-	-	-	-	-	1.5	.06	8	3.2	-	.50	5.3	3.2	-	1	7	9	+7	
Lk 24:1-7	14	3	-	.33	.67	.33	.33	.33	-	-	.50	.16	4	14	-	-	14.0	2.0	1.7	2	9	6	+5	
Jn 20:1,2	6	-	-	-	1	-	-	-	-	-	4.0	.20	1	-	-	1.0	3.0	3.0	-	1	6	10		
62. Mark's Longer Addition																								
Mk 16:9-20	24	3	.33	.33	1.0	-	-	1	-	.33	1.3	.19	4	12.0	-	-	24.0	1.8	3.7	1	10	6	+9	
63. Mark's Shorter Addition																								
	4	1	1	1	-	-	-	1	-	-	.00	.33	1	-	-	3.0	1.3	.4	-	-	9	8	+3	
Matthew's Resurrection Events																								
64. 28:9,10	5	1	-	-	1	-	-	-	-	-	3.0	-	1.0	5.0	-	1.0	5	2.5	3	2	5	10	+3	
65. 11-15	10	-	-	-	1	-	-	-	-	-	2.0	.08	2	10.0	-	1.0	5.0	1.3	-	-	8	9	+8	
66. 16-20	10	1	-	-	3.0	-	-	-	-	-	1.5	.14	4	10	-	1.0	10.0	1.7	2.0	1	8	8	+7	

CHART XV

Frequencies of the 17 Criteria in the Gospel Passion and Resurrection Accounts

Translation Frequencies	No. of lines of Greek text	No. of occur. of en	dia W. gen.	dia W. all cases	eis	W. accus.	kata W. all	Peri W. all cases	Pros W. dative	Hupo W. genitive	No. of occ. of kai for each occ. of de	Percent. of separ. articles	No. of dep. gen. post ea. prec. gen.	No. of lines ea. dep. gen. pers. pronoun	Lines ea. gen. pers. pron. dep. on anarth. subst.	No. of prec. attr. adj. for each attr. adj. post position	No. of lines ea. attrib. adjec.	No. of lines each adverb. participle	No. of dat. not used w. en for ea. occur. of en	Tot. no. of transl. Grk. frequencies	Tot. no. of orig. Grk. frequencies	No. of inst. where occ. of criter. are too few to indic.	Net original Grk. frequencies	Net translat. Grk. frequencies
			.06-/.01	.18-/.01	.49-/.01	.18-/.01	.19-/.01	.27-/.01	.024/.01	.07-/.01	2.1⁺	.05-	22⁺	9-	77-	.35-	10.1⁺	6⁺	2-	17				17
Luke's Resurrection		Events																						
67. 24:8-12	9	-	-	-	-	-	-	-	-	-	3.5	.15	2	9.0	-	1.0	9.0	2.3	4	2	6	9	+4	-
68. 13-27	32	6	-	-	.50	-	-	.50	-	-	2.2	.03	7	8.0	-	1.0	16.0	4.6	1.7	5	5	7	0	- 4
69. 28-35	16	5	.50	.50	.40	-	-	-	-	-	12.0	.00	2.0	5.3	12.0	-	16	2.5	1.2	6	2	9	0	0
70. 36-43	12	2	-	-	-	-	-	-	-	-	1.5	-	4.0	3.0	-	-	12.0	1.7	1.0	4	4	9		
71. 44-49	12	2	-	.50	.50	-	-	.50	-	-	1.0	.13	7.0	4.0	-	-	12	6.0	2.5	3	6	8	+3	3
72. 50-53	6	2	.50	.50	1.0	-	-	-	-	-	5.0	-	1	6.0	-	-	6.0	3.0	.00	3	6	8	+3	3
John's Resurrection		Events																						
73. 20:3-10	13	-	-	-	5	-	-	-	3.0	-	8.0	.17	1	13.0	-	3.0	4.3	2.2	-	1	7	9	+6	3
74. 11-18	20	1	-	-	2.0	-	-	-	-	-	3.5	-	7	3.3	6.7	-	20.0	2.9	5.0	4	5	8	+1	-
75. 19-23	10	1	-	1	1	-	-	-	-	-	5	.04	2	1.0	-	1.0	10.0	2.0	5	1	7	8	+6	3
76. 24-29	16	1	-	-	4.0	1	1	-	-	-	4.0	-	12.0	1.6	-	1.0	16.0	16.0	1.0	6	3	9	+3	-
77. 30, 31	5	2	-	-	-	-	-	-	-	-	.8	-	3	2.5	-	-	5.0	5.0	.00	3	5	8	+2	-
78. 21:1-14	33	1	-	-	6.0	-	-	-	-	-	2.5	.04	8	33.0	-	2.0	16.0	4.1	5.0	2	1	8	+5	3
79. 15-19	15	1	-	-	-	-	-	-	-	-	.50	-	7	3.8	-	-	11.0	7.5	-	4	6	12	-	-
80. 20-23	10	1	-	-	1.0	-	-	1	-	-	1.0	.17	1	10.0	-	-	15	3.3	1.0	1	1	10	+5	3
81. 24, 25	5	-	.50	-	-	1	1	1	-	-	1.0	-	.00	-	-	-	10	5	-	-	8	9	+8	-

CHAPTER III

The Johannine and Catholic Epistles

The Johannine Epistles

There is no general consensus on the relationship
of the Johannine Epistles to one another or to the
Fourth Gospel. Caird[200] has summarized the various
proposals well, indicating that some consider all to be
by the same writer;[201] others consider only the Gospel
and I John to have the same author;[202] some would
associate also II John with them;[203] and still others
propose one author for the Gospel and another for all 3
letters.[204] Caird concludes: "Amid this welter of
conflicting theories it is possible to make one
statement that will command universal agreement--that
the authorship of the Johannine letters is still very
much an open question.[205]

As Charts XVI and XIX below show, while both 1
John and 2 John fall deeply into the translation Greek

---

[200]"John, Letters of," IDB, Vol. 2, pp. 951f. Cf. detailed study in Brown,
Epistles, pp. 14-30.

[201]Cf. e.g. W. Kümmel, Introduction to the N.T. (1975), p. 450.

[202]Cf. Brooke, Epistles, p. lxxvii.

[203]E.g. Dodd distinguishes 3 John from the others: "...it is not profitable to
attempt any connection between 3 John and the other Johannine epistles. It remains an
isolated item..." Epistles, p. lx. Cf. also references in Brown, Epistles, pp. 15f.

[204]Cf. e.g. Bultmann, Epistles, p. 1; Brown, Epistles, p. 30.

[205]Op. cit., p. 952.

CHART XVI
Epistle Net Frequencies Compared to Those of Greek
Documents of More Than 50 Lines in Length

	No. of Lines	Net No. of Frequencies Characteristic of Original Greek																		Net No. of Frequencies Characteristic of Translation Greek													
		17	16	15	14	13	12	11	10	9	8	7	6	5	4	3	2	1	0	-1	-2	-3	-4	-5	-6	-7	-8	-9	-10	-11	-12	-13	-14
Plutarch - Selections	325		X																														
Polybius - Bks I,II	192			X																													
Epictetus - Bks III,IV	138	X																															
Bks I,II	349									X																							
Bks I,II,III,IV	487							X																									
Josephus - Selections	215		X																														
Papyri - Selections	630	X																															
II Maccabees 2:13-6:31	495	X																															
Philo - On Creation I-VIII	251									X																							
Hebrews	535		X																														
Acts 15:36-28:31	1056		X																														
Gospel of John	1756																				X												
John 14-17	237																							X									
1 John	236																										X						
James	211																				X												
1 Peter	196								X																								
2 Peter	145														X																		
Jude	62								X																								

	No. of Lines	Net No. of Frequencies Characteristic of Original Greek																		Net No. of Frequencies Characteristic of Translation Greek													
		17	16	15	14	13	12	11	10	9	8	7	6	5	4	3	2	1	0	-1	-2	-3	-4	-5	-6	-7	-8	-9	-10	-11	-12	-13	-14
Genesis 1-4,6,39	382																				X												
1 Samuel 3,4,22	194																										X						
1 Kings 17	58																							X									
2 Kings 13	71																											X					
Dan. - Hebrew - LXX	482																										X						
Hebrew - Theod.	460																									X							
Dan. - Aramaic - LXX	595																										X						
Aramaic - Theod.	634																											X					
Ezra - Hebrew	328																												X				
Aramaic	211																																X
Jer.-Prose A (Chaps 1,3,7,11,16)	201																										X						
Poetic A (Chaps 2,4,5,6,10)	357																									X							
Jer.-Prose B (Chaps 33-36)	216																																X
Poetic B (Chaps 30,31,37,38)	171																							X									
Ezek.-Prose A (Chaps 2-5)	200																							X									
Poetic A (Chaps 19,27)	74																																X
Ezek.-Prose B (Chaps 28,30-32)	203																										X						
Poetic B (Chaps 33-35)	132																											X					
I Maccabees (Chaps 1-5)	732																										X						

area,[206] 3 John falls just as deeply into the original
Greek area (Chart XIX).

Further, from those charts it can be seen that the
net frequencies of 1 and 2 John are more Semitic than
those of the Fourth Gospel as a whole, but similar to
those of some parts of that Gospel, e.g. particularly
chapters 14-17, the Final Discourse.

Chart XVII below shows that many of the smaller
sections of 1 John and 2 John fall into the clear
translation Greek area, whereas one of 3 John's smaller
units (vv. 13-15) falls into the clearly original Greek
area.

Further, it will be seen from Charts XVIII, XIX,
and XX that the pattern of net frequencies of the
smaller subsections of 1 and 2 John correspond to the
pattern of such smaller units of translated writings in
the Old Testament, and from Chart XX that all of the
smaller sub-units of 3 John correspond to the pattern
of such smaller units of the original Greek documents
studied.

All of this would seem to indicate that 3 John
has, indeed, as Dodd and others have suggested,[207] a
different origin than 1 and 2 John. This is not
surprising since, as has been frequently noted, 3 John
alone is "a true letter" while 1 and 2 John are more on
the order of church treatsies.[208]

---

[206]This accords with Beyer's statistics as indicated by Brown (Epistles, p. 24)
where he notes that "...I and II John have the highest percentage of Semitisms per page
in the N.T...". For the percentages on which the net frequencies for these charts and
subsequent ones concerning the Johannine Epistles see Chart XXV at the end of this
chapter and for the numerical count see Appendix 4.

[207]Cf. note 203 supra.

[208]Cf. Koester, Introduction, Vol. 2, p. 195. So also Bultmann, Epistles, pp. 1f.
(Footnote Continued)

CHART XVII
CLASSIFICATION OF MATERIAL IN 1,2,3 JOHN

	Locat.	Lines	Net Freq	Clear Orig.		Clear Trans.
1 John						
The Word of Life	1:1-4	10	+1		X	
God Is Light	1:5-10	14	-6			X
Christ Our Advocate	2:1-6	12	-2		X	
The New Commandment (A)	2:7-11	11	-3		X	
(B)	2:12-14	7	+2		X	
(C)	2:15-17	7	-2		X	
The Antichrist (A)	2:18-25	18	-2			X
(B)	2:26,27	5	+3	X		
Obedience in Action (A)	2:28,29	4	+1		X	
(B)	3:1-3	7	+2		X	
(C)	3:4-10	16	-7			X
Love in Action	3:11-18	17	-6			X
Confidence before God	3:19-24	13	-5			X
Test the Spirits	4:1-6	15	-4			X
The Source of Love (A)	4:7-12	13	-4			X
(B)	4:13-16a	7	-3		X	
(C)	4:16b-21	14	-3			X
Victory through Faith	5:1-5	11	-6			X
Witness about the Son	5:6-12	15	-1		X	
Certainties of Faith (A)	5:13-15	6	+4	X		
(B)	5:16,17	5	+2		X	
(C)	5:18-21	9	+1		X	
Larger Units (A)	1:5-2:27	74	-8			X
(B)	2:28-5:12	132	-9			X
(C)	5:13-21	20	-2			X
2 John						
Salutation	1-3	7	0		X	
Counsel and Warnings	4-11	17	-2			X
Conclusion	12,13	4	+4	X		
3 John						
Salutation	1-4	7	+5	X		
Encouragement for Gaius	5-8	6	+4		X	
Reproof for Diotrephes	9,10	6	+3		X	
Praise for Demetrius	11,12	5	+4		X	
Conclusion	13-15	4	+8	X		

While most consider 1 John to be a unity,[209]
Bultmann holds the view that "a prior written Source
(Vorlage) underlies the text of 1 John, which the
author annotated."[210] He finds this is 1:5-2:27 and
further considers 5:14-21 to have been added by a later
redactor.[211] If the three main sections of 1 John are
analyzed by Syntax Criticism, they all show up as clear
translation Greek, as can be seen at the end of the 1
John listing in Chart XVII.[212] This would make it
unlikely that 5:13-21 are the work of a later redactor
and further that 1 John is probably best understood as
a unity. The translation Greek net frequencies of 1
and 2 John certainly imply a Palestinian
Aramaic-speaking milieu.

James

While there is uncertainty concerning the author
and nature of the language of the Letter of James, it
is generally agreed that it has its roots in
Palestinian Jewish Christianity[213] and that it is

(Footnote Continued)
Kummel, however, considers 2 John also to be a "real" letter, but "addressed to a
community", Introduction, pp. 446f.

[209]Cf. e.g. Kummel, Introduction, pp. 45 and 440; Brown, Epistles, pp. 36ff.

[210]Epistles, p. 2.

[211]Ibid.

[212]For the percentages of these units see the end of Chart XXV for the Johannine
Epistles at the end of this chapter; the numerical count is found in Appendix 4 at the
end of "Numerical Summary II and III John." Note also that this larger unit 5:13-21
clarifies the net frequencies of the smaller sub units in that listing (5:13-15; 16,
17; 18-21) as clearly translation Greek.

[213]Cf. Koester, Introduction 2, p. 157; Martin, James, pp. 11f.

CHART XVIII
Epistle Net Frequencies Compared with Those of Greek
Documents of 31 to 50 Lines in Length

Name	No. of Units	17	16	15	14	13	12	11	10	9	8	7	6	5	4	3	2	1	0	-1	-2	-3	-4	-5	-6	-7	-8	-9	-10	-11	-12	-13	-14
		\<--- Original Greek ---\>																	\<--- Translation Greek ---\>														
Plutarch - Selections	4						3	1																									
Polybius - Books I,II	3							1	1	1																							
Epictetus - Bks III,IV	2					1			1																								
Bks I,II	2										1		1																				
Bks I,II,III,IV	4				1				1	1		1																					
Josephus - Selections	1							1																									
Papyri - Selections	3					1			1		1																						
II Maccabees 2:13-6:31	2			1			1																										
Philo - On Creation I-VIII	4					2				1	1																						
Hebrews	5		1		1	1				1	1																						
Acts 15:36-28:31	2									1	1																						
1 John	2																									1		1					
2 John	-																																
3 John	-																																
James	4														1	1	1											1					
1 Peter	4							1	1	1		1																					
2 Peter	2										1				1																		
Jude	-																																

Name	No. of Units	17	16	15	14	13	12	11	10	9	8	7	6	5	4	3	2	1	0	-1	-2	-3	-4	-5	-6	-7	-8	-9	-10	-11	-12	-13	-14
		\<--- Original Greek ---\>																	\<--- Translation Greek ---\>														
Genesis 1-4,6,39	4																			1	1		2										
1 Samuel 3,4,22	--																																
1 Kings 17	--																																
2 Kings 13	--																																
Dan. - Hebrew - LXX	1																1																
Hebrew - Theod.	1																								1								
Dan. - Aramaic - LXX	--																																
Aramaic - Theod.	--																																
Ezra - Hebrew	3																						1		1	1							
Aramaic	2																					1			1								
Jer. - Prose A	2																					1											1
Poetic A	1																															1	
Prose B	2																			1										1			
Poetic B	4																1					1	1	1									
Ezek. - Prose A	1																															1	
Poetic A	--																																
Prose B	--																																
Poetic B	--																																
I Maccabees 1-5	--																																

CHART XIX
Epistle Net Frequencies Compared with Those of Greek Documents of 16 to 30 Lines in Length

Name	No. of Units	Net No. of Frequencies Characteristic of Original Greek																	Net No. of Frequencies Characteristic of Translation Greek													
		17	16	15	14	13	12	11	10	9	8	7	6	5	4	3	2	1	0	-1	-2	-3	-4	-5	-6	-7	-8	-9	-10	-11	-12	-13	-14
Plutarch - Selections	7						1	1		1	1			2		1																	
Polybius - Books I,II	5							1	2	1	1																						
Epictetus - Bks III,IV	5							1		1	1	1	1																				
Bks I,II	10									1	1	2		3	3																		
Bks I,II,III,IV	15							1		2	2	3	1	3	3																		
Josephus - Selections	5								1			3		1																			
Papyri - Selections	12							2	2	3	3	1			1																		
II. Maccabees 2:13-6:31	15				3		5		5	1	1																						
Philo - On Creation I-VIII	4							1				1	1	1																			
Hebrews	9					1			1	2	2	1		1																			
Acts 15:36-28:31	27				1	1	1	2	3	3	8	2	2	1	3																		
1 John[1]	4																			1			1	2									
2 John[1]	2																			1		X											
3 John[1]	1				X																												
James	4								1						2		1																
1 Peter	3							1			1			1																			
2 Peter	4									1		1	2																				
Jude	1							1																									

1. X indicates the net frequencies of the letter as a whole.

Name	No. of Units	Net No. of Frequencies Characteristic of Original Greek																	Net No. of Frequencies Characteristic of Translation Greek													
		17	16	15	14	13	12	11	10	9	8	7	6	5	4	3	2	1	0	-1	-2	-3	-4	-5	-6	-7	-8	-9	-10	-11	-12	-13	-14
Genesis 1-4,6,39	5															1		2	1			1										
1 Samuel 3,4,22	4																	1	1	2												
1 Kings 17	--																															
2 Kings 13	1																	1														
Dan. - Hebrew - LXX	6														1		2	2	1													
Hebrew - Theod.	4																	2				2										
Dan. - Aramaic - LXX	10											1	1	2		3		1		1			1									
Aramaic - Theod.	13												1		1	2	1	3	2		1	1	1									
Ezra - Hebrew	10																			1	1	5		2								
Aramaic	7															1		1	1	2	2											
Jer. - Prose A	5																	2	1		1	1										
Poetic A	3																			1	1	1										
Jer. - Prose B	1																	1														
Poetic B	1													1																		
Ezek. - Prose A	4															1	1			1	1											
Poetic A	3																	1						2								
Ezek. - Prose B	6															2	1		1		1	1										
Poetic B	3																				1	1	1									
1 Maccabees 1-5	13														1		2	2	1	2		2	1	1		1						

CHART XX
Epistle Net Frequencies Compared with Those of Greek Documents of 4 to 15 Lines in Length

Name	No. of Units	17	16	15	14	13	12	11	10	9	8	7	6	5	4	3	2	1	0	-1	-2	-3	-4	-5	-6	-7	-8	-9	-10	-11	-12	-13	-14
		Net No. of Frequencies Characteristic of Original Greek																		Net No. of Frequencies Characteristic of Translation Greek													
Plutarch - Selection	49								1	5	3	6	12	8	4	6	2	2															
Polybius - Bks I,II	12							1	3	2	1	2	3																					
Epictetus - Bks III,IV	2							1							1																			
Bks I,II	30										3	2	4	5	7	5	2	1	1														
Bks I,II,III,IV	32									1	3	2	4	5	7	6	2	1	1														
Josephus - Selections	22											1	2	3	3	6	6	1															
Papyri - Selections	75							2	1	2	5	7	16	9	13	12	2	2	3	1													
II Maccabees 2:13-6:31	8				1	1	1	1	1	3		1																					
Philo - On Creation I-VIII	30										4	4	8	5	3	4		1	1														
Hebrews	46								2	5	1	5	3	6	7	4	6	4	1	2													
Acts 15:36-28:31	36								2	1	2	3	9	7	7	3	2																
1 John	19														1	1	3	3		1	2	3	2	1	2								
2 John	2																1				1												
3 John	5												1				1	2	1														
James	17													1			2	4	2	4	1	3											
1 Peter	17							1	2	1	2	1			2	2	4	1		1													
2 Peter	7												2			1	1	2	1														
Jude	5															2	2	1															

Name	No. of Units	17	16	15	14	13	12	11	10	9	8	7	6	5	4	3	2	1	0	-1	-2	-3	-4	-5	-6	-7	-8	-9	-10	-11	-12	-13	-14
		Net No. of Frequencies Characteristic of Original Greek																		Net No. of Frequencies Characteristic of Translation Greek													
Genesis 1-4,6,39	13															2	3	2		3		3											
1 Samuel 3,4,22	12																1	1	5				1	2	2								
1 Kings 17	5																1	1	1	1		1											
2 Kings 13	5																		1		1	1	1	1									
Dan. - Hebrew - LXX	35											1			1	3	2	5		7	8	4	3	1									
Hebrew - Theod.	37															2	3	3		2	7	8	10	2									
Dan. - Aramaic - LXX	38									1	1			3	4	3	4	6		3	6	4	2		1								
Aramaic - Theod.	36													2	5	1	4			6	3	6	5	3	1								
Ezra - Hebrew	15														1		2	3			2	2	2	2	1								
Aramaic	6														2					1	2	1											
Jer. - Prose A	12																1	2	2	1	1	5											
Poetic A	28																3	5	4	1	5	3	4	1	2								
Jer. - Prose B	19											1			1	1	2	1	2	3	1	1	3		2			1					
Poetic B	18																1	4	2	2	5	1	3										
Ezek.-Prose A	15																1	4		2	3	1	1	2		1							
Poetic A	2																					1		1									
Ezek. Prose B	12															1	2		2	1		3	1		2								
Poetic B	9																		1	3	2	1	1	1									
1 Maccabees 1-5	45																1	2		7	6	6	7	7	3	4	2						

basically of a parenetic genre.[214] It is "not...an actual letter to a specific person, church or group of churches. Rather it is a series of loosely connected moral and ethical admonitions and instructions"[215] best understood as a homily.

It is improbable that the author is, as Church tradition has claimed, James, the brother of Jesus;[216] however, the ascription to James may be the author's way of "indicating either that the origin of much of the tradition was in the Jerusalem church or that, in his opinion, some of the material went back to James, the leader of the Jerusalem church."[217]

The nature of the Greek of James has not been agreed upon. While most often it has been described as "fluent, even elegant Greek"[218] or "excellent"[219] or "very cultivated...elevated"[220] but also with more reserve as "a relatively good Greek,"[221] the Semitic nature of this Greek has also been noted by Dibelius-Greeven,[222] Kümmel.[223] Ward has correctly

---

[214]Cf. Dibelius-Greeven, p. 3.

[215]Martin, James, p. 10; cf also the detailed discussion in Dibelius-Greeven, pp. 1-11.

[216]Cf. Kümmel, Introduction, pp. 411-413; Dibelius-Greeven. pp. 11-21.

[217]Martin, James, p. 12. Cf also Reicke, James, p. 4.

[218]C.L. Mitton, The Epistle of James (1966), pp. 227,234.

[219]A.E. Barnett, "James, Letter of" in IDB, Vol. 2, p. 794.

[220]Kümmel, Introduction, p. 411.

[221]Dibelius-Greeven, p. 38.

[222]Ibid., pp. 36f.

[223]Introduction, p. 411.

called attention to the fact that "...James is also
characterized by many instances of Semitisms, including
direct, spontaneous Semitisms unrelated to the LXX."[224]
He further notes: "With reference to sentence syntax
James displays more Semitisms...per page of text than
any other N.T. letters except I-III John."[225]

This Semitic character of the Letter is so
pronounced that from time to time it has been suggested
that behind the present Letter is a Semitic original,
either Christian or Jewish.[226] While most commentaries
have rejected this theory, often because of the Greek
rhetorical style and techniques employed by the
writer,[227] Easton has continued to advocate the
proposal in a modified form.[228]

Chart XVI reveals that the net frequencies of the
Letter of James fall nearly into the clear translation
Greek area and are widely separated from the original
Greek documents studied. This suggests that most of
the subsections when analyzed will be found to have net
translation Greek frequencies as well. This is the
case as can be seen from the classification in Chart
XXI[229] below, where only one subsection shows up with
clear original Greek net frequencies (no. 9).

---

[224]R.B. Ward, "James, Letter of" in Supplement, p. 469.

[225]Ibid. Cf. also the discussion of this issue in Dibelius-Greeven, pp. 35-38.

[226]Cf. e.g. Kummel, Introduction, p. 406. Ropes, James, p. 27; and Dibelius-Greeven, note 128, p. 37.

[227]Cf. e.g. Dibelius-Greeven, pp. 17, 37; Ward, James, p. 469; Mayor, James, pp. cclx-cclxviii.

[228]James, pp. 9-12.

[229]For the percentages on which these net frequencies are based, see Chart XXV at the end of this chapter; for the numerical count see Appendix 4.

CHART XXI
CLASSIFICATION OF SMALLER UNITS IN JAMES

	Locat.	Lines	Net Freq	Clear Orig.				Clear Trans.
1. Value of Trials	1:1-8	13	0				X	
2. Poverty and Riches	1:9-11	6	0				X	
3. Temptations	1:12-15	8	+7	X				
4. Everything from God is Good	1:16-18	6	+2			X		
5. Importance of Hearing	1:19-21	6	+2			X		
6. Hearing and Doing	1:22-25	8	+4		X			
7. Importance of Right Action	1:26,27	5	-1					X
8. Evil of Partiality (A)	2:1-4	8	-3					X
9. (B)	2:5-13	16	+9	X				
10.Dead Faith	2:14-17	7	+3			X		
11.Two Kinds of Faith	2:18-26	16	+2				X	
12.Sins of the Tongue (A)	3:1-5a	10	+4		X			
13. (B)	3:5b-12	16	+2				X	
14.True Wisdom	3:13-18	11	+3		X			
15.Avoid Friendship with the World	4:1-10	18	-1					X
16.Avoid Speaking Evil of Others	4:11,12	5	+3		X			
17.Warning to the Arrogant	4:13-17	9	+3		X			
18.Warning to the Rich	5:1-6	12	-3					X
19.Patience! The Judge Is Near	5:7-12	14	0				X	
20.The Power of Prayer	5:13-18	13	-3					X
21.Concern for the Erring	5:19,20	4	0				X	

This suggested that it might be worthwhile to analyze specifically the proposal of Meyer, as modified by Easton,[230] of a Jewish Jacob Letter translated and interpreted by a Christian writer. The analysis, as can be seen in Chart XXII[231] below, shows that only 2 of the 4 "Christian interpolations" appear as clear original Greek and one of the interpolations has clear translation net frequencies. Further the basic core, the Jacob Letter, as proposed by them does not show up as translation Greek.

If 2 modifications are made in the proposal, however, a clearer demarcation of the material occurs. If the small "interpolation" 1:6-8 is omitted and then if the larger unit 2:1-13 is sub divided according to content into 2:1-7 and 2:8-13,[232] it will be seen from Chart XXII that 2:8-13 becomes clearly original Greek and the rest of the Letter of James as a whole (153 lines, -3 net frequencies) falls nearly into the area of clear translation Greek and is widely separated from original Greek documents of such large length (cf. Chart XVI). Further, even where the smaller units do not show up as clear translation Greek, their net frequencies fit within the outer limits of the ranges of smaller units of text of similar size of the translated writings of the Old Testament (cf. Charts XVII, XIX and XX).

Whether the original Semitic Letter was Jewish or Christian cannot be determined by Syntax Criticism.

---

[230] James, loc. cit.

[231] The percentages for this chart are found in Chart XXV at the end of this chapter and the numerical count in Appendix 4.

[232] So e.g. Moffatt, James, p. 34; Reicke, James, p. 26; Ropes, James, p. 197; Mitton, James, p. 89.

CHART XXII
THE THEORY OF A SEMITIC CORE LETTER

	Locat.	Lines	Net Freq	Clear Orig.		Clear Trans.
Meyer-Easton Theory						
Christian Interpolations	1:6-8	5	+2		X	X
	2:1-13	14	-3			
	2:14-26	23	+5	X		
	3:1-12	26	+5	X		
Jewish Letter of Jacob	Rest of James	133	+3		X	
Modified Theory						
Later Insertions	2:8-13	9	+8	X		
	2:14-26	23	+5	X		
	3:1-12	26	+5	X		
Original Semitic Letter	Rest of James	153	-3		X	
	1:1-11	19	0			X
	1:12-25	28	+3		X	
	1:26,27	5	-1			X
	2:1-7	15	0		X	
	3:13-18	11	+3		X	
	4:1-10	18	-1			X
	4:11-17	14	-1			X
	Chap. 5	43	-9			X

The Palestinian Aramaic speaking milieu, however, is
clear. It is also significant that even when a writer
of such good Greek (as the author of James is
considered to be[233]) is translating, this can be
detected by the 17 criteria of Syntax Criticism.

I Peter

The unity of 1 Peter has been questioned by
various scholars over the years.[234] There seems to be
a clear break after 4:11 with a benediction and then
4:12ff "seems to speak of suffering as a present
reality, while the preceding chapter discussed
suffering as [future] possibility."[235] Many have seen
the earlier part to have a very specific baptisimal
reference--either part of a homily or a liturgy.[236]
Some have suggested that 4:12-5:14 was added to an
earlier letter;[237] whereas Beare considers the
baptisimal homily to have been inserted into an earlier
letter, "possibly by a later editor, but more probably
by the writer himself."[238] Most scholars have,

---

[233]Cf. p. 103 supra.

[234]Cf. the surveys in Kümmel, Introduction, pp. 419f; J.N.D. Kelly, A Commentary
on the Epistles of Peter and Jude (1969), pp. 15-20.

[235]Koester, op. cit., p. 294.

[236]Cf. Kelly, op. cit., p. 16.

[237]E.g. Koester, loc. cit.

[238]F.W. Beare, The First Epistle of Peter (1961), p. 8.

however, rejected either view and consider the letter to be a unity.[239]

The net frequencies of 1 Peter as a whole fall into the clear original Greek area, as Chart XVI shows. However, if the net frequencies of each chapter and of the subsections are considered, as can be seen in Chart XXIII below, a significant fact appears: the net frequencies of chapter 5 are more Semitic than any of the others and so are the net frequencies of 4:12-19, the end of chapter 4. When these are combined 4:12-5:14 (the second of the two parts of 1 Peter suggested by earlier studies), the net frequencies become clear translation Greek and those of the first part 1:1-4:11 remain clear original Greek (cf. Chart XXIII).

One sub section of this larger unit (4:12-5:14) has, however, clear original Greek net frequencies -- 5:1-5. This very specific exhortation to the elders may be a separate piece of tradition or the final editor's own composition.[240] Thus a Semitic, Palestinian milieu seems to be behind most of 4:12-5:14.

Jude

The overwhelming view of scholarship is that Jude is a pseudonymous writing, to be dated close to the end of the 1st Christian century and was used by 2

---

[239]Cf. e.g. Kummel, op. cit., p. 420: "...the proposal that 1 Peter consists of the juxtaposition of two parts is unnecessary and improbable."

[240]Cf. discussions in Beare, 1 Peter, p. 172; Kelly, 1 Peter, p. 196.

CHART XXIII
CLASSIFICATION OF MATERIAL IN I PETER[1]

	Locat.	Lines	Net Freq	Clear Orig.				Clear Trans.
Salutation	1:1,2	5	+6			X		
The Risen Christ	1:3-9	15	+3				X	
Prophetic Witness	1:10-12	8	+11	X				
Holy Living	1:13-16	6	+4				X	
You Are Redeemed	1:17-21	10	+9		X			
You Are Reborn	1:22-25	5	+5			X		
The Living Stone	2:1-10	13	+12	X				
Glorify God	2:11,12	6	+4				X	
Obey the Government	2:13-17	9	+10		X			
Christ's Example	2:18-25	14	+4				X	
Duties of Spouses	3:1-7	16	+10	X				
Bless Revilers	3:8-12	4	+5			X		
Endure Persecution	3:13-22	21	+6		X			
Live As New People	4:1-6	12	+11	X				
The End Is Near	4:7-11	10	+9		X			
Suffering Is Coming	4:12-19	15	+1					X
The Role of Elders	5:1-5	10	+8		X			
Be Humble	5:6-11	11	+6			X		
Final Greetings	5:12-14	6	+4				X	
Chapter 1		49	+8		X			
Chapter 2		42	+9	X				
Chapter 3		41	+6			X		
Chapter 4		37	+10	X				
Chapter 5		27	+2					X
"Baptisimal" Section	1:1-4:11	154	+10		X			
Constancy in Trial	4:12-5:14	42	-1					X

---

[1]For the percentages on which the net frequencies of this chart are based see Chart XXV at the end of this chapter and for the numerical count see Appendix 4.

Peter,[241] where in chapter 2 Jude appears almost "in
its entirety.[242] All commentators remark the good
quality of the Greek of Jude.[243]

When Jude is analyzed by the criteria of Syntax
Criticism the net frequencies of it as a whole are
found to be in the area of clear original Greek (62
lines, +10) as can be seen in Chart XVI. When the
individual sub sections are studied they are seen to
be conformable to the pattern of such sub sections in
documents that are known to be original Greek as Charts
XIX and XX show and radically different from the
pattern of such sub sections in translated writings of
the Greek Old Testament.

2 Peter

The Greek of 2 Peter is unique in the New
Testament, as Koester indicates:

"Finally, the language of the writing is
the written idiom of second century Christianity,
a thoroughly Hellenized literary language...
Borrowings from Atticistic rhetoric clearly
distinguish 2 Peter from the Greek Koine of
almost all other early Christian writings."[244]

It has been characterized variously as "pompous,"

---

[241]Cf. the surveys in Kümmel, Introduction, pp. 427f; Kelly, op. cit., pp. 225-227
and 231-234.

[242]Koester, Introduction, Vol. 2, p. 246. A few consider both Jude and 2 Peter to
be dependent, rather on a common source. Cf. Kümmel, op. cit., p. 431, note 2 and
Reicke, Jude, pp. 189f.

[243]Kümmel, Introduction, p. 428.

[244]Op. cit., p. 295.

"pretentious," "bombastic," "florid."[245] This is a style which was beginning to come in in the second Christian century.[246]

As Kummel indicates it is "widely acknowledged" that 2 Peter is pseudepigraphical and to be dated at the end of the 1st Christian century or later.[247]

As Chart XVI indicates, the net frequencies of 2 Peter as a whole fall nearly in the exact center, between clear original Greek and clear translation Greek. This normally indicates that some of the subsections would show up clearly as translation Greek and some clearly as original Greek.

From Chart XXIV which follows it will be seen that a number of subsections do show up clearly as original Greek (nos. 2,6,8,9) but none show up clearly as translation Greek. Further the other units which do not show up clearly as original do fall within the range of similarly-sized smaller units of original Greek (cf. Chart XIX for nos. 4,7 and Chart XX for nos. 1,3,5,10,11).

Thus it is most likely that 2 Peter is, in its entirety and in its sub sections, original Greek. The ambigious net frequency figure for the entire letter (+2, 145 lines) is mostly due to the lessened use of prepositions other than en in the document. This has

---

[245]Cf. Kelly, op. cit., p. 228; Moffatt, op. cit., p. 174; R.J. Bauckham, Jude, 2Peter. Vol. 50 of Word Commentary (1983), p. 137.

[246]Reicke, op. cit., pp. 146f.

[247]Op. cit., p. 433 (cf. note 6 for a list of modern dissenters from this view). Cf also Kelly, op. cit., p. 235 and the long discussion in Bauckham, op. cit., pp. 158-162.

CHART XXIV
CLASSIFICATION OF MATERIAL IN II PETER[248]

	Locat.	Lines	Net Freq	Clear Orig.			Clear Trans.
1. Salutation	1:1,2	4	+4			X	
2. Grow in True Knowledge	1:3-11	21	+5	X			
3. The Writer's Purpose	1:12-15	8	+5		X		
4. The Source of Knowledge	1:16-21	16	+4	X			
5. False Prophets	2:1-3	8	+3			X	
6. Punishment of Error	2:4-10a	14	+8	X			
7. Nature of the Deceivers	2:10b-16	16	+4	X			
8. Fate of the Deceivers	2:17-22	15	+8	X			
9. Scoffers in Last Days	3:1-7	16	+8	X			
10. Live in Expectation	3:8-13	14	+6		X		
11. Final Exhortation	3:14-18	13	+4			X	

been remarked by various scholars[249] and may be
understood either as the writer's idiosyncratic style
or, most likely, reflecting the development of the
Koine (from the 2nd Christian century onward) which

---

[248]For the percentages on which the net frequencies of this chart are based see
Chart XXV at the end of this chapter; for the numerical count see Appendix 4.

[249]Cf. e.g. N. Turner, Style, Vol. 4 of Moulton's New Testament Greek Grammar
(1976), p. 141.

tends to do this very thing.[250] If the data for Second
Peter in Chart XXV at the end of this study is
examined, it will be seen that the criteria which come
out with translation Greek frequencies are those
related to the use of prepositions particularly (the
first 9 criteria and the final one[251]).

---

[250]Cf. N. Turner, Syntax, Vol. 3 of Moulton's Grammar (1963), p. 277: "...the
number [of prepositions used] was decreasing...the variety in the use of each
preposition has also diminished. On the other hand, en, eis, ek are much more widely
used." This suggests that some of the criteria of Syntax Criticism will not be valid
for documents which are datable in the second Christian century or later (cf. the first
9 which present the frequency of prepositions in relation to the frequency of en and
the final one which presents the frequency of the dative not used with en in relation
to the frequency of en).

[251]Either in their infrequency in relation to the frequency of en; or in not
occurring at all; whereas in 1st century Koine they would appear and would normally
have relatively higher frequencies.

CHART XXV

Frequencies of the 17 Criteria in the Johannine Epistles

	No. of lines of Greek text	No. of occur. of en	W. gen.	W. all cases (dia)	eis	W. accus.	W. all cases (kata)	Peri w. all cases	Pros w. dative	HupO w. genitive	No. of occ. of kai for each occ. of de	Percent. of separ. articles	No. of dep. gen. post ea. prec. dep. gen.	No. of lines ea. dep. gen. pers. pronoun	Lines ea. gen. pers. pron. dep. on anarth. subst.	No. of prec. attr. adj. for each attr. adj. post position	No. of lines ea. attrib. adjec.	No. of lines each adverb. participle	No. of dat. not for w. en pstn ea. occur. of en	Tot. no. of transl. Grk. frequencies	Tot. no. of orig. Grk. frequencies	No. of inst. where occ. of criter. are too few to be indic.	Net original Grk. frequencies	Net transl. Grk. frequencies
			.06- .01	.18- .01	.49- .01	.18- .01	.19- .01	.27- .01	.024- .01	.07- .01	2.1-	.05-	22-	9-	77-	.35-	10.1-	6+	2-					
Translation Frequencies:																								
I John Entire	236	79	.03	.06	.11	.01	.01	.01	-.01	.01	6.1	.02	30.3	1.5	26.3	.33	4.0	26.3	.37	17	1	2		17
1:1-4	10	1	-	-	-	-	-	.13	-	-	3.0	-	5	2.5	-	-	5.0	10	4	3	4	10		-13
5-10	14	6	-	-	-	-	-	1	-	-	6.0	-	5	3.5	14.0	-	14	14	.33	7	1	9	+1	-6
Chapter 1	24	6	-	-	-	-	-	.17	-	-	4.5	.00	10	3.0	24.0	-	12.0	24	1.0	8	1	8		7
2:1-6	12	6	-	-	-	-	-	.50	-	-	2.0	-	5.0	3.0	12.0	-	12.0	12	.17	5	3	9		-2
7-11	11	8	-	1.0	-	-	-	-	-	-	1.0	.05	4	2.8	-	.00	2.2	11	.25	6	3	8	+2	-3
12-14	7	1	-	-	-	-	-	-	-	-	-	-	2	7.0	-	-	7	7	7.0	2	4	11		
15-17	7	3	-	-	.33	-	-	-	-	-	1.0	.05	6	7.0	-	-	7	7	.00	5	3	9	+3	-2
18-25	18	4	-	-	-	-	-	-	-	-	4	.00	-	18	-	2.0	6.0	18	.50	5	3	10	+1	-2
26, 27	5	2	-	-	-	-	-	1.0	-	-	5	.33	.00	7.0	-	-	5	5	.50	2	5	10		
28, 29	4	2	-	-	-	-	-	-	-	-	-	-	1	4.0	-	-	5	4	.00	3	4	10		
Chapter 2	64	26	-	.04	.04	.01	.01	.19	-	-	4.0	.03	9.0	5.8	64.0	.29	7.1	64	.50	10	2	5	+2	8
3:1-3	7	-	-	1	.25	-	-	-	-	-	3	-	2	-	-	1.0	7.0	7	-	2	4	11		7
4-10	16	4	-	-	.20	-	-	-	-	-	4	.03	6	8.0	16.0	-	16	16	.00	8	1	8		-6
11-18	17	5	-	.20	-	-	-	-	-	-	2.5	.00	10	2.4	-	-	17.0	8.5	.60	7	1	9		-5
19-24	13	5	-	.20	-	-	-	-	-	-	9.5	-	8.0	1.9	-	-	13	13	.00	6	1	10		
Chapter 3	53	14	-	.07	.14	-	-	-	-	-	9.5	.01	26.0	3.3	53.0	1.0	26.5	26.5	.36	10	1	6		9
4:1-6	15	5	-	.20	.20	-	-	-	-	-	5	.00	4	-	-	-	15	15	.20	6	2	9		-4
7-12	13	5	.20	.20	.20	-	-	.20	-	-	-	.00	5	3.3	-	-	13.0	13	.00	7	3	7		-4

CHART XXV

Frequencies of the 17 Criteria in the Johannine Epistles

	No. of lines of Greek text	No. of occur. of en	dia W. gen.	dia W. all cases	eis	kata W. accus.	kata W. all cases	Peri w. all cases	Pros w. dative	Hupo w. genitive	No. of occ. of kai for each occ. of de	Percent. of separ. articles	No. of dep. gen. post ea. prec. dep. gen.	No. of lines ea. dep. gen. pers. pronoun	Lines ea. gen. pers. pron. dep. on anarth. subst.	No. of prec. attr. adj. for each attr. adj. post position	No. of lines ea. attrib. adjec.	No. of lines each adverb. participle	No. of dat. not used w. en for ea. occur. of en	Tot. no. of transl. Grk. frequencies	Tot. no. of orig. Grk. frequencies	No. of inst. where occ. of criter. are too few to be indic.	Net original Grk. frequencies	Net transl. Grk. frequencies
Translation Frequencies			.06-.01	.18-.01	.49-.01	.18-.01	.19-.01	.27-.01	.024 -.01	.07-.01	2.1 !	.05-	22 +	9-	77-	.35-	10.1 !	6 !	2-	17				17
4:13-16a	7	6	-	-	-	-	-	-	-	-	3	-	3	7.0	-	-	7	7	.00	5	2	10		- 3
16b-21	14	8	-	-	-	-	-	-	-	-	3.0	.13	4	4.7	-	1.0	14.0	14	.00	6	3	8		- 3
Chapter 4	49	24	.04	.08	.08	-	-	.04	-	-	11.0	.04	16	6.1	-	1.0	24.5	49	.04	10	2	5		- 8
5:1-5	11	1	-	-	-	-	-	-	-	-	3.0	.00	7	2.8	-	-	11	11	.00	7	1	9		- 6
6-12	15	5	.20	.20	.60	-	-	.40	-	-	3	.00	8	5.0	-	-	15.0	15	.20	6	5	6		- 1
13-15	6	-	-	-	1	1	1	-	-	-	2	-	3	6.0	-	-	6.0	6	-	2	6	9	+ 4	
16, 17	5	-	-	-	-	-	-	.20	-	-	2	-	1	5.0	-	-	5	5.0	-	2	4	11	+ 2	
18-21	9	3	-	-	-	-	-	-	-	-	2.0	.07	2	9.0	-	.50	3.0	9	.00	4	5	8	+ 1	
Chapter 5	46	9	.11	.11	.44	.11	.11	.33	-	-	6.0	.01	21	4.6	-	.25	9.2	46.0	.44	10	4	3		- 6
II John Entire	28	8	.13	.25	.38	.13	.13	-	-	-	3	.00	9	4.7	-	.25	5.6	14.0	.75	9	4	4		- 5
VV. 1-3	7	3	-	.33	.33	-	-	-	-	-	2	-	2	7.0	-	1.0	7.0	7	1.0	4	4	9		
VV. 4-11	17	5	-	-	.40	.20	.20	-	-	-	-	.00	4	5.7	-	.00	5.7	17.0	.40	6	4	7	0	- 2
VV. 12, 13	4	-	1	1	-	-	-	-	-	-	-	-	3	2.0	-	-	4.0	4.0	-	1	5	11	+ 4	
III John Entire	28	3	.33	.67	.33	.33	.33	.33	-	.67	2.0	.07	.33	28.0	-	.50	9.3	4.7	3.3	1	14	2	+13	
VV. 1-4	7	3	-	-	-	-	-	.33	-	-	-	.17	.00	-	-	1.0	3.5	2.3	.67	1	6	10	+ 5	
VV. 5-8	6	-	-	-	1	-	-	-	-	-	-	-	.00	-	-	-	6	3.0	-	-	4	13	+ 4	
VV. 9, 10	6	-	-	1	-	-	-	-	-	-	-	.17	-	-	-	-	6.0	6.0	3	1	4	12	+ 3	
VV. 11, 12	5	-	-	-	-	-	-	-	-	2	1.0	-	1	5.0	-	-	5	5	-	1	5	11	+ 4	

CHART XXV

Frequencies of the 17 Criteria in the Johannine Epistles

Criterion					
No. of lines of Greek text	4	74	132	20	
No. of occur. of en	–	30	46	3	
dia — W. gen.	.06-	.01	1	--	.04	--
dia — W. all cases	.18-	.01	1	.03	.09	--
eis	.49-	.01	-	.03	.15	.33
kata — W. accus.	.18-	.01	1	--	--	.33
kata — W. all cases	.19-	.01	1	--	--	.33
Peri — W. all cases	.27-	.01	-	.16	.07	.33
Pros — W. dative	.024	.01	-	--	--	--
Hupe — W. genitive	.07-	.01	-	--	--	--
No. of occ. of kai for each occur. of de	2.1-	1.0	4.2	2.3	6.0	
Percent. of separ. article	.05-	-	.03	.02	.04	
No. of dep. gen. post ea. prec. dep. gen.	22-	-	11.0	58.0	6	
No. of lines ea. dep. gen. pers. pronoun	9.	-	5.3	4.1	6.7	
Lines ea. gen. pers. pron. dep. on anarth. subst.	77-	-	37.0	32.0	--	
No. of prec. attr. adj. for each attr. adj. post position	.35-	-	.29	.67	.33	
No. of criter. ea. attrib. adjec.	10.1'	4	8.2	26.4	5.0	
No. of lines each adverb. participle	6'	4	30	66.0	20.0	
No. of dat. not used w. en used w. en for ea. occur. of en	2-	3	.50	.15	1.0	
Tot. no. of transl. Grk. frequencies	17	-	10	11	7	
Tot. no. of orig. Grk. frequencies	8	2	2	5		
No. of inst. where occ. of criter. are too few to be indic.	9	5	4	5		
Net original Grk. frequencies	8	+				
Net translat. Grk. frequencies	17	-8	-9	-2		

No. of occur. of prepositions/ea. occur. of en — Dependent genitives

Translation Frequencies VV. 13-15

1 John - 3 main sections
1:5 - 2:27
2:28 - 5:12
5:13 - 21

118

CHART XXV

Frequencies of the 17 Criteria in James

Translation Frequencies	Greek text No. of lines	No. of occur. of en	dia W. gen.	dia W. all	eis	kata W. accus.	kata W. all	Peri w. all cases	Pros w. dative	Hupo w. genitive	No. of occ. of de per kai	% separ. articles	No. of dep. gen. post ea. prec.	pers. pronoun gen. dep. (lines ea.)	Lines ea. gen. on anarth. subst.	adj. post position	attrib. adjec. (lines ea.)	adverb. participle (lines each)	No. of dat. not used w. en	Tot. no. of transl. Grk. freq.	Tot. no. of orig. Grk. freq.	No. of inst. occ. too few to be indic.	Net original Grk. freq.	Net translat. Grk. freq.
James Entire	211	38	.06- / .03	.18- / .05	.49- / .37	.18- / .08	.19- / .13	.27- / .01	.024- / -.01	.07- / .13	2.1 / 1.4	.05- / .10	22 / 12.4	9- / 3.9	77- / 12.4	.35- / .84	10.1 / 4.6	6+ / 6.6	2- / .89	17	—	2		17
1:1-8	13	4	.01	.01	.01	.08	.01	.01	-.01	.01	3.0	.36	1.7	4.3 / 1.2	6.5	.00	4.3	3.3 / 6	.75 / .33	9	6	2	+7	3
9-11	6	3	—	—	—	—	—	—	—	—	1.5	.08	.7	—	—	—	6.0	—	—	5	5	7	+2	—
12-15	8	—	—	—	1	—	—	—	—	—	.00	.43	1	6.0	6.0	1.0	8.0	1.3 / 6	—	4	4	9	+2	0
16-18	6	1	—	—	3.0	—	—	—	—	—	.00	.25	2.0	3.0	6.0	.00	2.0	3.0	.00	—	—	10	+4	0
19-21	6	1	—	—	.50	—	—	—	—	—	1.0	.20	5	4.0	—	1.0	3.0	6.0	.50	3	3	9		—
22-25	8	2	—	—	—	—	—	—	—	—	—	.17	3.0	1.7	2.5	—	4.0	4.0	—	4	5	7		—
26, 27	5	1	—	—	—	—	—	—	—	—	1.0	—	—	—	—	—	2.5	2.5	.50	2	6	9		—
Chapter 1	52	11	—	—	.45	—	.29	—	—	.09	.55	.22	5.4	3.2	8.7	.17	3.7	3.1	.91	5	6	10	+1	3
2:1-4	8	4	—	—	.25 / .50	—	—	—	—	.50	.50	—	7	2.0 / 16.0	4.0 / 16.0	.25 / .50	1.6 / 5.3	8.0 / 8	.00 / 1.5	6	3	8	+9	—
5-13	16	2	—	—	—	.33	.33	—	—	.33	.40	.20	4	7.0 / 4.0	16.0	.50	7.0	7.0	.00	3	12	—	+3	—
14-17	7	1	—	—	—	—	.25	—	—	—	.33	.14	2	4.0	—	1.0	7.0	5.3	.00	4	7	6	+2	—
18-26	16	—	—	—	—	—	—	—	—	—	2.5	.00	—	4.0	2.5	—	8.0	5.3 / 4	.50	3	5	9	+3	—
Chapter 2	47	7	.14	.14	.29	.29	.29	—	—	.14	.75	.08	18.0	4.7	11.8	.57	4.3	7.8	1.0	6	9	2	+1	—
3:1-5a	10	1	—	—	2.0	—	—	—	—	2.0	1.0	—	3.0	5.0 / 5.3	10.0	4.0	1.6	3.3	1.0	3	7	7	+4	—
5b-12	16	3	—	—	—	.33	.33	—	—	.33	3.0	.19	11	5.3	16.0 / 8.0	2.0	2.5	16	.33	5	7	5	+2	—
13-18	11	4	—	—	.25	—	.25	—	—	—	.33	.29	4	5.2	—	1.0	2.8	11	.25	3	6	8	+3	—
Chapter 3	37	8	—	—	.25 / .38	.13	.25	—	—	.38	1.0	.16	18.0	5.3	12.3	2.0	2.7	12.3	.38	6	7	4	+1	—

CHART XXV

Frequencies of the 17 Criteria in James and Jude

	No. of lines of Greek text	No. of occur. of ēn	dia W. gen.	dia W. all cases	eis	W. accus.	W. all cases	Peri w. all cases	Pros W. dative	Hupo W. genitive	No. of occ. of kai for each occ. of dē	Percent of separ. articles	No. of dep. occ. post ea. prec. dep. gen.	No. of lines ea. dep. gen. pers. pronoun	Lines ea. gen. dep. pers. pron. on anarth. subst.	No. of prec. attr. adj. for each attr. post position	No. of lines ea. attrib. adjec.	No. of lines each adverb. participle	No. of dat. not used w. ēn for ea. occur.	Tot. no. of transl. Grk. frequencies	Tot. no. of orig. Grk. frequencies	No. of inst. where occ. of criter. are too few to be indic.	Net original Grk. frequencies	Net translat. Grk. frequencies
Translation Frequencies		4	.06/.01	.18/.01	.47/.01	.18/.01	.19/.01	.27/.01	.024/.01	.07/.01	2.1+	.05-	22.	.9.	77.	.35-	10.1+	6+	2-	17				17
4:1-10	18	4	-	.25	.50	-	-	-	-	-	3.5	-	8	4.5	-	1.0	18.0	18	1.0	5	4	8	3	-1
11, 12	5	1	-	-	-	-	-	-	-	-	.50	-	2	5.0	-	-	5	5	-	1	4	12	3+	-
13-17	9	1	-	-	-	-	-	-	-	-	2.0	-	2	4.5	-	-	9.0	4.5	1.0	.2	5	10	2+	-
Chapter 4	32	5	-	.20	.60	-	-	-	-	-	2.0	.00	12	4.6	-	1.0	16.0	16.0	1.0	4	6	7	2+	3
5:1-6	12	2	-	-	1.0	-	1.0	-	-	-	5	.00	12	1.5	-	1.0	12.0	12.0	1.5	6	3	8		-1
7-12	14	1	-	-	-	-	-	-	-	-	.50	.05	10.0	7.0	14.0	3.0	4.7	14.0	1.0	5	5	7		0
13-18	13	3	-	-	-	-	-	-	-	-	10	-	5	13.0	-	-	13	6.5	1.7	5	2	10		-1
19, 20	4	1	-	-	-	-	-	-	-	-	1	-	5	1.3	1.3	-	4	4	.00	4	4	9		0
Chapter 5	43	7	-	-	.29	-	.14	-	-	-	8.5	.02	32.0	3.1	10.8	4.0	10.8	10.8	1.3	10	1	6		-1
Jude 1,2	(3)	1	-	-	-	-	-	-	-	-	.00	.00	1.0	-	-	-	3	.3	3.0	1	6	10	(+5)	
3,4	7	-	-	.2	-	-	-	1	-	-	-	.63	1.0	3.5	-	3.0	2.3	2.3	3	1	8	8	+7	
5-7	9	1	-	.50	-	-	1	-	-	-	-	.57	1.0	-	-	1.0	1.5	1.8	-	-	7	10	+7	
8-13	16	2	-	.33	.33	1.0	.50	.50	-	.50	.00	.31	.75	16.0	-	.20	2.7	2.0	3.0	1	10	6	+9	
14-16	9	1	1.0	1.0	1.0	.33	.33	2.0	-	.33	1.0	-	.4	2.3	9.0	.67	4.5	3.0	.33	3	8	6	+5	
17-23	13	3	-	-	.33	-	-	-	-	-	.25	.23	2.5	6.5	-	1.0	2.6	1.9	1.0	3	9	5	+6	
24,25	5	1	-	-	1.0	-	-	-	-	-	.00	.20	3	1.7	5.0	-	5.0	5	-	3	9	5	+6	
Jude Entire	62	8	.13	.13	.75	.25	.50	.63	-	.25	.15	.35	2.8	5.2	31.0	.92	2.7	2.4	2.1	3	13	1	+10	

CHART XXV

Frequencies of the 17 Criteria in James—Theory of a Jacob Letter

	No. of lines of Greek text	No. of occur. of en	W. gen.	die W all cases	s/s	W accus.	kata W all cases	Peri W all cases	Pros W dative	Hupo W genitive	No. of occ. of kai for each occ. of de	Percent. of separ. articles	No. of dep. gen. post ea. prec.	No. of lines ea. dep. gen.	pers. pronoun dep. gen.	Lines ea. gen. pers. pron. dep. on anarth. subst.	No. of prec. attr. adj. for each attr. adj. post position	No. of lines ea. attrib. adjec.	No. of lines each adverb. participle	No. of dat. not used w. en for ea. occur.	Tot. no. of transl. Grk. frequencies	Tot. no. of orig. Grk. frequencies	No. of inst. where occ. of criter. are too few to be indic.	Net original Grk. frequencies	Net translat. Grk. frequencies
Translation Frequencies			.06 / .01	18 / .01	42 / .01	18 / .01	19 / .01	27 / .01	.024 / .01	.07 / .01	2.1 / .01	.05	22.	9.		77.	.35	10.1	6.	2.	17				17
Meyer-Easton Theory Christian Interpolations																									
1:6-8	5	2	-- / .17	-- / .17	-- / .33	-- / .17	-- / .17	--	--	-- / .17	.00	.25	2	5.0 / 2.8	5.0	--	--	5.0	5.0 / 7.0	.50 / .50	3	5	9	+2	
2:1-13	14	6									.42	.13	11	4.6	2.8	4.7	.33	1.8	5.8	.50	9	6	2	+5	
2:14-26	23	1		1.0		1.0	1.0				1.2	.04	7.0		4.6	23.0	2.0	7.7	5.8	4.0	3	8	6	+5	
3:1-12	26	4	.50		.50	.25	.25			.75	2.0	.13	14.0	5.2	5.2	8.7	2.7	8.7	8.7	.50	4	9	4	+3	
Jewish Letter of Jacob																									
Rest of James	133	25	-- / .04	.04	.40	--	.08	--	--	.04	1.7	.09	11.1	3.5	3.5	13.3	.64	5.8	6.0	.96	8	5	4	+3	-3
Modified Theory Later Insertions																									
2:8-13	9	1	1.0 / 1.0	1.0	--	1.0	1.0	--	--	1.0	.25	.33	2	9	9	--	--	9.0	4.5	1.0	2	10	5	+8	0
2:14-26	23		See Above	See Above																					
3:1-12	26		See Above	See Above																					
Original Semitic Letter																									
1:1-11	19	7	--	--	1.7	--	--	--	--	--	.80	.21	4.0	2.4	2.4	9.5	.00	4.8	4.8	.57	5	5	7	+3	
1:12-25	28	3							.33	.33	.27	8.5	5.6	5.6	14.0	.33	3.5	2.5	1.3	4	7	6		
1:26,17	5		See Frequencies for all of James																						
2:1-7	15	5	--	--	.40	--	--	--	--	--	.67	.06	9	3.0	3.0	5.0	.40	2.1	15	.40	5	5	7		0
3:13-18	11		See Frequencies for all of James																						
4:1-10	18		See Frequencies for all of James																						
4:11-17	14	1	--	--	1.0	--	--	--	--	--	1.0	--	4	4.7	4.7	--	--	14.0	7.0	1.0	4	3	10		-1
Chap. 5	43		See Frequencies for all of James																						
Total	153	32	-- / .03	.03 / .38	.38	--	.06	--	--	.06	1.5	.09	12.7	3.5	3.5	11.1	.55	4.9	6.7	.84	8	5	4		-3

CHART XXV

Frequencies of the 17 Criteria in 1 Peter

Translation Frequencies	No. of lines of Greek text	No. of occur. of en	dip W. gen.	dip W. all cases	s-s	kata W. accus.	kata W. all cases	Peri w. all cases	Pros w. dative	Hupo w. genitive	No. of occ. of kai for each occ. of de	Percent of separ. articles	No. of dep. gen. post ea. prec. dep. gen.	No. of lines ea. dep. gen. pers. pronoun	Lines ea. dep. pers. pron. on anarth. subst.	No. of prec. attr. adj. for each attr. adj. post position	No. of lines ea. attrib. adjec.	No. of lines each adverb. participle	No. of dat. not used w. en for ea. occur. of en	Tot. no. of transl.	Tot. no. of orig. Grk. frequencies	No. of inst. where occ. of criter. are too few to be indic.	Net original Grk. frequencies	Net translat. Grk. frequencies
1 Peter Entire	196	47	.30	.38	.81	.19	.21	.11	.01	.02	.26	.31	2.9	9.3	196	1.8	3.9	2.9	1.5	17	13	1	+10	17
1:1,2	5	1	-	-	1.0	1.0	1.0	-	-	-	-	-	11	-	-	1.0	5.0	5	2.0	3	7	9	+6	
3-9	15	6	.50	.50	1.0	.17	.17	-	-	-	.00	.30	4.5	7.5	-	.11	1.5	2.5	.17	1	8	4	+3	
10-12	8	1	1.0	1.0	4.0	-	-	2.0	-	-	.00	.83	-	-	-	1.0	4.0	4.0	5.0	5	11	6	+11	
13-16	6	3	-	-	-	.33	.33	-	-	-	-	.33	5	3.0	-	1.0	6	2.0	.67	0	6	9	+4	
17-20	10	1	1.0	2.0	2.0	1.0	1.0	-	-	-	1.0	.56	2.0	5.0	-	-	2.5	10.0	.00	2	11	4	+9	
22-25	5	1	1.0	1.0	2.0	-	1.0	-	-	-	.00	-	3	5.0	-	-	2.5	2.5	.00	2	7	8	+5	
Chapter 1	49	13	.46	.55	1.1	.31	.31	.15	-	.50	.20	.42	7.0	7.0	-	.36	2.6	3.5	1.1	3	11	3	+8	
2:1-10	13	2	.50	.50	2.0	-	.33	-	-	-	.20	.50	.00	13	-	2.0	2.2	4.3	2.5	0	12	5	+12	
11,12	6	3	-	-	-	-	-	-	-	-	-	.33	2	6.0	-	2.0	3.0	3.0	.00	2	6	9	+4	
13-17	9	-	1	2	1	-	-	-	-	-	1.0	.25	2.0	-	-	2.0	4.5	4.5	.4	1	10	7	+10	
18-25	14	2	.29	.50	.50	-	-	-	-	-	.00	-	5	3.5	-	-	.14	1.4	4.5	2	6	9	+4	
Chapter 2	42	7	.29	.57	.86	.14	.14	-	-	.14	.29	.21	3.7	8.4	-	4.0	4.2	2.5	2.6	2	11	4	+9	
3:1-7	16	2	.50	.50	1.0	.50	.50	-	-	-	.00	.40	1.6	8.0	-	8.0	2.0	2.0	3.0	1	11	5	+10	
8-12	4	-	-	-	1	-	-	-	-	-	1.0	1.0	-	-	-	-	4	2.0	-	0	5	12	+5	
13-22	21	8	.25	.38	.38	-	-	.25	-	-	.50	.27	1.2	21.0	-	.50	2.7	.90	.75	3	9	5	+6	
Chapter 3	41	10	.20	.40	.60	.10	.10	.20	-	-	.25	.38	1.4	13.7	-	4.5	3.7	2.2	1.2	4	10	3	+6	

CHART XXV

Frequencies of the 17 Criteria in 1 Peter

Translation Frequencies	No. of lines of Greek text	No. of occur. of en	dis W. gen.	dis W. all cases	eis	kata W. accus.	kata W. all cases	Peri w. all cases	Pros w dative	Hupo w genitive	No. of occ. of kai for each occ. of de	Percent. of separ. articles	No. of dep. gen. post ea prec.	No. of lines ea. dep. gen. pers. pronoun	Lines ea. gen. dep. pers. pron. on anarth. subst.	No. of prec. attr. adj. for each adj. post position	No. of lines ea. attrib. adjec.	No. of lines each adverb. participle	No. of dat. not used w. en for ea. occur. of en	Tot. no. of transl. Grk. frequencies	Tot. no. of orig. Grk. frequencies	No. of inst. where occ. of criter. are too few to be indic.	Net original Grk. frequencies	Net translat. Grk. frequencies
			.06·	.18·	.42·	.18·	.12·	.27·	.024	.07·	.21′	.05·	.22′	.9·	.77·	.35·	.10.1′	.6′	.2·	17				17
4:1-6	12	3	.06/.01	.18/.01	.42/.01	.18/.01	.12/.01	.27/.01	.024/.01	.07/.01	.00	.60	1.0	12	-	2.0	6.0	3.0	4.0	0	11	6	+11	
7-11	10	1	-/1.0	-/1.0	1.0	.67	.67	-	-	-	.00	.13	5.0	10	-	2.0	5.0	5.0	1.0	1	10	6	+9	
12-19	15	5	.11	.11	5.0	-/.20	-/.20	-	-	-	.33	.21	2.3	5.0	15.0	1.0	15.0	7.5	1.2	5	6	6	+1	
Chapter 4	37	9			.79	.33	.33	-	-	-	.20	.29	2.3	12.3	37.0	5.0	7.4	4.5	2.1	2	12	3	+10	
5:1-5	10	2	-	-	-	.50	.50	-	-	-	1.0	.43	1.0	10	-	1.0	10.0	2.5	1.0	1	9	7	+8	
6-11	11	3	.67	.67	.67	-	-	.33	-	-	.00	.29	2.5	5.5	-	2.0	5.5	2.8	1.7	2	8	7	+6	
12-14	6	3	.25	.25	.33	-	-	-	-	-	-	.40	3	6.0	-	2.0	3.0	3.0	.67	3	7	7	+4	
Chapter 5	27	8			.38	.13	.13	.13	-	-	.50	.36	2.2	9.0	-	5.	5.4	2.7	1.1	6	8	3	+2	
1:1 - 4:11	154	34	.35/.15	.47/.15	1.0/.23	.21/.15	.24/.15	.18/.08	-/-	.03/-	.22	.34	3.2	10.3	154	1.4	3.5	2.8	1.7	3	13	1	+10	-1
4:12 - 5:14	42	13	.15	.15	1.2						.40	.30	2.2	7.0	42.0	6	7.0	3.5	1.2	8	7	2		

CHART XXV

Frequencies of the 17 Criteria in 2 Peter

	Net translat. Grk. frequencies	Net original Grk. frequencies	No. of inst. where occ. of criter. are too few to be indic.	Tot. no. of orig. Grk. frequencies	Tot. no. of transl. Grk. frequencies	No. of dat. not used w. en for ea. occur. of en	No. of lines each adverb. participle	No. of lines ea. attrib. adjec.	No. of prec. attr. adj. adj. for each attr. adj. post position	Dep. gen. — Lines ea. subst. pers. dep. on anarth. subst.	Dep. gen. — No. of lines ea. dep. gen. pers. pronoun	Dep. gen. — No. of dep. gen. post ea. prec. dep. gen.	Percent. of separ. articles	No. of occ. of kai for each occur. of de	Hupo w genitive	Pros w dative	Peri w all cases	kata W all cases	kata W accus.	eis	dia W all cases	dia W gen.	No. of occur. of en	No. of lines of Greek text
Translation Frequencies	17					2·	6·	10.1·	.35·	77·	9·	22·	05·	.1·	.07/.01	.024/.01	.27/.01	.12/.01	.18/.01	.42/.01	.18/.01	.06/.01		
1:1, 2		+4	9	6	2	1.5	4	4.0	1.0	—	2.0	7	.25	—	—	—	—	—	—	—	—	—	2	4
3–11		+5	6	8	3	.78	2.6	3.5	6.0	—	5.3	3.0	.21	.00	—	—	.33	—	—	.22	.33	.33	9	21
12–15		+5	8	7	2	.33	2.7	8.0	1.0	—	4.0	3.0	.43	.00	—	—	—	—	—	—	—	—	3	8
16–21		+4	7	7	3	2.0	2.0	2.3	2.5	—	4.0	3.0	.50	.2	.67	—	.06	—	—	.33	—	—	3	16
Chapter 1		+3	4	8	5	1.0	2.6	3.3	6.5	—	6.1	4.2	.30	.22	.12	—	—	—	—	.18	.18	.18	17	49
2:1–3		+3	8	6	3	1.0	4.0	4.0	2.0	—	8.0	3.0	.14	3.0	—	—	—	—	—	—	.33	—	3	8
4–10a		+8	7	9	1	1.7	2.0	3.5	3.0	—	14	3.5	.40	.00	.33	—	—	—	—	.67	—	—	3	14
10b–16		+4	7	7	3	1.0	1.2	2.7	2.0	—	8.0	2.0	.25	.00	—	—	.20	.20	—	.20	—	—	5	16
17–22		+8	7	9	1	2.7	2.1	3.8	1.0	—	15.0	10	.27	1.0	.33	—	—	—	—	—	—	—	3	15
Chapter 2		+4	5	8	4	1.5	1.8	3.3	2.2	—	13.3	4.3	.23	.67	.14	—	—	.07	—	.33	.07	—	14	53
3:1–7		+8	3	11	3	1.7	2.5	4.0	4.0	—	5.3	3.7	.56	.00	.33	—	—	.33	.33	.33	.67	.67	3	16
8–13		+6	5	9	3	.20	2.0	14.0	1.0	—	14.0	3.0	.29	.25	—	—	.20	.20	.20	.40	.20	—	5	14
14–18		+4	5	8	4	1.0	3.3	2.6	4.0	—	6.5	1.0	.58	.00	—	—	.08	.20	.20	.20	—	—	5	13
Chapter 3		+7	2	11	4	.85	2.5	4.3	9.0	—	7.2	2.3	.51	.17	.08	—	—	.23	.23	.31	.23	.15	13	43
All of 2 Peter	17	+2	1	9	7	1.1	2.2	3.5	4.1	145	6.6	3.5	.35	.33	.11	—	.05	.09	.07	.25	.16	.11	44	145

APPENDIX 1
Numerical Summary of
the Gospel of John

Numerical Summary - John

	LINES	EN	DIA		(') EIS	KATA		PERI T	PROS D	HUPO G	KAI	DE	ARTICLE		DEPENDENT GENITIVES					ATTRIBUTIVE ADJECTIVES		ADVERB. PARTICIPLES	DATIVES
			G	T		A	T						UN-SEP.	SEP.	PREC.	ART. c GS D S	ART. c GS D P	No ART. c GS D S	No ART. c GS D P	PREC.	POST		
1:1-5	6	4	1	1	-	-	-	-	-	-	6	-	11	-	-	1	-	-	-	-	-	-	-
6-13	12	1	2	2	4	-	-	2	-	-	3	1	13	-	-	-	1	3	-	-	1	-	1
14-18	10	1	2	2	1	-	-	1	-	-	4	-	9	1	-	1	2	2	-	-	-	1	-
19-28	17	2	-	-	-	-	-	1	-	-	10	-	15	1	1	2	-	-	-	-	-	1	1
29-34	13	3	-	1	-	-	-	-	-	-	7	-	14	-	-	3	-	-	-	-	1	6	2
35-42	17	-	-	-	-	-	-	-	-	-	5	2	19	1	-	3	1	-	-	-	-	8	6
43-51	19	2	-	-	1	-	-	1	-	-	8	1	19	1	-	4	-	2	-	-	-	3	3
Chap 1	94	13	5	6	6	-	-	5	-	-	43	4	100	4	1	14	4	7	-	-	2	19	13
2:1-12	24	2	-	-	3	1	1	-	-	-	13	5	35	3	-	3	8	3	-	3	-	3	4
13-22	19	3	-	-	1	-	-	1	-	-	12	1	25	2	1	3	4	1	-	-	-	2	3
23-25	6	4	-	1	1	-	-	1	-	-	-	2	7	1	1	-	1	-	-	-	-	1	1
Chap 2	49	9	-	1	5	1	1	2	-	-	25	8	67	6	2	6	13	4	-	3	-	6	8
3:1-15	30	2	-	-	3	-	-	-	-	-	13	1	33	1	-	6	3	1	-	-	1	1	1
16-21	14	1	1	1	5	-	-	-	-	-	1	3	26	4	2	2	1	-	-	1	2	-	-
22-30	18	1	-	1	2	-	-	1	-	-	6	3	19	2	-	3	1	-	-	1	1	-	3
31-36	11	1	-	-	1	-	-	-	-	-	3	1	21	3	1	2	2	-	-	-	1	-	1
Chap 3	73	5	1	2	11	-	-	1	-	-	23	8	99	10	3	13	7	1	-	2	5	1	5
4:1-6	10	-	1	1	2	-	-	-	-	-	1	2	13	1	-	-	2	2	-	-	-	1	1
7-15	20	1	-	-	3	-	-	-	-	-	5	1	23	1	-	1	4	1	-	-	3	3	1
16-26	21	6	-	-	-	-	-	-	-	-	6	-	21	1	1	-	2	-	-	1	-	-	6
27-30	7	-	-	-	1	-	-	-	-	-	5	-	7	-	-	-	2	-	-	-	-	-	1
31-38	15	2	-	-	2	-	-	-	-	-	4	1	18	-	1	1	2	-	-	1	1	1	1
39-42	8	-	-	3	1	-	-	-	-	-	3	1	8	2	-	2	1	1	-	1	-	1	2
43-45	6	3	-	-	3	-	-	-	-	-	-	1	5	2	-	-	-	-	-	1	-	1	-
46-54	19	4	-	-	3	-	-	-	-	-	4	2	27	-	1	1	6	-	-	-	-	4	2
Chap 4	106	16	1	4	15	-	-	-	-	-	28	8	122	7	3	5	19	4	-	4	4	11	14
Prologue 1:1-18	28	6	5	5	5	-	-	3	-	-	13	1	33	1	-	2	3	5	-	-	1	1	1
The Writer's Witness 3:1-13, 31-36	28	1	-	-	4	-	-	-	-	-	15	2	49	4	1	7	5	1	-	-	1	1	2
3:14-21	16	3	1	1	5	-	-	-	-	-	2	3	31	4	2	3	1	-	-	1	3	-	-

Numerical Summary - John

	LINES	EN	DIA G	DIA T	KATA EIS	KATA A	KATA T	PERI T	PROS D	HUPO G	KAI	DE	ART UN-SEP	ART SEP	PREC	ART c GS D S	ART c GS D P	No ART c GS D S	No ART c GS D P	ATTR PREC	ATTR POST	ADVERB. PARTICIPLES	DATIVES
5:1-9a	14	4	-	-	2	-	-	-	-	-	5	3	14	-	-	-	3	5	-	-	-	3	3
9b-18	18	4	-	2	-	-	-	-	-	-	7	4	22	3	-	-	3	-	-	-	1	2	6
19-29	25	4	-	-	4	-	-	-	-	-	4	1	33	4	-	2	2	3	-	1	1	1	3
30-40	22	3	-	-	-	-	-	6	-	-	7	3	22	2	-	1	3	-	2	-	3	1	2
41-47	12	3	-	-	1	-	-	1	-	-	2	1	10	3	1	2	1	-	-	2	1	1	4
Chap 5	91	18	-	2	7	-	-	7	-	-	25	12	101	12	1	5	12	8	2	3	6	8	18
6:1-15	29	1	-	-	4	-	-	-	-	-	3	6	32	3	1	3	3	1	-	-	2	6	3
16-21	11	-	-	-	4	-	-	-	-	-	5	2	11	1	-	-	1	-	-	-	1	5	-
22-33	27	1	-	-	5	-	-	-	-	-	4	-	45	1	-	4	5	-	-	1	3	3	4
34-40	15	2	-	-	2	-	-	-	-	-	3	1	19	2	-	3	1	-	-	2	2	-	-
41-51	20	3	-	-	1	-	-	1	-	-	4	1	33	4	1	2	2	-	-	1	1	-	-
52-59	16	5	-	2	1	-	-	-	-	-	4	-	22	4	5	2	3	-	-	3	1	2	1
60-65	13	1	-	1	-	-	-	1	-	-	1	1	15	-	-	1	2	-	-	-	-	3	-
66-71	10	-	-	-	1	-	-	-	-	-	3	1	10	-	-	2	1	2	-	-	1	1	2
Chap 6	141	13	-	3	18	-	-	2	-	-	27	12	187	15	7	17	18	3	-	7	11	20	10
7:1-9	16	5	-	-	4	-	-	1	-	-	3	4	22	2	1	1	4	-	-	1	2	1	1
10-13	7	3	-	1	1	-	-	2	-	-	2	2	8	1	-	1	1	-	-	-	-	-	1
14-24	21	4	-	1	1	1	1	1	-	-	6	2	19	4	-	2	1	-	-	2	1	3	2
25-31	14	1	-	-	1	-	-	-	-	-	8	2	10	1	-	-	1	-	-	-	-	2	1
32-36	12	-	-	-	1	-	-	1	-	-	6	-	11	-	-	1	-	-	-	-	1	1	-
37-39	7	1	-	-	2	-	-	1	-	-	2	2	8	1	-	1	1	1	-	1	1	1	-
40-44	7	1	-	1	-	-	-	-	-	-	-	2	12	-	-	-	-	-	-	-	-	1	-
45-52	13	-	-	1	1	-	-	-	-	-	1	-	15	-	-	-	1	-	-	-	-	-	1
Chap 7	97	15	-	4	11	1	1	6	-	-	28	14	105	9	1	6	9	1	-	4	5	9	6
8:12-20	20	4	-	-	-	1	1	4	-	-	4	3	24	2	1	2	6	-	-	-	2	2	1
21-30	21	3	-	-	2	-	-	1	-	-	5	-	19	-	-	1	3	-	-	-	-	1	1
31-38	14	3	-	-	2	-	-	-	-	-	4	1	18	2	-	-	-	3	1	-	2	-	4
39-47	22	2	-	3	-	-	-	1	-	-	2	2	31	-	-	4	4	1	1	-	2	-	2
48-59	25	-	-	-	2	-	-	-	-	-	10	3	20	1	-	-	8	-	1	1	1	-	1
Chap 8	102	12	-	3	6	1	1	6	-	-	25	9	112	5	1	7	21	4	3	1	7	3	9

Numerical Summary - John

	L I N E s	DIA			KATA			PERI T	PROS D	HUPO G	KAI	DE	ARTICLE		DEPENDENT GENITIVES					ATTRIBUTIVE ADJECTIVES		ADVERB. PARTI-CIPLES	DATIVES
		EN	G	T	EIS	A	T						UN-SEP.	SEP.	PREC.	ART.cGS DS	DP	NoART.cGS DS	DP	PREC.	POST		
7:53 - 8:11	21	3	-	-	5	1	1	-	-	-	9	11	20	1	-	1	2	-	-	-	-	11	4
9:1-12	23	2	-	-	2	-	-	-	-	-	9	-	22	1	3	3	3	1	-	-	-	7	1
13-17	12	2	-	-	-	-	1	-	-	-	3	4	13	1	4	-	-	-	-	1	1	-	-
18-23	14	-	-	1	-	-	2	-	-	-	2	1	11	-	1	-	6	-	-	-	-	1	-
24-34	21	2	-	-	-	-	-	-	-	-	8	2	12	-	4	-	1	2	-	-	-	1	2
35-39	9	-	-	-	4	-	-	-	-	-	6	1	9	-	-	1	-	-	-	-	-	1	1
40-41	4	-	-	-	-	-	-	-	-	-	1	1	3	1	-	-	1	-	-	-	-	-	-
Chap 9	83	6	-	1	6	-	-	3	-	-	29	9	70	3	12	4	11	3	-	1	1	10	4
10:1-6	12	-	2	2	1	1	1	-	-	-	4	3	15	2	1	1	2	1	-	1	-	-	3
7-18	25	-	1	2	-	-	1	-	-	-	12	-	32	-	-	1	5	-	-	-	3	1	1
19-21	5	1	-	1	-	-	-	-	-	-	1	1	3	-	1	1	-	-	-	-	-	-	-
22-30	15	4	-	-	1	-	-	1	-	-	9	-	25	-	-	3	5	-	-	-	3	-	3
31-39	16	3	-	1	1	-	-	2	-	-	2	1	18	-	1	2	3	1	-	2	1	1	6
40-42	5	-	-	-	2	-	-	1	-	-	5	1	3	-	-	-	-	-	-	-	-	-	-
Chap 10	78	8	3	6	5	1	1	5	-	-	33	6	96	2	3	8	15	2	-	3	7	2	13
11:1-16	29	4	1	2	1	-	-	2	-	-	3	7	37	-	-	6	6	-	-	-	-	2	3
17-27	18	4	-	-	4	-	-	1	-	-	1	3	27	3	-	1	2	-	-	1	-	1	1
28-37	20	2	-	-	2	-	-	-	-	-	6	3	18	3	2	1	1	-	-	-	-	8	4
38-44	15	1	-	1	1	-	-	-	-	-	4	3	15	1	-	2	1	-	-	-	1	3	5
45-53	18	-	-	-	3	-	-	-	-	-	5	3	20	-	1	1	-	-	-	-	-	1	1
54-57	10	2	-	-	4	-	-	-	-	-	3	2	13	1	-	1	-	-	-	-	-	1	2
Chap 11	110	13	1	3	15	-	-	3	-	-	22	21	130	8	3	12	10	-	-	1	1	16	16
12:1-8	16	-	-	1	2	-	-	1	-	-	3	5	20	4	-	3	4	3	-	-	2	2	4
9-11	6	-	-	2	1	-	-	-	-	-	1	1	8	-	-	-	-	1	-	-	-	-	-
12-19	14	-	-	1	3	-	-	-	-	-	2	1	19	1	1	2	-	-	-	-	-	2	5
20-26	15	2	-	-	2	-	-	-	-	-	5	3	22	1	-	2	2	1	-	-	2	3	5
27-36a	20	2	-	3	3	-	-	-	-	-	5	1	26	1	1	3	1	2	-	2	-	1	2
36b-43	11	-	-	2	2	-	-	1	-	-	2	1	9	-	-	3	1	-	-	1	-	2	-
44-50	14	2	-	-	5	-	-	-	-	-	4	1	16	2	1	-	2	-	-	1	1	-	-
Chap 12	96	6	-	9	18	-	-	2	-	-	22	13	120	9	3	13	10	7	-	4	5	10	16

Numerical Summary - John

	LINES	DIA EN	DIA G	DIA T	EIS	KATA A	KATA T	PERI T	PROS D	HUPO G	KAI	DE	ARTICLE UN-SEP.	ARTICLE SEP.	DEP. GEN. PREC.	ART. c GS D S	ART. c GS D P	No ART. c GS D S	No ART. c GS D P	ATTR. ADJ. PREC.	ATTR. ADJ. POST	ADVERB. PARTICIPLES	DATIVES
13:1-11	24	1	-	1	5	-	-	-	-	-	6	2	30	-	3	2	1	1	-	-	-	6	1
12-20	16	-	-	-	-	-	-	1	-	-	1	1	14	1	2	-	3	-	-	-	-	-	1
21-30	19	1	-	-	3	-	-	2	-	-	3	2	20	-	-	2	1	2	-	-	-	5	2
31-35	10	5	-	-	-	-	-	-	-	-	4	-	6	-	-	1	-	-	-	-	1	-	1
36-38	7	-	-	1	-	-	-	-	-	-	-	1	3	-	-	-	2	-	-	-	-	-	3
Chap 13	76	7	-	2	8	-	-	3	-	-	14	6	73	1	5	5	7	3	-	-	1	11	8
14:1-14	27	9	1	2	3	-	-	-	-	-	9	3	31	1	1	1	5	-	-	1	-	1	7
15-24	21	5	-	-	1	-	-	-	-	1	10	2	20	2	-	1	6	-	-	1	1	-	5
25-31	15	2	-	-	-	-	-	-	-	-	4	1	13	2	2	-	1	-	-	-	2	1	3
Chap 14	63	16	1	2	4	-	-	-	-	1	23	6	64	5	3	2	12	-	-	2	3	2	15
15:1-10	20	14	-	1	1	-	-	-	-	-	7	-	23	-	-	1	6	-	-	-	2	2	2
11-17	13	2	-	-	-	-	-	-	-	-	1	1	13	-	1	-	6	-	1	1	2	-	3
18-25	17	2	-	2	1	-	-	1	-	-	-	3	19	2	-	-	7	-	-	-	-	-	-
26,27	4	-	-	-	-	-	-	1	-	-	-	1	5	-	-	1	-	-	-	-	-	-	-
Chap 15	54	18	-	3	2	-	-	2	-	-	8	5	60	2	1	2	19	-	1	1	4	2	5
16:1-4	6	-	-	-	-	-	-	-	-	-	1	-	4	-	-	-	1	-	-	-	-	1	1
5-11	12	-	-	-	1	-	-	6	-	-	2	5	9	-	1	1	-	-	-	-	-	1	1
12-15	8	1	-	1	-	-	-	-	-	-	1	1	7	-	-	1	-	-	-	-	-	-	3
16-24	22	3	-	1	2	-	-	1	-	-	9	3	18	1	1	-	7	-	-	-	-	-	-
25-33	18	8	-	-	2	-	-	2	-	-	6	-	15	-	-	-	2	-	-	-	-	-	3
Chap 16	66	12	-	2	5	-	-	9	-	-	19	9	53	1	2	2	10	-	-	-	-	2	8
17:1-5	10	-	-	-	1	-	-	-	-	-	2	1	9	3	1	-	1	1	-	3	1	2	3
6-19	28	9	-	-	2	-	-	3	-	-	16	1	30	-	1	1	4	-	-	-	3	-	3
20-26	16	7	1	1	2	-	-	2	-	-	5	2	10	-	-	-	2	1	-	-	2	-	1
Chap 17	54	16	1	1	5	-	-	5	-	-	23	4	49	3	2	1	7	2	-	3	6	2	7

130

Numerical Summary - John

Lines	L I N E S	DIA EN	DIA G	DIA T	KATA EIS	KATA A	KATA T	PERI T	PROS D	HUPO G	KAI	DE	Article UN-SEP.	Article SEP.	Dep. Gen. PREC.	Art. c GS D S	Art. c GS D P	No Art. c GS D S	No Art. c GS D P	Attr. Adj. PREC.	Attr. Adj. POST	Adverb. Participles	Datives
18:1-11	23	-	-	-	3	-	-	-	-	-	4	4	27	2	2	1	3	-	-	-	1	4	3
12-14	6	-	-	-	-	-	-	-	-	-	2	1	9	1	-	1	-	1	-	-	-	-	1
15-18	11	-	-	-	1	-	-	-	1	-	4	5	20	2	-	3	-	-	-	1	2	1	4
19-24	13	3	-	-	-	-	-	3	-	-	1	2	13	1	-	-	2	1	-	-	-	3	4
25-27	6	1	-	-	-	-	-	-	-	-	2	1	5	-	-	1	1	-	-	-	-	-	-
28-38a	28	-	-	-	6	1	2	1	-	-	5	2	40	-	1	2	1	-	-	1	5	1	3
38b-40	6	2	-	-	-	-	-	-	-	-	2	2	6	-	-	1	-	-	-	-	-	2	3
Chap 18	93	6	-	-	10	1	2	4	1	-	20	17	120	6	3	9	7	2	-	2	8	11	18
19:1-7	16	2	-	-	-	1	1	-	-	-	8	-	14	2	1	1	-	1	-	2	1	3	3
8-12	12	-	-	1	1	-	1	-	-	-	2	2	10	3	-	-	-	1	-	1	-	1	2
13-16a	9	-	-	-	1	-	-	-	-	-	2	2	8	1	-	-	2	1	-	-	-	1	1
16b-22	14	-	-	-	1	-	-	-	-	-	3	3	21	-	1	3	-	2	-	-	-	1	5
23-27	13	-	1	1	1	-	-	1	-	-	2	2	24	2	-	3	5	-	-	1	1	3	2
28-30	6	-	-	-	-	-	-	-	-	-	1	-	8	-	2	-	-	1	-	-	-	3	2
31-37	14	1	-	-	-	-	-	-	-	-	6	1	18	2	5	2	-	1	-	1	-	1	2
38-42	13	3	-	2	-	-	-	-	-	-	4	4	21	-	-	4	1	2	-	-	1	2	2
Chap 19	97	6	1	4	4	1	2	1	-	-	28	14	124	10	9	13	8	9	-	5	3	15	19
20:1-10	19	-	-	-	6	-	-	-	-	-	12	2	23	5	-	1	1	-	-	4	1	8	2
11-18	20	1	-	-	2	-	-	-	3	-	7	2	16	-	-	1	3	-	3	-	1	7	5
19-23	10	-	-	1	1	-	-	-	-	-	5	-	14	-	-	2	-	-	-	-	1	5	5
24-29	16	1	-	-	4	-	-	-	-	-	8	2	25	1	1	2	10	-	-	1	-	1	1
30,31	5	2	-	-	-	-	-	-	-	-	-	1	7	-	-	1	2	-	-	1	-	1	-
Chap 20	70	4	-	1	13	-	-	-	3	-	32	7	85	6	1	7	16	-	3	6	3	22	13
21:1-14	33	1	-	-	6	-	-	-	-	-	9	5	43	2	-	5	1	2	-	2	1	8	5
15-19	15	-	-	-	-	-	-	-	-	-	5	2	10	-	-	-	4	3	-	-	-	2	2
20-23	10	1	-	-	1	-	-	-	-	-	1	2	13	-	-	-	1	-	-	-	-	3	1
24-25	5	-	-	-	-	1	1	1	-	-	1	1	5	1	1	-	-	-	-	-	-	-	-
Chap 21	63	2	-	-	7	1	1	1	-	-	16	10	71	3	1	5	6	5	-	2	1	13	8
John Entire	17?6	22	14,59	18	7	9	67	4	1		513	2?2	208	127	67	156	241	65	9	54	83	195	22?

APPENDIX 2

Numerical Summaries of the
Passion and Resurrection Accounts

Numerical Summaries of the Passion and Resurrection Accounts

	LINES	EN	DIA G	DIA T	KATA EIS	KATA A	KATA T	PERI T	PROS D	HUPO G	KAI	DE	ART UN-SEP	ART SEP	DEP GEN PREC	ART c GS D S	ART c GS D P	NO ART c GS D S	NO ART c GS D P	ATTR ADJ PREC	ATTR ADJ POST	ADVERB PARTICIPLES	DATIVES
1. The Triumphal Entry																							
Mk 11: 1-11	21	1	-	-	8	-	-	-	-	-	17	2	22	2	-	2	4	-	-	-	-	7	1
Mt 21: 1-11	19	3	1	1	5	-	-	-	-	-	8	7	24	3	1	1	1	1	-	1	-	9	3
Lk 19: 28-38	19	4	-	1	3	-	-	1	1	-	5	5	23	1	1	3	2	1	-	-	1	12	2
Jn 12: 12-19	14	-	-	1	3	-	-	-	-	-	2	1	19	1	1	2	-	-	-	-	-	2	5
2. Crying Stones																							
Lk 19: 39-44	11	2	-	-	-	-	-	-	-	-	8	1	11	-	-	1	4	1	1	-	-	3	2
3. Cursing of the Fig Tree																							
Mk 11: 12-14	6	1	-	-	1	-	-	-	-	-	5	-	3	1	-	1	1	-	-	-	-	4	1
Mt 21: 18,19	4	1	-	-	2	-	-	-	-	-	4	1	4	-	-	-	-	-	-	-	-	2	1
4. Cleansing of the Temple																							
Mk 11: 15-19	11	1	1	1	2	-	-	-	-	-	7	1	15	-	-	2	1	-	-	-	-	1	1
Mt 21: 12-17	13	3	-	-	2	-	-	-	-	-	8	3	17	1	-	2	-	-	-	-	-	2	2
Lk 19: 45-48	6	1	-	-	1	1	1	-	-	-	3	2	9	1	-	1	-	-	-	-	-	3	-
Jn 2: 13-17	10	1	-	-	1	-	-	-	-	-	7	-	15	2	1	2	2	1	-	-	-	2	-
5. Lesson from Withered Fig Tree																							
Mk 11: 20-26	12	2	-	-	1	1	-	1	-	-	5	-	11	-	-	-	3	1	-	-	-	5	4
Mt 21: 20-22	7	1	-	-	1	-	-	-	-	-	2	1	8	-	-	1	-	-	-	-	-	4	-
6. Authority of Jesus Questioned																							
Mk 11: 27-33	15	4	-	-	1	1	-	-	-	-	8	1	11	1	-	1	-	-	-	-	-	3	5
Mt 21: 23-27	13	4	-	-	1	1	-	-	-	-	3	3	12	-	-	2	-	-	-	-	-	6	3
Lk 20: 1-8	14	4	-	-	1	-	-	-	-	-	6	3	12	-	-	1	-	1	-	-	-	6	2
7. Parable of Two Sons																							
Mt 21: 28-32	12	2	-	-	1	-	-	-	-	-	3	7	16	1	-	2	-	1	-	-	-	6	5

Numerical Summaries of the Passion and Resurrection Accounts

LINES	EN	DIA G	T	EIS	KATA A	T	PERF T	PROG D	HUPO G	KAI	DE	ARTICLE UN-SEP	SEP	PREC	ART c GS D S	D P	No ART c GS D S	D P	PREC	POST	ADVERB PARTICIPLES	DATIVES
8. Parable of Vineyard and Tenants																						
Mk 12: 1-12 — 19	1	-	-	-	-	-	-	-	-	16	2	17	-	-	2	1	-	-	1	2	6	1
Mt 21: 33-46 — 26	3	-	1	1	-	-	1	-	-	12	6	31	1	-	3	9	-	-	3	-	6	2
Lk 20: 9-19 — 24	1	-	-	-	-	-	-	-	-	9	9	29	1	-	3	1	-	-	1	2	9	2
9. Parable of the Banquet																						
Mt 22: 1-14 — 26	1	-	-	6	-	-	-	-	-	10	8	34	6	1	3	9	2	-	2	-	11	2
Lk 14: 15-24 — 22	1	-	1	2	-	-	-	-	-	13	2	24	-	2	3	3	3	-	-	1	6	2
10. Paying Taxes to Caesar																						
Mk 12: 13-17 — 12	-	-	-	1	-	-	1	-	-	4	4	14	1	1	3	-	3	-	-	-	2	4
Mt 22: 15-22 — 14	2	-	-	1	-	-	1	-	-	5	2	16	-	-	4	2	1	-	-	-	5	5
Lk 20: 20-26 — 13	-	-	-	-	-	-	-	-	-	4	3	14	-	3	4	1	-	-	-	-	4	2
11. Question about the Resurrection																						
Mk 12: 18-27 — 16	3	-	1	-	-	-	1	-	-	6	1	15	1	-	2	-	3	2	-	-	5	1
Mt 22: 23-33 — 15	4	-	-	-	-	-	1	-	1	4	4	23	-	-	4	3	2	-	-	-	7	4
Lk 20: 27-40 — 22	1	-	-	-	-	-	-	-	-	4	6	22	2	2	1	2	5	1	-	-	5	3
12. The Great Commandment																						
Mk 12: 28-34 — 10	-	-	-	-	-	-	-	-	-	4	-	10	-	-	1	1	1	-	1	-	5	1
Mt 22: 34-40 — 7	3	-	-	-	-	-	-	-	-	1	3	7	3	-	-	1	-	-	1	-	2	1
13. Question about David's Son																						
Mk 12: 35-37 — 5	2	-	-	-	-	-	-	-	-	3	-	6	1	1	-	-	1	-	-	1	2	-
Mt 22: 41-45 — 5	1	-	-	-	-	1	-	-	-	-	1	4	-	-	-	-	-	1	-	-	3	1
Lk 20: 41-44 — 3	1	-	-	-	-	-	-	-	-	1	1	1	-	2	-	-	1	-	-	-	-	-
14. The Denouncing of the Scribes																						
Mk 12: 38-40 — 6	5	-	-	-	-	-	-	-	-	1	-	9	-	-	1	1	=	=	1	=	=	1
Mt 23: 1-10 — 18	3	-	-	-	1	1	-	-	1	4	7	26	1	3	1	5	-	1	-	2	1	3
Lk 20: 45-47 — 7	4	-	-	-	-	-	-	-	-	-	1	9	-	-	1	1	-	-	1	-	1	1

Numerical Summaries of the Passion and Resurrection Accounts

	LINES	EN	DIA G	DIA T	DIA KIS	KATA A	KATA T	PER T	PROS D	HUPO G	KAI	DE	ARTICLE UN-SEP	ARTICLE SEP	DEP. GEN. PREC	ART. c GS D S	ART. c GS D P	No ART. c GS D S	No ART. c GS D P	ATTR. ADJ. PREC	ATTR. ADJ. POST	ADVERB. PARTICIPLES	DATIVES
15. Various Sins																							
Mt 23: 11-36	53	16	-	1	1	-	-	-	-	-	9	10	70	3	2	15	4	6	-	-	5	-	9
16. Lament over Jerusalem																							
Mt 23: 37-39	5	-	-	-	-	-	-	-	-	-	1	-	6	-	-	-	2	-	-	-	-	-	-
Lk 13: 34,35	5	-	-	-	-	-	-	-	-	-	1	1	5	1	1	-	1	-	-	-	-	-	-
17. Widow's Offering																							
Mk 12: 41-44	9	-	-	-	2	-	-	-	-	-	4	1	11	-	-	-	3	-	-	-	2	3	1
Lk 21: 1-4	7	-	-	-	2	-	-	-	-	-	1	3	8	1	-	-	2	-	-	1	2	1	1
18. Destruction of Temple Foretold																							
Mk 13: 1,2	5	-	-	-	-	-	-	-	-	-	2	-	3	1	-	1	-	-	-	3	-	1	-
Mt 24: 1,2	5	-	-	-	-	-	-	-	-	-	2	1	6	-	-	1	1	-	-	-	-	2	1
Lk 21: 5,6	3	1	-	-	-	-	-	1	-	-	1	-	1	-	-	-	-	-	-	-	1	1	3
19. Beginning of Woes (A)																							
Mk 13: 3-8	11	-	-	-	1	2	2	-	-	-	2	2	6	1	-	1	1	2	-	-	-	2	1
Mt 24: 3-8	11	-	-	-	-	2	2	-	-	-	3	3	9	1	-	2	1	3	-	1	-	4	2
Lk 21: 7-11	11	-	-	-	-	1	1	-	-	-	-	3	5	-	-	-	1	-	-	-	2	2	1
20. Beginning of Woes (B)																							
Mk 13: 9-13	12	1	-	1	6	-	-	-	-	1	8	2	7	1	-	-	1	-	-	-	1	1	1
Mt 24: 9-14	10	1	-	2	3	-	-	-	-	1	10	1	11	1	-	1	2	-	-	-	-	-	1
Lk 21: 12-19	12	2	-	1	2	-	-	-	-	2	4	2	9	-	-	-	7	-	-	-	-	2	3
21. Great Tribulation (A)																							
Mk 13: 14-20	11	3	-	1	3	-	-	-	-	-	3	4	17	2	-	-	2	-	-	-	-	1	2
Mt 24: 15-22	11	5	-	2	1	-	-	-	-	-	2	3	22	-	-	1	3	1	-	-	2	-	3
Lk 21: 20-24	11	5	-	-	3	-	-	-	-	2	5	1	14	1	-	-	1	3	1	-	1	1	4

Numerical Summaries of the Passion and Resurrection Accounts

	LINES	EN	G	T	EIS	A (KATA)	T (KATA)	PERI T	PROS D	HUPO G	KAI	DE	UN-SEP	SEP	PREC	Art c GS D S	Art c GS D P	No Art c GS D S	No Art c GS D P	Adj PREC	Adj POST	Adverb Participles	Datives
22. Great Tribulation (B)																							
Mk 13: 21-23	5	-	-	-	-	-	-	-	-	-	2	1	3	-	-	-	-	-	-	-	-	-	-
Mt 24: 23-25	6	-	-	-	-	-	-	-	-	-	1	-	2	-	-	-	-	-	-	-	1	-	-
23. Great Tribulation (C)																							
Mt 24: 26-28	5	2	-	-	-	-	-	-	-	-	-	-	8	-	-	2	-	-	-	-	-	-	-
Lk 17: 23,24	4	1	-	-	1	-	-	-	-	-	2	-	7	-	-	1	1	-	-	-	-	1	-
24. Coming of the Son of Man																							
Mk 13: 24-27	5	1	-	-	-	-	-	-	-	-	3	-	5	1	-	-	1	2	-	-	-	-	-
Mt 24: 29-31	7	1	-	-	-	-	-	-	-	-	5	1	8	1	-	3	2	1	1	-	1	-	-
Lk 21: 25-28	7	2	-	-	-	-	-	-	-	-	3	1	5	-	-	-	2	5	-	-	-	2	3
25. Lesson of the Fig Tree																							
Mk 13: 28-31	7	-	-	-	-	-	-	-	-	-	-	2	8	1	-	-	2	-	-	-	-	1	1
Mt 24: 32-35	7	-	-	-	-	-	-	-	-	-	-	2	8	1	-	-	2	-	-	-	-	-	1
Lk 21: 29-33	8	-	-	-	-	-	-	-	-	-	1	1	8	1	-	1	1	-	-	-	-	2	-
26. The Unknown Day and Hour																							
Mk 13: 32-37	10	1	-	-	-	-	-	1	-	-	1	2	13	-	-	1	3	-	-	-	-	4	1
Mt 24: 36-44	16	3	-	1	1	-	-	1	-	-	4	3	26	-	-	7	2	-	-	-	-	1	1
27. Exhortation to Watch																							
Lk 21: 34-36	7	2	-	-	-	-	-	-	-	-	1	2	7	-	1	1	-	1	-	-	1	1	3
28. The Faithful or the Unfaithful Servant																							
Mt 24: 45-51	12	4	-	-	-	-	-	-	-	-	2	2	18	2	1	2	6	-	-	2	1	2	3
Lk 12: 42-46	12	4	-	-	-	-	-	-	-	-	4	1	18	1	-	1	6	-	-	1	1	2	2
29. Parable of the Ten Virgins																							
Mt 25: 1-13	21	1	-	-	3	-	-	-	-	-	4	9	23	4	-	1	6	2	1	1	-	7	5

Numerical Summaries of the Passion and Resurrection Accounts

	LINES	DIA EN	DIA G	DIA T	DIA EIS	KATA A	KATA T	PERI T	PROS D	HUPO G	KAI	DE	ARTICLE UN-SEP	ARTICLE SEP	DEP GEN PREC	ART.c GS D S	ART.c GS D P	NoART.c GS D S	NoART.c GS D P	ATTR ADJ PREC	ATTR ADJ POST	ADVERB. PARTICIPLES	DATIVES
30. Parable of the Talents																							
Mt 25: 14-30	34	2	-	-	3	1	1	-	-	-	12	8	28	15	-	5	9	-	-	5	6	13	2
Lk 19: 11-27	33	4	-	2	1	-	-	-	-	-	13	6	20	4	1	1	6	-	1	2	4	14	3
31. The Judgment of the Nations																							
Mt 25: 31-40	20	3	-	-	-	-	-	-	-	-	15	4	16	3	-	2	3	3	3	-	1	5	4
41-46	13	2	-	-	3	-	-	-	-	-	7	1	8	1	-	-	1	1	-	-	3	4	5
32. Jesus Lodges on the Mt. of Olives																							
Lk 21: 37,38	3	2	-	-	1	-	-	-	-	-	1	2	5	2	-	-	-	-	-	-	-	1	-
33. Plot to Kill Jesus																							
Mk 14: 1,2	4	2	-	-	-	-	-	-	-	-	1	1	6	-	-	-	-	1	-	-	-	1	-
Mt 26: 1-5	8	2	-	-	2	-	-	-	-	-	3	1	15	1	-	3	1	-	-	-	-	-	1
Lk 22: 1,2	3	-	-	-	-	-	-	-	-	-	1	1	6	1	-	1	-	-	-	-	-	-	-
Jn 11: 45-53	18	-	-	-	3	-	-	-	-	-	5	3	20	-	1	1	-	-	-	-	-	1	1
34. Anointing at Bethany																							
Mk 14: 3-9	15	3	-	-	4	-	-	-	-	-	3	4	13	1	1	2	1	1	1	1	3	3	3
Mt 26: 6-13	13	3	-	-	3	-	-	-	-	-	1	4	12	1	-	-	2	2	1	-	2	6	2
Jn 12: 1-8	16	-	-	1	2	-	-	1	-	-	3	5	20	4	-	3	4	3	-	-	2	2	4
35. Judas' Agreement to Betray																							
Mk 14: 10,11	4	-	-	-	-	-	-	-	-	-	3	1	4	-	-	1	-	-	-	-	-	1	-
Mt 26: 14-16	4	-	-	-	-	-	-	-	-	-	2	-	2	1	-	-	-	1	-	-	-	1	1
Lk 22: 3-6	6	-	-	-	1	-	-	-	-	-	5	1	5	1	-	1	-	-	-	-	-	1	2
36. Preparations for Passover																							
Mk 14: 12-16	12	-	-	-	2	-	-	-	-	-	11	-	14	1	-	1	4	2	-	-	2	2	5
Mt 26: 17-19	7	-	-	-	1	-	-	-	-	-	3	2	14	1	-	1	2	-	-	-	-	1	4
Lk 22: 7-13	12	1	-	-	3	-	-	-	-	-	4	4	15	-	-	2	1	1	-	-	1	5	4

Numerical Summaries of the Passion and Resurrection Accounts

	LINES	DIA EN	DIA G	DIA T	DIA EIS	KATA A	KATA T	PERI T	PROS D	HUPO G	KAI	DE	ART UN-SEP	ART SEP	PREC	ART c GS D S	ART c GS D P	No ART c GS D S	No ART c GS D P	ATTR ADJ PREC	ATTR ADJ POST	ADVERB PARTICIPLES	DATIVES
37. Betrayal Foretold																							
Mk 14: 17-21	9	-	1	1	1	-	1	1	-	-	2	2	11	1	-	2	-	-	-	-	-	3	2
Mt 26: 20-25	11	1	1	1	-	-	-	1	-	-	2	4	11	1	-	2	-	-	-	-	1	5	2
Lk 22: 14,21-23	6	-	1	1	-	1	1	-	-	-	2	-	10	1	-	1	1	-	-	-	-	-	2
Jn 13: 21-30	19	1	-	-	3	-	-	2	-	-	3	2	20	-	-	2	1	2	-	-	-	5	2
38. Institution of Lord's Supper																							
Mk 14: 22-26	9	1	-	-	1	-	-	-	-	-	6	-	11	-	-	4	2	-	-	-	-	6	-
Mt 26: 26-30	10	1	-	-	2	-	-	1	-	-	3	2	12	1	-	4	3	1	-	-	-	8	-
Lk 22: 15-20	13	2	-	-	2	-	-	-	-	-	5	-	13	5	-	3	2	-	-	2	-	6	1
1 Cor.11 23-25	8	2	-	-	2	-	-	-	-	-	1	-	8	4	1	-	-	-	-	4	-	2	-
39. Dispute about Greatness																							
Lk 22: 24-30	13	5	-	-	-	-	-	-	-	-	3	5	19	1	-	2	4	-	2	-	-	1	2
40. Peter's Denial Foretold																							
Mk 14: 27-31	8	-	-	-	1	-	-	-	-	-	2	3	6	1	-	-	-	-	-	-	-	-	2
Mt 26: 31-35	9	4	-	-	1	-	-	-	-	-	-	2	9	-	-	-	-	-	-	-	-	1	1
Lk 22: 31-34	7	-	-	-	2	-	-	1	-	-	1	3	7	-	-	-	2	-	-	-	-	1	-
Jn 13: 36-38	7	-	-	1	-	-	-	-	-	-	-	1	3	-	-	-	2	-	-	-	-	-	3
41. Purse, Bag and Sword																							
Lk 22: 35-38	9	1	-	-	-	-	-	1	-	-	3	4	9	-	-	-	1	-	-	-	-	-	-
42. Prayer in Gethsemane																							
Mk 14: 32-42	22	-	-	-	3	-	-	-	-	-	15	1	20	3	1	2	2	-	-	-	-	6	2
Mt 26: 36-46	24	-	-	-	3	-	-	-	-	-	11	1	15	4	1	2	2	1	3	-	-	13	-
Lk 22: 39-46	11	-	-	-	3	1	1	-	-	-	5	2	12	-	1	1	1	-	-	-	-	8	1

Numerical Summaries of the Passion and Resurrection Accounts

	LINES	EN	G	T	EIS	A	T	PERI T	PROS D	HUPO G	KAI	DE	UN-SEP	SEP	PREC	Art c GS D S	Art c GS D P	No Art c GS D S	No Art c GS D P	Attr PREC	Attr POST	Adverb Participles	Datives
43. Betrayal and Arrest of Jesus																							
Mk 14:43-50	15	1	-	-	-	1	1	-	-	-	9	3	15	-	1	1	-	2	-	-	-	8	2
Mt 26:47-56	22	3	-	-	1	1	1	-	-	-	8	3	25	2	1	2	4	4	-	-	-	8	2
Lk 22:47-53	15	2	-	-	-	1	1	1	-	-	4	4	18	2	2	2	1	2	-	-	1	5	2
Jn 18:1-11	23	-	-	-	3	-	-	-	-	-	4	4	27	2	2	1	3	-	-	-	1	4	3
44. Young Man Who Fled																							
Mk 14:51,52	3	-	-	-	-	-	-	-	-	-	2	1	2	-	-	-	-	-	-	-	-	1	1
45. Jesus Before the Council (A)																							
Mk 14:53-61a	16	-	1	1	3	-	3	-	-	-	10	2	20	1	-	1	1	-	-	-	1	5	1
Mt 26:57-63a	12	-	1	1	-	-	1	-	-	-	3	5	14	3	-	2	-	-	-	-	-	5	1
Lk 22:54,55	4	1	-	-	1	-	-	-	-	-	1	3	4	1	-	1	-	1	1	-	-	3	-
Jn 18:13,14	4	-	-	-	-	-	-	-	-	-	1	1	5	-	-	-	-	1	-	-	-	-	1
46. Jesus Before the Council (B)																							
Mk 14:61b-65	9	-	-	-	-	-	-	-	-	-	3	3	8	3	1	1	1	-	-	-	-	1	3
Mt 26:63b-68	10	-	-	-	1	-	1	-	-	-	2	2	13	-	-	1	2	-	-	-	-	3	2
Lk 22:63-71	13	-	-	-	2	-	-	-	-	-	5	6	13	-	-	2	2	-	-	-	-	5	1
Jn 18:19-24	13	3	-	-	-	-	-	3	-	-	1	2	13	1	-	2	1	-	-	-	-	3	4
47. Peter's Denial of Jesus																							
Mk 14:66-72	15	1	-	-	1	-	-	-	-	-	9	3	19	-	-	1	-	1	-	-	-	7	1
Mt 26:69-75	13	1	-	-	1	-	-	-	-	-	6	4	13	1	-	1	1	-	-	-	-	5	1
Lk 22:56-62	13	-	-	-	-	-	-	-	-	-	6	4	8	1	-	1	-	-	-	-	-	10	3
Jn 18:15-18, 25-27	17	1	-	-	1	-	-	-	1	-	6	6	25	2	-	4	1	-	-	1	2	1	4
48. Jesus Brought Before Pilate																							
Mk 15:1-5	9	-	-	-	-	-	-	-	-	-	4	3	10	2	-	1	-	-	-	-	-	4	-
Mt 27:1,2,11-14	11	1	-	-	-	-	1	-	-	1	5	3	13	2	-	2	-	-	-	-	-	3	1
Lk 23:1-5	11	1	-	-	-	-	1	-	-	-	1	5	13	2	-	1	2	-	-	-	-	10	-
Jn 18:28-38a	28	-	-	-	6	1	2	1	-	-	5	2	40	-	1	2	1	-	-	1	5	1	3

Numerical Summaries of the Passion and Resurrection Accounts

	LINES	DIA EN	DIA G	DIA T	KATA EIS	KATA A	KATA T	PERI T	PROS D	HUPO G	KAI	DE	ARTICLE UN-SEP	ARTICLE SEP	DEP. GEN. PREC	ART. c GS D S	ART. c GS D P	No ART. c GS D S	No ART. c GS D P	ATTR. ADJ. PREC	ATTR. ADJ. POST	ADVERB. PARTICIPLES	DATIVES
49. Death of Judas																							
Mt 27: 3-10	11	-	1	1	3	-	-	-	-	-	2	3	14	2	-	1	-	2	-	-	1	9	3
50. Jesus Before Herod																							
Lk 23: 6-12	15	5	-	1	-	-	-	1	-	1	4	5	14	2	-	1	1	-	-	1	2	9	3
51. Jesus Sentenced to Die (A)																							
Lk 23: 13-17	7	1	-	-	-	-	1	-	-	-	2	1	6	-	-	-	-	-	-	-	-	3	2
52. Jesus Sentenced to Die (B)																							
Mk 15: 6-15	16	1	-	1	-	1	1	-	-	-	2	9	16	6	-	2	-	-	-	-	-	6	6
Mt 27: 15-26	23	-	-	2	-	2	2	-	-	-	1	11	25	5	-	-	3	-	-	-	1	10	6
Lk 23: 18-25	13	3	-	2	1	-	-	-	-	-	2	8	11	2	-	-	3	1	-	-	1	5	4
Jn 18: 38b-40; 19:4-16a	38	4	-	1	2	1	2	-	-	-	10	6	32	6	-	1	2	3	-	3	-	6	8
53. Soldiers Mock Jesus																							
Mk 15: 16-20	9	-	-	-	-	-	-	-	-	-	10	1	6	1	1	-	1	1	-	1	1	2	5
Mt 27: 27-31	11	1	-	-	4	-	-	-	-	-	8	-	13	-	-	1	4	1	-	-	1	6	3
Jn 19: 1-3	5	-	-	-	-	-	-	-	-	-	4	-	6	-	1	1	-	-	-	-	1	1	1
54. Crucifixion of Jesus (A)																							
Mk 15: 21-26	8	-	-	-	-	-	-	-	-	-	7	2	6	1	1	4	3	-	-	1	-	1	-
Mt 27: 32-37	8	-	-	-	1	-	-	-	-	-	4	2	5	-	1	1	4	-	-	-	-	6	1
Lk 23:26 32-38	14	-	-	-	-	-	-	-	-	-	3	7	14	2	1	2	-	-	-	-	1	4	6
Jn 19: 16b-24	21	-	1	1	1	-	-	1	-	-	4	4	28	2	1	3	1	2	-	1	-	2	6
55. Crucifixion of Jesus (B)																							
Mk 15: 27-32	10	1	-	-	-	-	-	-	-	-	3	-	11	-	-	-	1	-	1	-	-	4	2
Mt 27: 38-44	11	1	-	-	-	-	-	-	-	-	2	2	9	2	1	-	-	1	-	-	-	2	2
Lk 23: 39-43	8	3	-	-	-	-	-	-	-	-	2	3	5	2	-	-	1	1	-	-	-	3	1
56. Women Weeping																							
Lk 23: 27-31	8	3	-	-	-	-	-	-	-	-	-	2	6	1	-	-	1	2	-	1	-	1	1

Numerical Summaries of the Passion and Resurrection Accounts

	Lines	en	DIA G	DIA T	eis	KATA A	KATA T	PERI T	PROS D	HUPO G	KAI	DE	Article Un-sep.	Article Sep.	Dep. Gen. Prec.	Art. c GS D S	Art. c GS D P	No Art. c GS D S	No Art. c GS D P	Attr. Adj. Prec.	Attr. Adj. Post	Adverb. Participles	Datives
57. Death of Jesus																							
Mk 15: 33-41	16	2	-	-	2	-	-	-	-	-	6	4	12	3	2	1	-	2	1	-	3	10	6
Mt 27: 45-51, 54-56	18	1	-	-	1	-	-	1	-	-	2	7	14	7	3	3	-	1	-	-	2	12	5
Lk 23: 44-49	11	-	-	-	-	-	-	-	-	-	4	4	15	1	-	1	-	-	-	-	1	7	3
Jn 19: 25-30	12	-	-	-	1	-	-	-	-	-	2	1	25	-	2	3	4	1	-	-	1	5	3
58. Earthquake																							
Mt 27: 51b-53	4	-	-	-	1	-	-	-	-	-	6	-	5	2	-	-	1	1	-	1	-	1	1
59. Burial of Jesus																							
Mk 15: 42-47	13	1	-	-	-	-	-	-	-	-	7	2	14	3	-	4	-	-	-	1	-	7	2
Mt 27: 57-61	9	3	-	-	-	-	-	-	-	-	3	2	13	2	2	2	-	-	-	2	3	4	3
Lk 23: 50-56	12	1	-	-	-	-	-	-	-	-	5	2	12	-	-	2	2	2	-	-	3	4	5
Jn 19: 31-42	27	4	-	2	-	-	-	-	-	-	10	5	39	2	5	6	1	3	-	1	1	3	4
60. Guard at the Tomb																							
Mt 27: 62-66	11	-	-	-	-	-	-	-	-	-	1	2	14	4	-	-	1	-	-	1	-	4	1
61. Women Visit the Empty Tomb																							
Mk 16: 1-8	17	1	-	-	2	-	-	-	-	-	8	1	21	-	-	3	1	-	-	-	1	7	2
Mt 28: 1-8	16	-	-	-	2	-	-	-	-	-	6	4	17	1	-	-	5	3	-	1	2	5	2
Lk 24: 1-7	14	3	-	-	2	1	1	1	-	-	2	4	16	3	-	3	-	1	-	-	1	7	5
Jn 20: 1,2	6	-	-	-	1	-	-	-	-	-	4	1	8	2	-	1	-	-	-	1	1	2	1

Numerical Summary - Mark's Passion and Resurrection Account

LINES	EN	DIA G	DIA T	EIS	KATA A	KATA T	PERI T	PROS D	HUPO G	KAI	DE	Article UN-SEP.	Article SEP.	Dep. Gen. PREC.	Art. c GS D S	Art. c GS D P	No Art. c GS D S	No Art. c GS D P	Attr. Adj. PREC.	Attr. Adj. POST	ADVERB. PARTICIPLES	DATIVES
Triumphal Entry to Preparation for Passover (11:1-14:16)																						
11:1-11	21	1	-	-	8	-	-	-	-	-	17	2	22	2	-	2	4	-	-	-	-	7	1
12-14	6	1	-	-	1	-	-	-	-	-	5	-	3	1	-	1	1	-	-	-	-	4	1
15-19	11	1	1	1	2	-	-	-	-	-	7	1	15	-	-	2	1	-	-	-	-	1	1
20-26	12	2	-	1	1	-	1	-	-	-	5	-	11	-	-	-	3	1	-	-	-	5	4
27-33	15	4	-	1	1	-	-	-	-	-	8	1	11	1	-	1	-	-	-	-	-	3	5
12:1-12	19	1	-	-	-	-	-	-	-	-	16	2	17	-	-	2	1	-	-	1	2	6	1
13-17	12	-	-	-	1	-	-	1	-	-	4	4	14	1	1	3	-	3	-	-	-	2	4
18-27	16	3	-	1	-	-	-	1	-	-	6	1	15	1	-	2	-	3	2	-	-	5	1
28-34	10	-	-	-	-	-	-	-	-	-	4	-	10	-	-	1	1	1	-	1	-	5	1
35-37	5	2	-	-	-	-	-	-	-	-	3	-	6	1	1	-	-	1	-	-	1	2	-
38-40	6	5	-	-	-	-	-	-	-	-	1	-	9	-	-	1	1	-	-	1	-	-	1
41-44	9	-	-	-	2	-	-	-	-	-	4	1	11	-	-	-	3	-	-	-	2	3	1
13:1,2	5	-	-	-	-	-	-	-	-	-	2	-	3	1	-	1	-	-	-	3	-	1	-
3-8	11	-	-	-	1	2	2	-	-	-	2	2	6	1	-	1	1	2	-	-	-	2	1
9-13	12	1	-	1	6	-	-	-	-	1	8	2	7	1	-	-	1	-	-	-	1	1	1
14-20	11	3	-	1	3	-	-	-	-	-	3	4	17	2	-	-	2	-	-	-	-	1	2
21-23	5	-	-	-	-	-	-	-	-	-	2	1	3	-	-	-	-	-	-	-	-	-	-
24-27	5	1	-	-	-	-	-	-	-	-	3	-	5	1	-	-	1	2	-	-	-	-	-
28-31	7	-	-	-	-	-	-	-	-	-	-	2	8	1	-	-	2	-	-	-	-	1	1
32-37	10	1	-	-	-	-	-	1	-	-	1	2	13	-	-	1	3	-	-	-	-	4	1
14:1,2	4	2	-	-	-	-	-	-	-	-	1	1	6	-	-	-	-	1	-	-	-	1	-
3-9	15	3	-	-	4	-	-	-	-	-	3	4	13	1	1	2	1	1	1	1	3	3	3
10,11	4	-	-	-	-	-	-	-	-	-	3	1	4	-	-	1	-	-	-	-	-	1	-
12-16	12	-	-	-	2	-	-	-	-	-	11	-	14	1	-	1	4	2	-	-	2	2	5
11:1-14:16	243	31	1	6	32	2	3	3	-	1	119	31	243	16	3	22	30	17	3	7	11	60	35

Mark's Passion and Resurrection Account

Lines		EN	G (DIA)	T	EIS	A (KATA)	T	PERI T	PROS D	HUPO G	KAI	DE	UN-SEP (ART.)	SEP.	PREC.	ART. c GS D S	ART. c GS D P	No Art. c GS D S	No Art. c GS D P	PREC. (Attr. Adj.)	POST	ADVERB. PARTICIPLES	DATIVES
Last Supper to Burial (14:17-15:47)																							
14:17-21	9	-	1	1	1	-	1	1	-	-	2	2	11	1	-	2	-	-	-	-	-	3	2
22-26	9	1	-	-	1	-	-	-	-	-	6	-	11	-	-	4	2	-	-	-	-	6	-
27-31	8	-	-	-	1	-	-	-	-	-	2	3	6	1	-	-	-	-	-	-	-	-	2
32-42	22	-	-	-	3	-	-	-	-	-	15	1	20	3	1	2	2	-	-	-	-	6	2
43-50	15	1	-	-	-	1	1	-	-	-	9	3	15	-	1	1	-	2	-	-	-	8	2
51,52	3	-	-	-	-	-	-	-	-	-	2	1	2	-	-	-	-	-	-	-	-	1	1
53-61a	16	-	1	1	3	-	3	-	-	-	10	2	20	1	-	1	1	-	-	-	1	5	1
61b-65	9	-	-	-	-	-	-	-	-	-	3	3	8	3	1	1	1	-	-	-	-	1	3
66-72	15	1	-	-	1	-	-	-	-	-	9	3	19	-	-	1	-	1	-	-	-	7	1
15:1-5	9	-	-	-	-	-	-	-	-	-	4	3	10	2	-	1	-	-	-	-	-	4	-
6-15	16	1	-	1	-	1	1	-	-	-	2	9	16	6	-	2	-	-	-	-	-	6	6
16-20	9	-	-	-	-	-	-	-	-	-	10	1	7	1	1	-	1	1	-	1	1	2	5
21-26	8	-	-	-	-	-	-	-	-	-	7	2	6	1	1	4	3	-	-	1	-	1	-
27-32	10	1	-	-	-	-	-	-	-	-	3	-	11	-	-	-	1	-	1	-	-	4	2
33-41	16	2	-	-	2	-	-	-	-	-	6	4	12	3	2	1	-	2	1	-	3	10	6
42-47	13	1	-	-	-	-	-	-	-	-	7	2	14	3	-	4	-	-	-	1	-	7	2
14:17-15:47	187	8	2	3	12	2	6	1	-	-	97	39	189	25	7	24	10	6	2	3	5	71	35
Resurrection Accounts (Chapter 16)																							
Markan Ending																							
16:1-8	17	1	-	-	2	-	-	-	-	-	8	1	21	-	-	3	1	-	-	-	1	7	2
Longer Ending																							
16:9-11	5	-	-	-	-	-	-	-	-	1	1	1	1	1	=	-	-	1	-	-	-	5	3
12-18	14	3	-	-	2	-	-	-	-	-	6	4	11	1	-	-	2	-	-	-	1	5	8
19,20	5	-	1	1	1	-	-	-	-	-	1	1	5	2	-	-	-	1	-	-	-	3	-
16:9-20	24	3	1	1	3	-	-	-	-	1	8	6	17	4	-	-	2	2	-	-	1	13	11
Shorter Ending	4	-	1	1	-	-	-	1	-	-	-	2	4	2	-	1	-	-	-	3	-	-	1
Triumphal to Prep	243	31	1	6	32	2	3	3	-	1	119	31	243	16	3	22	30	17	3	7	11	60	35
Passover to Burial	187	8	2	3	12	2	6	1	-	-	97	39	189	25	7	24	10	6	2	3	5	71	35
Resurrection	17	1	-	-	2	-	-	-	-	-	8	1	21	-	-	3	1	-	-	-	1	7	2
Mark 11:1-16:8	447	40	3	9	46	4	9	4	-	1	224	71	353	41	10	49	41	23	5	10	17	138	72

Numerical Summary - Matthew's Passion and Resurrection Account

	LINES	EN	DIA G	DIA T	DIA EIS	KATA A	KATA T	PERI T	PROS D	HUPO G	KAI	DE	ART Un-SEP	ART SEP	GEN PREC	Art. c GS D S	Art. c GS D P	No Art. c GS D S	No Art. c GS D P	ADJ PREC	ADJ POST	ADVERB. PARTICIPLES	DATIVES
Triumphal Entry to Preparation for Passover (21:1 to 26:19)																							
21:1-11	19	3	1	1	5	-	-	-	-	-	8	7	24	3	1	1	1	1	-	1	-	9	3
12-17	13	3	-	-	2	-	-	-	-	-	8	3	17	1	-	2	-	-	-	-	-	2	2
18,19	4	1	-	-	2	-	-	-	-	-	4	1	4	-	-	-	-	-	-	-	-	2	1
20-22	7	1	-	-	1	-	-	-	-	-	2	1	8	-	-	1	-	-	-	-	-	4	-
23-27	13	4	-	1	1	-	-	-	-	-	3	3	12	-	-	2	-	-	-	-	-	6	3
S 28-32	12	2	-	-	1	-	-	-	-	-	3	7	16	1	-	2	-	1	-	-	-	6	5
33-46	26	3	-	1	1	-	-	1	-	-	12	6	31	1	-	3	9	-	-	3	-	6	2
Q22:1-14	26	1	-	-	6	-	-	-	-	-	10	8	34	6	1	3	9	2	-	2	-	11	2
15-22	14	2	-	-	1	-	-	1	-	-	5	2	16	-	-	4	2	1	-	-	-	5	5
23-33	15	4	-	-	-	-	-	1	-	1	4	4	23	-	-	4	3	2	-	-	-	7	4
34-40	7	3	-	-	-	-	-	-	-	-	1	3	7	3	-	-	1	-	-	1	-	2	1
41-45	5	1	-	-	-	-	-	1	-	-	-	1	4	-	-	-	-	-	1	-	-	3	1
46	2	-	-	-	-	-	-	-	-	-	1	-	1	-	-	-	-	-	-	-	-	-	1
23:1-10	18	3	-	-	-	1	1	-	-	1	4	7	26	1	3	1	5	-	1	-	2	1	3
Q 11-36	53	16	-	1	1	-	-	-	-	-	9	10	70	3	2	15	4	6	-	-	5	-	9
Q 37-39	5	-	-	-	-	-	-	-	-	-	1	-	6	-	-	-	2	-	-	-	-	-	-
24:1,2	5	-	-	-	-	-	-	-	-	-	2	1	6	-	-	1	1	-	-	-	-	2	1
3-8	11	-	-	-	-	2	2	-	-	-	3	3	9	1	-	2	1	3	-	1	-	4	2
9-14	10	1	-	2	3	-	-	-	-	1	10	1	11	1	-	1	2	-	-	-	-	-	1
15-22	11	5	-	2	1	-	-	-	-	-	2	3	22	-	-	1	3	1	-	-	2	-	3
23-25	6	-	-	-	-	-	-	-	-	-	1	-	2	-	-	-	-	-	-	-	1	-	-
Q 26-28	5	2	-	-	-	-	-	-	-	-	-	-	8	-	-	2	-	-	-	-	-	-	-
29-31	7	1	-	-	-	-	-	-	-	-	5	1	8	1	-	3	2	1	1	-	1	-	-
32-35	7	-	-	-	-	-	-	-	-	-	-	2	8	1	-	-	2	-	-	-	-	-	1
36-44	16	3	-	1	1	-	-	1	-	-	4	3	26	-	-	7	2	-	-	-	-	1	1
Q 45-51	12	4	-	-	-	-	-	-	-	-	2	2	18	2	1	2	6	-	-	2	1	2	3
S25:1-13	21	1	-	-	3	-	-	-	-	-	4	9	23	4	-	1	6	2	1	1	-	7	5
14-30	34	2	-	-	3	1	1	-	-	-	12	8	28	15	-	5	9	-	-	5	6	13	2
31-46	33	5	-	-	3	-	-	-	-	-	22	5	24	4	-	2	4	4	3	-	4	9	9
26:1-5	8	2	-	-	2	-	-	-	-	-	3	1	15	1	-	3	1	-	-	-	-	-	1
6-13	13	3	-	-	3	-	-	-	-	-	1	4	12	1	-	-	2	2	1	-	?	6	?
14-16	4	-	-	-	-	-	-	-	-	-	2	-	2	1	-	-	-	1	-	-	-	1	1
17-19	7	-	-	-	1	-	-	-	-	-	3	2	14	1	-	1	2	-	-	-	-	1	4
21:1-26:19	449	76	1	9	41	4	4	5	-	3	151	108	535	52	8	69	78	27	8	16	24	110	78

Matthew's Passion and Resurrection Account

	Lines	EN	DIA G	DIA T	EIS	KATA A	KATA T	PERI T	PROS D	HUPO G	KAI	DE	Art. Un-sep.	Art. Sep.	Dep. Gen. Prec.	Art. c GS D S	Art. c GS D P	No Art. c GS D S	No Art. c GS D P	Attr. Adj. Prec.	Attr. Adj. Post	Adverb. Participles	Datives
Last Supper to Burial (26:20-27:66)																							
26:20-25	11	1	1	1	-	-	-	1	-	-	2	4	11	1	-	2	-	-	-	-	1	5	2
26-30	10	1	-	-	2	-	-	1	-	-	3	2	12	1	-	4	3	1	-	-	-	8	-
31-35	9	4	-	-	1	-	-	-	-	-	-	2	9	-	-	-	-	-	-	-	-	1	1
36-46	24	-	-	-	3	-	-	-	-	-	11	1	15	4	1	2	2	1	3	-	-	13	-
47-56	22	3	-	-	1	1	1	-	-	-	8	3	25	2	1	2	4	4	-	-	-	8	2
57-63a	12	-	1	1	-	-	1	-	-	-	3	5	14	3	-	2	-	-	-	-	-	5	1
63b-68	10	-	-	-	1	-	1	-	-	-	2	2	13	-	-	1	2	-	-	-	-	3	2
69-75	13	1	-	-	1	-	-	-	-	-	6	4	13	1	-	1	1	-	-	-	-	5	1
27:1,2, 11-14	11	1	-	-	-	-	1	-	-	1	5	3	13	2	-	2	-	-	-	-	-	3	1
3-10	11	-	1	1	3	-	-	-	-	-	2	3	14	2	-	1	-	2	-	-	1	9	3
15-26	23	-	-	2	-	2	2	-	-	-	1	11	25	5	-	-	3	-	-	-	1	10	6
27-31	11	1	-	-	4	-	-	-	-	-	8	-	13	-	-	1	4	1	-	-	1	6	3
32-37	8	-	-	-	1	-	-	-	-	-	4	2	5	-	1	1	4	-	-	-	-	6	1
38-44	11	1	-	-	-	-	-	-	-	-	2	2	9	2	1	-	-	1	-	-	-	2	2
45-51, 54-56	18	1	-	-	1	-	-	1	-	-	2	7	14	7	3	3	-	1	-	-	2	12	5
51b-53	4	-	-	-	1	-	-	-	-	-	6	-	5	2	-	-	1	1	-	1	-	1	1
57-61	9	3	-	-	-	-	-	-	-	-	3	2	13	2	2	2	-	-	-	2	3	4	3
62-66	11	-	-	-	-	-	-	-	-	-	1	2	14	4	-	-	1	-	-	1	-	4	1
26:20-27:66	228	17	3	5	19	3	6	3	-	1	69	55	237	38	9	24	25	12	3	4	9	105	35
Resurrection Accounts (Chapter 28)																							
28:1-8	16	-	-	-	2	-	-	-	-	-	6	4	17	1	-	-	5	3	-	1	2	5	2
9,10	5	-	-	-	1	-	-	-	-	-	3	1	5	-	1	-	1	-	-	-	-	2	3
11-15	10	-	-	-	1	-	-	-	-	-	4	2	11	1	-	-	1	1	-	1	1	8	2
16-20	10	1	-	-	3	-	-	-	-	-	3	2	12	2	-	4	-	-	-	1	-	6	2
28:9-20	25	1	-	-	5	-	-	-	-	-	10	5	28	3	1	4	2	1	-	2	1	16	7
Triumph. to Prep. Last Supper	449	76	1	9	41	4	4	5	-	3	151	108	535	52	8	69	78	27	8	16	24	110	78
to Burial	228	17	3	5	19	3	6	3	-	1	69	55	237	38	9	24	25	12	3	4	9	105	35
Resurrection	41	1	-	-	7	-	-	-	-	-	16	9	45	4	1	4	7	4	-	3	3	21	9
21:1-28:20	718	94	4	14	67	7	10	8	-	4	236	172	817	94	18	97	110	43	11	23	36	236	122

Numerical Summary-Luke's Passion and Resurrection Account

Triumphal Entry to Preparation for Passover (Luke 19:28 - 22:13)

	LINES	EN	DIA G	DIA T	EIS	KATA A	KATA T	PERI T	PROS D	HUPO G	KAI	DE	ART Un-SEP.	ART SEP.	DEP.GEN PREC.	ART c GS D S	ART c GS D P	No ART c GS D S	No ART c GS D P	ATTR ADJ PREC.	ATTR ADJ POST	ADVERB. PARTICIPLES	DATIVES
19:28-38	19	4	-	1	3	-	-	1	1	-	5	5	23	1	1	3	2	1	-	-	1	12	2
39-44	11	2	-	-	-	-	-	-	-	-	8	1	11	-	-	1	4	1	1	-	-	3	2
45-48	6	1	-	-	1	1	1	-	-	-	3	2	9	1	-	1	-	-	-	-	-	3	-
20:1-8	14	4	-	1	-	-	-	-	-	-	6	3	12	-	-	1	-	1	-	-	-	6	2
9-19	24	1	-	-	-	-	-	-	-	-	9	9	29	1	-	3	1	-	-	1	2	9	2
20-26	13	-	-	-	-	-	-	-	-	-	4	3	14	-	3	4	1	-	-	-	-	4	2
27-40	22	1	-	-	-	-	-	-	-	-	4	6	22	2	2	1	2	5	1	-	-	5	3
41-44	3	1	-	-	-	-	-	-	-	-	1	1	1	-	2	-	-	1	-	-	-	-	-
45-47	7	4	-	-	-	-	-	-	-	-	-	1	9	-	-	1	1	-	-	1	-	1	1
21:1-4	7	-	-	-	2	-	-	-	-	-	1	3	8	1	-	-	2	-	-	1	2	1	1
5,6	3	1	-	-	-	-	-	1	-	-	1	-	1	-	-	-	-	-	-	-	1	1	3
7-11	11	-	-	-	-	1	1	-	-	-	-	3	5	-	-	-	1	-	-	-	2	2	1
12-19	12	2	-	1	2	-	-	-	-	2	4	2	9	-	-	-	7	-	-	-	-	2	3
20-24	11	5	-	-	3	-	-	-	-	2	5	1	14	1	-	-	1	3	1	-	1	1	4
25-28	7	2	-	-	-	-	-	-	-	-	3	1	5	-	-	-	2	5	-	-	-	2	3
29-33	8	-	-	-	-	-	-	-	-	-	1	1	8	1	-	1	1	-	-	-	-	2	-
34-36	7	2	-	-	-	-	-	-	-	-	1	2	7	-	1	1	-	1	-	-	1	1	3
37,38	3	2	-	-	1	-	-	-	-	-	1	2	5	2	-	-	-	-	-	-	-	1	-
22:1,2	3	-	-	-	-	-	-	-	-	-	1	1	6	1	-	1	-	-	-	-	-	-	-
3,6	6	-	-	-	1	-	-	-	-	-	5	1	5	1	-	1	-	-	-	-	-	1	2
7-13	12	1	-	-	3	-	-	-	-	-	4	4	15	-	-	2	1	1	-	-	1	5	4
19:28-22:13	209	33	-	3	16	2	2	2	1	4	67	52	218	12	9	21	26	19	3	3	11	62	38

Numerical Summary-Luke's Passion and Resurrection Account

	LINES	DIA EN	DIA G	DIA T	DIA EIS	KATA A	KATA T	PERI T	PROS D	HUPO G	KAI	DE	ARTICLE UN-SEP.	ARTICLE SEP.	DEP. GEN. PREC.	Art. c GS D S	Art. c GS D P	No Art. c GS D S	No Art. c GS D P	ATTR. ADJ. PREC.	ATTR. ADJ. POST	ADVERB. PARTICIPLES	DATIVES
Passover to Burial																							
22:14, 21-23	6	-	1	1	-	1	1	-	-	-	2	-	10	1	-	1	1	-	-	-	-	-	2
15-20	13	2	-	-	2	-	-	-	-	-	5	-	13	5	-	3	2	-	-	2	-	6	1
24-30	13	5	-	-	-	-	-	-	-	-	3	5	19	1	-	2	4	-	2	-	-	1	2
31-34	7	-	-	-	2	-	-	1	-	-	1	3	7	-	-	-	2	-	-	-	-	1	-
35	2	-	-	-	-	-	-	-	-	-	1	1	1	-	-	-	-	-	-	-	-	-	-
36-46	11	-	-	-	3	1	1	-	-	-	5	2	12	-	1	1	1	-	-	-	-	8	1
47-53	15	2	-	-	-	1	1	1	-	-	4	4	18	2	2	2	1	2	-	-	1	5	2
54,55	4	1	-	-	1	-	-	-	-	-	1	3	4	1	-	1	-	1	1	-	-	3	-
56-62	13	-	-	-	-	-	-	-	-	-	6	4	8	1	-	1	-	-	-	-	-	10	3
63-71	13	-	-	-	2	-	-	-	-	-	5	6	13	-	-	2	2	-	-	-	-	5	1
23:1-5	11	1	-	-	-	1	-	-	-	-	1	5	13	2	-	1	2	-	-	-	-	10	-
6-12	15	5	-	1	-	-	1	-	1	-	4	5	14	2	-	1	1	-	-	1	2	9	3
13-17	7	1	-	-	-	1	-	-	-	-	2	1	6	-	-	-	-	-	-	-	-	3	2
18-25	13	3	-	2	1	-	-	-	-	-	2	8	11	2	-	-	3	1	-	-	1	5	4
26, 32-38	14	-	-	-	-	-	-	-	-	-	3	7	14	2	1	2	-	-	-	-	1	4	6
27-31	8	3	-	-	-	-	-	-	-	-	-	2	6	1	-	-	1	?	-	1	-	1	1
39-43	6	3	-	-	-	-	-	-	-	-	2	3	5	2	-	-	1	1	-	-	-	3	1
44-49	11	-	-	-	-	-	-	-	-	-	4	4	15	1	-	1	-	-	-	-	1	7	3
50-56	12	1	-	-	-	-	-	-	-	-	5	2	12	-	-	2	2	2	-	-	3	4	5
22:14-23:56	214	27	1	4	11	3	5	3	-	1	59	72	216	24	5	22	23	10	3	4	10	89	43
Resurrection Accounts (Chap. 24)																							
24:1-7	14	3	-	-	2	1	1	1	-	-	2	4	16	3	-	3	-	1	-	-	1	7	5
8-12	9	-	-	-	-	-	-	-	-	-	7	2	11	2	-	1	1	-	-	1	-	4	4
13-27	32	6	-	-	3	-	-	3	-	-	13	6	29	1	-	-	4	3	-	1	1	7	10
28-35	16	5	-	-	2	-	-	-	-	-	12	1	17	-	1	1	1	-	-	-	-	6	6
36-43	12	2	-	1	-	-	-	-	-	-	6	4	5	-	1	-	3	-	1	-	1	7	2
44-49	12	2	-	-	1	-	-	1	-	-	2	2	13	2	1	2	3	2	-	-	-	2	5
50-53	6	2	1	1	2	-	-	-	-	-	5	1	4	-	-	-	1	-	-	-	1	2	-
8-53	87	17	1	2	8	-	-	4	-	-	45	16	79	5	3	4	13	5	1	2	3	28	27
24:1-53	101	20	1	2	10	1	1	5	-	-	47	20	95	8	3	7	13	6	1	2	4	35	32

Numerical Summary-Luke's Passion and Resurrection Account

	LINES	EN	DIA G	DIA T	EIS	KATA A	KATA T	PER T	PROS D	HUPO G	KAI	DE	ARTICLE Un-Sep.	ARTICLE Sep.	Prec.	Art. c GS D S	Art. c GS D P	No Art. c GS D S	No Art. c GS D P	Attr. Adj. Prec.	Attr. Adj. Post	Adverb. Participles	Datives
Triump. E. to Pass. Pre.	209	33	-	3	16	2	2	2	1	4	67	52	218	12	9	21	26	19	3	3	11	62	38
Passover to Bur.	214	27	1	4	11	3	5	3	-	1	59	72	216	24	5	22	23	10	3	4	10	89	43
Resurr.	101	20	1	2	10	1	1	5	-	-	47	20	95	8	3	7	13	6	1	2	4	35	32
Total 19-28: 24:53	524	80	2	9	37	6	8	10	1	5	173	144	529	44	17	50	62	35	7	9	25	186	113

APPENDIX 3
Various Regroupings of
Gospel Material

Various Re-groupings of Gospel Material

Translation Frequencies	No. of lines of Greek text	No. of occur. of en	dia W. gen.	dia W. all cases	eis	W. accus.	kata W. all	Peri w. all	Pros w. dative	Hupo w. genitive	No. of occ. of kai for each occ. of de	Percent. of separ. articles	No. of dep. gen. post/ea. prec. dep. gen.	No. of lines ea. dep. gen. pers. pronoun	Lines/ea. gen. dep. pers. pron. on anarth. subst.	No. of prec. attr. adj. for each attr. adj. post position	No. of lines/ea. attrib. adjec.	No. of lines/each adverb. participle	No. of dat. not used w. en for en. occur. ea.	Tot. no. of transl. Grk. frequencies	Tot. no. of orig. Grk. frequencies	No. of inst. where occ. of criter. are too few to be indic.	Net original Grk. frequencies	Net translat. Grk. frequencies
(reference)			.06-/.01	.18-/.01	.49-/.01	.18-/.01	.19-/.01	.27-/.01	.024/-.01	.07-/.01	2.1+	.05-	22+	9-	77-	.35-	10.1+	6+	2-	17				17
Group 1																								
Mark 11:1-16:8	447	40	.08/.01	.23/.01	1.2/.01	.10/.01	.23/.01	.10/.01	—	.03/.01	3.2	.10	11.8	9.7	89.4	.59	16.6	3.2	1.8	6	10	—	+4	—
Matt 21-28	718	94	.04/.04	.15/.01	.71/.01	.07/.01	.11/.01	.08/.01	—	.04/.01	1.4	.10	14.5	5.9	65.3	.64	12.2	3.0	1.3	10	6	1	—	-4
Luke 19:28-24:53	524	80	.03/.01	.11/.01	.46/.01	.08/.01	.10/.01	.13/.01	.01	.06/.01	1.2	.08	9.1	7.6	74.9	.36	15.4	2.8	1.4	12	5	1	—	-7
John 12-21	732	93	.03/.01	.26/.01	.82/.01	.03/.04	.05/.01	.29/.01	.04	.01/.01	2.3	.05	6.4	6.9	183.0	.74	12.4	8.1	1.3	10	7	—	—	-3
John 12,13,18-21	495	31	.03/.01	.51/.01	1.9/.01	.10/.13	.16/.01	.35/.01	.13	—	2.0	.06	6.1	8.7	165.0	.90	12.4	6.0	2.6	6	10	1	+4	-8
John 14-17	237	62	.03/.01	.13/.01	.26/.01	—	—	.26/.01	—	.02	3.0	.05	7.3	4.8	237.0	.46	12.5	29.6	.56	11	3	3	—	—
Group 2																								
Luke 22:43-45a	4	1	—	—	—	—	—	—	—	—	3.0	—	2.0	4.0	—	—	4	1.0	1.0	3	3	10	—	-1
Group 3																								
Matt 26:52-54	6	1	—	—	1.0	—	—	—	—	—	1	—	4	2.0	—	—	6	.6	1.0	4		8	+1	
Matt 47-51,55,56	16	2	—	—	—	.50	.50	—	—	—	2.3	.09	6.0	16.0	—	—	16	2.0	.50	6		4	+3	
Group 4																								
Lk 23:1-25	46	10	—	.30	.10	—	.20	.10	—	.10	.47	.12	9	7.7	—	.33	11.5	1.7	.90	6	7	4	+1	-1

Various Re-groupings of Gospel Material

Translation Frequencies	No. of lines of Greek text	No. of occur. of en	dia W. gen. (.06-/.01)	dia W. all cases (.18-/.01)	eis (.49-/.01)	kata W. accus. (.18-/.01)	kata W. all (.19-/.01)	Peri W. all cases (.27-/.01)	Pros W. dative (.024-/.01)	Hupo W. genitive (.07-/.01)	No. of occ. of kai for each occur. of de (2.1+)	Percent of separ. articles (.05-)	No. of dep. gen, post ea. prec. dep. gen. (22+)	No. of lines/ea. dep. gen, pers. pronoun (9-)	Lines/ea. gen, pers. pron. dep. on anarth. subst. (77-)	No. of prec. attr. adj./for each attr. adj., post position (.35-)	No. of lines/ea. attrib. adjec. (10.1+)	No. of lines/each adverb. participle (6+)	No. of dat. not used w. en for ea. occur. of en (2-)	Tot. no. of transl. Grk. frequencies (17)	Tot. no. of orig. Grk. frequencies (—)	No. of Inst. where occ. of criter. are too few to be indic. (—)	Net original Grk. frequencies	Net transl. Grk. frequencies (17)
Group 5																								
Mk 15:21-32	18	1	--	--	--	--	--	--	--	--	5.0	.05	9.0	2.0	18.0	1.0	18.0	3.6	2.0	7	3	7		-4
Mt 27:32-44	19	1	--	--	1.0	--	--	--	--	--	1.5	.13	3.0	4.8	--	--	19	2.4	3.0	2	6	9	+4	
Lk 23:26,32-43	22	3	--	--	--	.33	.33	.33	--	--	.50	.17	4.0	22.0	--	--	22.0	3.1	2.3	2	6	9	+4	
Taylor Prim Mk	22	1	--	--	--	2	2	--	--	--	2.3	.16	11.0	4.4	22.0	.50	7.3	1.8	3.0	4	6	7	+2	
Group 6																								
Lk 24:1-12	23	3	--	--	.67 / 8.0	--	--	.25	--	--	1.5	.16	6	23.0	--	1.0	11.5	2.1	3.0	1	11	5	+10	
Jn 20:1-18	39	1	--	--	--	--	--	--	3.0	--	4.8	.11	9	6.8	13.0	2.0	6.5	2.6	7.0	3	8	6	+5	-1
1 Cor 15:3b-7	6	--	--	--	--	2	2	--	--	--	3.0	--	--	6.0	--	--	6	6	5	2	5	10	+3	
Group 7																								
Lk 24:36-49	24	1	--	--	1.0	--	--	.25	--	--	1.3	.10	5.5	3.4	24.0	--	24.0	2.7	1.8	6	5	6	+9	
Mt 28:9-20	25	--	--	--	--	--	--	--	--	--	2.0	.10	7.0	12.5	--	2.0	8.3	1.6	7.0	--	9	8		
Group 8																								
Jn 21:15-23	25	1	--	.75	1.0	--	--	.50	--	--	1.5	.00	8	5.0	--	--	25	5.0	3.0	3	5	9	+2	-1
Group 9																								
Jn 12:20-36a	35	4	--	--	1.3 / 3.5	--	--	--	--	--	2.5	.04	11.0	11.7	--	1.0	8.8	8.8	1.8	4	6	7	+2	
Jn 12:36b-50	25	2	--	--	--	--	--	--	--	--	3.0	.07	6.0	8.3	--	2.0	8.3	12.5	.00	4	6	7	+2	

Various Regroupings of Gospel Materials

	No. of lines of Greek text	No. of occur. of en	dia W. gen.	dia W. all cases	eis	kata W. accus.	kata W. all cases	Peri W. all cases	Pros W. dative	Hupo W. genitive	No. of occ. of kai for each occ. of de	Percent of separ. articles	No. of dep. gen. post ea. prec.	No. of lines ea. dep. gen. pers. pronoun	Lines/ea. gen. dep. pers. pron. on anarth. subst.	No. of prec. attr. adj. for each attr. adj. post position	No. of lines ea. attrib. adjec.	No. of lines/each adverb. participle	No. of dat. not used w. en for ea. occur. of en	Tot. no. of transl. Grk. frequencies	Tot. no. of orig. Grk. frequencies	No. of inst. where occ. of criter. are too few to be indic.	Net original Grk. frequencies	Net translat. Grk. frequencies
Translation Frequencies			.06- .01	.18- .01	.49- .01	.18- .01	.19- .01	.27- .01	.024 .01	.07- .01	2.1+	.05-	22+	9.	77.	.35.	10.1+	6+	2-	17		—		17
Group 10 Jn 13:1-20	40	1	—	1.0	5.0	—	—	1.0	—	—	2.3	.02	1.4	10.0	—	—	40	6.7	2.0	5	5	7	0	0
Group 11 Jn 15:18 -16:15	47	3	—	1.0	.67	—	—	2.7	—	—	.40	.04	11.0	5.9	—	—	47	23.5	1.7	5	5	7	0	0
Group 12 Jn 17:6-26	44	16	.06	.06	.25	—	—	.31	—	—	7.0	.00	8.0	7.3	—	.00	8.3	16	.25	9	3	5	0	-6

NUMERICAL SUMMARIES OF REGROUPED MATERIAL

	LINES	EN	DIA G	DIA T	EIS	KATA A	KATA T	PER D	PROS D	HUPO G	KAI	DE	ARTICLE UN-SEP	ARTICLE SEP	DEP. GEN. PREC	ART.c GS DS	ART.c GS DP	No ART.c GS DS	No ART.c GS DP	ATTR.ADJ PREC	ATTR.ADJ POST	ADVERB. PARTICIPLES	DATIVES
Group 1																							
Mk 11:1-16:8	447	40	3	9	46	4	9	4	-	1	224	71	353	41	10	49	41	23	5	10	17	138	72
Mt 21-28	718	94	4	14	67	7	10	8	-	4	236	172	817	94	18	97	110	43	11	23	36	236	122
Lk 19:28-24:53	524	80	2	9	37	6	8	10	1	5	173	144	529	44	17	50	62	35	7	9	25	186	113
Jn 12-21	732	93	3	24	76	3	5	27	4	1	205	91	819	46	30	59	102	28	4	25	34	90	117
Jn 12,13; 18-21	495	31	1	16	60	3	5	11	4	-	132	67	593	35	22	52	54	26	3	19	21	82	82
Jn 14-17	237	62	2	8	16	-	-	16	-	1	73	24	226	11	8	7	48	2	1	6	13	8	35
Group 2																							
Lk 22:43-45a	4	1	-	-	-	-	-	-	-	-	3	1	3	-	-	-	1	1	-	-	-	4	1
Group 3																							
Mt 26:52-54	6	1	-	-	1	-	-	-	-	-	1	-	6	-	-	-	3	1	-	-	-	-	1
Mt 26:47-51, 54,55	16	2	-	-	-	1	1	-	-	-	7	3	19	2	1	2	1	3	-	-	-	8	1
Group 4																							
Lk 23:1-25	46	10	-	3	1	-	2	1	-	1	9	19	44	6	-	2	6	1	-	1	3	27	9
Group 5																							
Mk 15:21-32	18	1	-	-	-	-	-	-	-	-	10	2	17	1	1	4	4	-	1	1	-	5	2
Mt 27:32-44	19	1	-	-	1	-	-	-	-	-	6	4	14	2	2	1	4	1	-	-	-	8	3
Lk 23:26,32, 43	22	3	-	-	-	-	-	-	-	-	5	10	19	4	1	2	1	1	-	-	1	7	7
Taylor Mk	22	1	-	-	-	-	-	-	-	-	9	4	16	3	1	4	4	2	1	1	2	12	3
Group 6																							
Lk 24:1-12	23	3	-	-	2	1	1	1	-	-	9	6	27	5	-	4	1	1	-	1	1	11	9
Jn 20:1-18	39	1	-	-	8	-	-	-	3	-	19	4	39	5	-	2	4	-	3	4	2	15	7
I Cor 15: 3b-7	6	-	-	-	-	2	2	-	-	-	3	1	8	-	-	-	1	-	-	-	-	-	5
Group 7																							
Lk 24:36-49	24	4	-	1	1	-	-	1	-	-	8	6	18	2	2	2	6	2	1	-	1	9	7
Mt 28:9-20	25	1	-	-	5	-	-	-	-	-	10	5	28	3	1	4	2	1	-	2	1	16	7

NUMERICAL SUMMARIES OF REGROUPED MATERIAL

	LINES	EN	DIA G	DIA T	EIS	KATA A	KATA T	PLEI (T)	PROS D	HUPO G	KAI	DE	ARTICLE UN-SEP.	ARTICLE SEP.	PREC.	ART. c GS D S	ART. c GS D P	No ART. c GS D S	No ART. c GS D P	ATTRIB. ADJ. PLEC.	ATTRIB. ADJ. POST	ADVERB. PARTI-CIPLES	DATIVES
Group 8																							
Jn 21:15-23	25	1	-	-	1	-	-	-	-	-	6	4	23	-	-	-	5	3	-	-	-	5	3
Group 9																							
Jn 12:20-36a	35	4	-	3	5	-	-	-	-	-	10	4	48	2	1	5	3	3	-	2	2	4	7
Jn 12:36b-50	25	2	-	-	7	-	-	1	-	-	6	2	25	2	1	3	3	-	-	2	1	2	-
Group 10																							
Jn 13:1-20	40	1	-	1	5	-	-	1	-	-	7	3	44	1	5	2	4	1	-	-	-	6	2
Group 11																							
Jn 15:18-16:15	47	3	-	3	2	-	-	8	-	-	4	10	44	2	1	3	8	-	-	-	-	2	5
Group 12																							
Jn 17:6-26	44	16	1	1	4	-	-	5	-	-	21	3	40	-	1	1	6	1	-	-	5	-	4

APPENDIX 4

Numerical Summaries of the
Johannine Epistles,
James, Jude, 1 and 2 Peter

Numerical Summary 1 John

Lines	L I N E S	DIA EN	DIA G	DIA T	DIA EIS	KATA A	KATA T	PERI T	PROS D	HUPO G	KAI	DE	Article Un-sep.	Article Sep.	Dep. Gen. Prec.	Art. c GS D S	Art. c GS D P	No Art. c GS D S	No Art. c GS D P	Attr. Adj. Prec.	Attr. Adj. Post	Adverb. Participles	Datives
1:1-4	10	-	-	-	-	-	-	1	-	-	3	1	13	-	-	1	4	-	-	-	2	-	4
5-10	14	6	-	-	-	-	-	-	-	-	6	1	12	-	-	1	3	-	1	-	-	-	2
Chap 1	24	6	-	-	-	-	-	1	-	-	9	2	25	-	-	2	7	-	1	-	2	-	6
2:1-6	12	6	-	-	-	-	-	3	-	-	4	2	12	-	1	1	3	-	1	-	1	-	1
7-11	11	8	-	-	-	-	-	-	-	-	1	1	18	1	-	-	4	-	-	-	5	-	2
12-14	7	1	-	1	-	-	-	-	-	-	-	-	9	-	-	1	1	-	-	-	-	-	7
15-17	7	3	-	-	1	-	-	-	-	-	1	1	21	1	-	5	1	-	-	-	-	-	-
18-25	18	4	-	-	-	-	-	-	-	-	4	-	21	-	-	-	-	-	-	2	1	-	2
26-27	5	2	-	-	-	-	-	2	-	-	5	-	2	1	1	-	-	-	-	-	-	-	1
28-29	4	2	-	-	-	-	-	-	-	-	1	-	3	-	-	-	1	-	-	-	-	-	-
Chap 2	64	26	-	1	1	-	-	5	-	-	16	4	86	3	2	7	10	-	1	2	7	-	13
3:1-3	7	-	-	1	-	-	-	-	-	-	3	-	4	-	-	-	-	2	-	1	-	-	2
4-10	16	4	-	-	1	-	-	-	-	-	4	-	28	1	-	4	1	-	1	-	-	-	-
11-18	17	5	-	-	1	-	-	-	-	-	5	2	25	-	-	3	7	-	-	-	1	2	3
19-24	13	5	-	-	-	-	-	-	-	-	7	-	15	-	1	1	7	-	-	-	-	-	-
Chap 3	53	14	-	1	2	-	-	-	-	-	19	2	72	1	1	8	15	2	1	1	1	2	5
4:1-6	15	5	-	1	1	-	-	-	-	-	5	-	26	-	-	4	-	-	-	-	-	-	1
7-12	13	5	1	1	1	-	-	1	-	-	-	-	21	-	-	1	4	-	-	-	1	-	-
13-16a	7	6	-	-	-	-	-	-	-	-	3	-	9	-	-	1	1	1	-	-	-	-	-
16b-21	14	8	-	-	-	-	-	-	-	-	3	1	21	3	-	1	3	-	-	1	-	-	-
Chap 4	49	24	1	2	2	-	-	1	-	-	11	1	77	3	-	7	8	1	-	1	1	-	1
5:1-5	11	1	-	-	-	-	-	-	-	-	3	1	26	-	-	3	4	-	-	-	-	-	-
6-12	15	5	1	1	3	-	-	2	-	-	3	-	40	-	-	5	3	-	-	-	1	-	1
13-15	6	-	-	-	1	1	1	-	-	-	2	-	7	-	-	2	1	-	-	-	1	-	2
16,17	5	-	-	-	-	-	-	1	-	-	2	-	2	-	-	-	1	-	-	-	-	1	1
18-21	9	3	-	-	-	-	-	-	-	-	2	1	14	1	-	1	1	-	-	1	2	-	-
Chap 5	46	9	1	1	4	1	1	3	-	-	12	2	89	1	-	11	10	-	-	1	4	1	4
Entire 1 John	236	79	2	5	9	1	1	10	-	-	67	11	349	8	3	35	50	3	3	5	15	3	29

Numerical Summary II John, III John

	LINES	EN	DIA G	DIA T	KIS	KATA A	KATA T	PERI T	PROS D	HUPO G	KAI	DE	ARTICLE Un-sep.	ARTICLE Sep.	PREC.	Art. c GS D S	Art. c GS D P	No Art. c GS D S	No Art. c GS D P	Attr. Adj. Prec.	Attr. Adj. Post	Adverb. Participles	Datives
II John																							
1-3	7	3	-	1	1	-	-	-	-	-	1	-	9	-	-	1	1	-	-	1	-	-	3
4-11	17	5	-	-	2	1	1	-	-	-	2	-	20	-	-	1	3	-	-	-	3	1	2
12,13	4	-	1	1	-	-	-	-	-	-	-	-	4	-	-	1	2	-	-	-	1	1	1
II John Entire	28	8	1	2	3	1	1	-	-	-	3	-	33	-	-	3	6	-	-	1	4	2	6
III John																							
1-4	7	3	-	-	-	-	-	1	-	-	-	-	5	1	2	-	-	-	-	1	1	3	2
5-8	6	-	-	-	1	-	-	-	-	-	-	-	7	-	1	-	-	-	-	-	-	2	1
9,10	6	-	-	1	-	-	-	-	-	-	2	-	5	1	-	-	-	-	-	-	1	1	3
11,12	5	-	-	-	-	-	-	-	-	2	1	1	8	-	-	-	1	-	-	-	-	-	1
13-15	4	-	1	1	-	1	1	-	-	-	1	1	2	-	-	-	-	-	-	-	-	-	3
III John Entire	28	3	1	2	1	1	1	1	-	2	4	2	27	2	3	-	1	-	-	1	2	6	10
I John - 3 Main Sections																							
1:5 -2:27	74	30	-	1	1	-	-	5	-	-	21	5	95	3	2	8	12	-	2	2	7	-	15
2:28-5:12	132	46	2	4	7	-	-	3	-	-	37	4	218	4	1	23	31	3	1	2	3	2	7
5:13-21	20	3	-	-	1	1	1	1	-	-	6	1	23	1	-	3	3	-	-	1	3	1	3

Numerical Totals - James

Lines	EN	DIA G	DIA T	EIS	KATA A	KATA T	PERI T	PROS D	HUPO G	KAI	DE	Article UN-SEP.	Article SEP.	Dep.Gen. PREC.	Art.c GS D S	Art.c GS D P	NoArt.c GS D S	NoArt.c GS D P	Attr.Adj. PREC.	Attr.Adj. POST	Adverb. Participles	Datives
1:1-8	4	-	-	-	-	-	-	-	-	1	3	7	4	3	1	1	1	2	-	3	4	3
9-11	3	-	-	-	-	-	-	-	-	3	2	12	1	-	1	5	1	-	-	1	-	1
12-15	-	-	-	-	-	-	-	-	1	-	3	4	3	-	1	-	-	-	1	-	6	1
16-18	-	-	-	1	-	-	-	-	-	-	-	3	1	2	1	-	2	1	-	3	2	2
19-21	1	-	-	3	-	-	-	-	-	-	1	4	1	-	-	1	3	1	1	1	1	-
22-25	2	-	-	1	-	-	-	-	-	2	2	5	1	-	2	2	3	-	-	2	2	1
26,27	1	-	-	-	-	-	-	-	-	-	-	4	-	1	-	1	-	2	-	2	2	2
Chap. 1 (52)	11	-	-	5	-	-	-	-	1	6	11	39	11	6	6	10	10	6	2	12	17	10
2:1-4	4	-	-	1	-	-	-	-	-	1	2	8	-	-	2	2	1	2	1	4	-	-
5-13	2	1	1	1	1	1	-	-	1	2	5	12	3	-	-	-	3	1	1	2	2	3
14-17	1	-	-	-	1	1	-	-	-	1	3	6	1	-	1	-	-	1	1	-	1	-
18-26	-	-	-	-	-	-	-	-	-	5	2	20	-	1	-	4	1	-	1	1	3	4
Chap. 2 (47)	7	1	1	2	2	2	-	-	1	9	12	46	4	1	3	6	5	4	4	7	6	7
3:1-5a	1	-	-	2	-	-	-	-	2	1	1	10	-	1	1	1	-	1	4	1	3	1
5b-12	3	-	-	-	1	1	-	-	1	3	1	17	4	-	2	1	6	2	4	2	-	1
13-18	4	-	-	-	-	1	-	-	-	1	3	5	2	-	-	2	2	-	2	2	-	1
Chap. 3 (37)	8	-	-	2	1	2	-	-	3	5	5	32	6	1	3	4	8	3	10	5	3	3
4:1-10 (18)	4	-	1	2	-	-	-	-	-	7	2	17	-	-	1	4	3	-	1	-	-	4
11,12 (5)	-	-	-	-	-	-	-	-	-	1	2	5	-	-	-	1	1	-	-	-	-	-
13-17 (9)	1	-	-	1	-	-	-	-	-	2	1	7	-	-	-	2	-	-	-	1	2	1
Chap. 4 (32)	5	-	1	3	-	-	-	-	-	10	5	29	-	-	1	7	4	-	1	1	2	5
5:1-6 (12)	2	-	-	2	-	-	-	-	-	5	-	20	-	-	3	8	1	-	1	-	1	3
7-12 (14)	1	-	-	-	-	1	-	-	-	1	2	20	1	1	6	1	2	1	3	-	1	1
13-18 (13)	3	-	-	-	-	-	-	-	-	10	-	14	-	-	3	1	1	-	-	-	2	5
19,20 (4)	1	-	-	-	-	-	-	-	-	1	-	2	-	-	-	-	2	3	-	-	-	-
Chap. 5 (43)	7	-	-	2	-	1	-	-	-	17	2	56	1	1	12	10	6	4	4	-	4	9
James Entire (211)	38	1	2	14	3	5	-	-	5	47	35	202	22	9	25	37	33	17	21	25	32	34

NUMERICAL TOTALS - JAMES

	Lines	EN	DIA G	DIA T	DIA EIS	KATA A	KATA T	PERI T	PROS D	HUPO G	KAI	DE	ARTICLE UN-SEP	ARTICLE SEP	GEN PREC	Art. c GS D S	Art. c GS D P	No Art. c GS D S	No Art. c GS D P	ATTR. ADJ. PREC	ATTR. ADJ. POST	ADVERB. PARTICIPLES	DATIVES
MEYER-EASTON THEORY																							
CHRISTIAN INTERPOLATIONS																							
1:6-8	5	2	-	-	-	-	-	-	-	-	-	1	3	1	-	-	1	1	-	-	1	1	1
2:1-13	14	6	1	1	2	1	1	-	-	1	3	7	20	3	-	2	2	4	3	2	6	2	3
2:14-26	23	1	-	-	-	1	1	-	-	-	6	5	26	1	1	1	4	1	1	2	1	4	4
3:1-12	26	4	-	-	2	1	1	-	-	3	4	2	27	4	1	3	2	6	3	8	3	3	2
Letter of Jacob																							
	133	25	-	1	10	-	2	-	-	1	34	20	126	13	7	19	28	21	10	9	14	22	24
MODIFIED THEORY																							
LATER INSERTIONS																							
2:8-13	9	1	1	1	-	1	1	-	-	1	1	4	4	2	-	-	-	2	-	-	1	2	1
2:14-26	See Above																						
3:1-12	See Above																						
Original Semitic Letter																							
1:1-11	19	7	-	-	-	-	-	-	-	-	4	5	19	5	3	2	6	2	2	-	4	4	4
1:12-25	28	3	-	-	5	-	-	-	-	1	2	6	16	6	2	4	3	8	2	2	6	11	4
1:26,27	See Numerical Totals - James																						
2:1-7	15	5	-	-	2	-	-	-	-	-	2	3	16	1	-	2	2	2	3	2	5	-	2
3:13-18	See Numerical Totals - James																						
4:1-10	See Numerical Totals - James																						
4:11-17	14	1	-	-	1	-	-	-	-	-	3	3	12	-	-	-	3	1	-	-	1	2	1
Chap.5	See Numerical Totals - James																						
Total	153	32	-	1	12	-	2	-	-	2	36	24	145	15	7	21	31	24	13	11	20	23	27

Numerical Totals - Jude

LINES	EN	DIA G	DIA T	EIS	KATA A	KATA T	PERI T	PROS D	HUPO G	KAI	DE	ARTICLE UN-SEP.	ARTICLE SEP.	DEP. GEN. PREC.	Art. c GS D S	Art. c GS D P	No Art. c GS D S	No Art. c GS D P	ATTR. ADJ. PREC.	ATTR. ADJ. POST	ADVERB. PARTICIPLES	DATIVES
1,2	1	-	-	-	-	-	-	-	-	-	1	-	1	1	-	-	1	-	-	-	-	3
3,4	-	-	-	2	-	-	1	-	-	-	-	3	5	2	-	2	-	-	3	-	3	3
5-7	-	-	-	1	-	-	1	-	-	-	1	3	4	2	-	-	2	-	3	3	5	2
8-13	2	-	-	1	-	-	1	-	1	-	5	11	5	2	4	1	2	-	1	5	8	6
14-16	1	-	-	-	1	3	2	-	-	1	1	5	-	-	1	3	-	1	1	1	3	1
17-23	3	-	-	1	1	1	-	-	1	1	4	10	3	2	2	2	1	-	2	3	7	1
24,25	1	1	1	1	-	-	-	-	-	-	1	4	1	-	-	2	-	1	1	-	-	1
Jude Entire	8	1	1	6	2	4	5	-	2	2	13	36	19	9	7	10	6	2	11	12	26	17

(LINES totals: 1,2 = 3; 3,4 = 7; 5-7 = 9; 8-13 = 16; 14-16 = 9; 17-23 = 13; 24,25 = 5; Jude Entire = 62)

Numerical Summary 1 Peter

	LINES	EN	DIA G	DIA T	KATA KIS	KATA A	KATA T	PERI T	PROS D	HUPO G	KAI	DE	ART UN-SEP	ART SEP	DEP GEN PREC	Art. c GS D S	Art. c GS D P	No Art. c GS D S	No Art. c GS D P	ADJ PREC	ADJ POST	ADVERB. PARTICIPLES	DATIVES
1:1,2	5	1	-	-	1	1	1	-	-	-	-	-	-	-	-	-	-	11	-	1	-	-	2
3-9	15	6	3	3	6	1	1	-	-	-	-	2	7	3	2	2	2	5	-	1	9	6	1
10-12	8	1	1	1	4	-	-	2	-	-	-	1	1	5	-	1	-	-	-	1	1	2	5
13-16	6	3	-	-	-	1	1	-	-	-	-	-	4	2	-	1	2	2	-	-	-	3	2
17-20	10	1	1	2	2	1	1	-	-	-	1	1	4	5	3	-	2	4	-	2	2	1	4
22-25	5	1	1	1	2	-	-	-	-	-	-	1	5	-	-	1	1	1	-	-	2	2	-
Total	49	13	6	7	15	4	4	2	-	-	1	5	21	15	5	5	7	23	-	5	14	14	14
2:1-10	13	2	1	1	4	-	-	-	-	1	1	5	3	3	1	-	-	-	-	4	2	3	5
11,12	6	3	-	-	-	1	-	-	-	-	-	-	4	2	-	-	1	1	-	2	-	2	-
13-17	9	-	1	2	1	-	-	-	-	-	1	1	8	2	2	1	-	3	-	2	-	2	4
18-25	14	2	-	1	1	-	-	-	-	-	-	1	12	-	-	-	-	4	1	-	-	10	9
Total	42	7	2	4	6	-	1	-	-	1	2	7	27	7	3	1	5	5	-	8	2	17	18
3:1-7	16	2	1	1	2	1	1	-	-	-	-	-	12	8	5	1	2	5	-	8	-	8	6
8-12	4	-	-	-	1	-	-	-	-	-	-	2	-	2	-	-	-	-	-	-	-	2	-
13-22	21	8	2	3	3	-	-	2	-	-	1	2	11	4	5	1	1	4	-	1	2	9	6
Total	41	10	3	4	6	1	1	2	-	-	1	4	23	14	10	2	3	9	-	9	2	19	12
4:1-6	12	3	-	-	3	2	2	-	-	-	-	1	4	6	2	1	-	1	-	2	-	4	12
7-11	10	1	1	1	5	-	-	-	-	-	-	1	7	1	1	1	-	4	-	2	-	2	1
12-19	15	5	-	-	-	1	1	-	-	-	1	3	19	5	4	5	2	1	1	1	-	2	6
Total	37	9	1	1	8	3	3	-	-	-	1	5	30	12	7	7	2	6	1	5	-	8	19
5:1-5	10	2	-	-	-	1	1	-	-	-	1	1	8	6	3	1	-	2	-	1	-	4	2
6-11	11	3	-	-	2	-	-	1	-	-	-	1	10	4	2	3	2	-	-	2	-	4	5
12-14	6	3	2	2	1	-	-	-	-	-	-	-	3	2	-	-	1	2	-	2	-	2	2
Chap. 5	27	8	2	2	3	1	1	1	-	-	1	2	21	12	5	4	3	4	-	5	-	10	9
1 Peter Entire	196	47	14	18	38	9	10	5	-	1	6	23	122	60	30	19	20	47	1	32	18	68	72
1:1-4:11	154	34	12	16	35	7	8	4	-	1	4	18	82	43	21	10	15	42	-	26	18	56	57
4:12-5:14	42	13	2	2	3	2	2	1	-	-	2	5	40	17	9	9	5	5	1	6	-	12	15

Numerical Summary 2 Peter

	L I N E S	DIA EN	DIA G	DIA T	KATA EIS	KATA A	KATA T	PERI T	PROS D	HUPO G	KAI	DE	ARTICLE UN-SEP.	ARTICLE SEP.	DEP. GEN. PREC.	ART. c GS D S	ART. c GS D P	No ART. c GS D S	No ART. c GS D P	ATTR. ADJ. PREC.	ATTR. ADJ. POST	ADVERB. PARTICIPLES	DATIVES
1:1,2	4	2	-	-	-	-	-	-	-	-	-	-	3	1	-	-	2	5	-	1	-	-	3
3-11	21	9	3	3	2	-	-	-	-	-	-	7	23	6	3	3	4	2	-	6	-	8	7
12-15	8	3	-	-	-	-	-	1	-	-	-	2	4	3	1	1	2	-	-	1	-	3	1
16-21	16	3	-	-	1	-	-	-	-	2	2	-	5	5	2	-	4	2	-	5	2	8	6
Chap. 1	49	17	3	3	3	-	-	1	-	2	2	9	35	15	6	4	12	9	-	13	2	19	17
2:1-3	8	3	-	1	-	-	-	-	-	-	3	1	6	1	1	1	1	1	-	2	-	2	3
4-10a	14	3	-	-	2	-	-	-	-	1	-	2	3	2	2	-	-	7	-	3	1	7	5
10b-16	16	5	-	-	1	-	1	-	-	-	-	2	6	2	3	2	2	2	-	4	2	13	5
17-22	15	3	-	-	1	-	-	-	-	1	1	1	11	4	-	4	1	5	-	2	2	7	8
Chap. 2	53	14	-	1	4	-	1	-	-	2	4	6	26	9	6	7	4	15	-	11	5	29	21
3:1-7	16	3	2	2	1	1	1	-	-	1	-	1	8	10	3	3	3	5	-	4	-	6	5
8-13	14	5	-	1	2	1	1	-	-	-	1	4	5	2	1	1	1	1	-	1	-	7	1
14-18	13	5	-	-	1	1	1	1	-	-	-	1	5	7	4	-	2	2	-	4	1	4	5
Chap. 3	43	13	2	3	4	3	3	1	-	1	1	6	18	19	8	4	6	8	-	9	1	17	11
2 Peter Entire	145	44	5	7	11	3	4	2	-	5	7	21	79	43	20	15	22	32	-	33	8	65	49

APPENDIX 5

The Methodology of "Syntax Criticism" and Criticisms of It

The methodology "Syntax Criticism" has been
developed in a number of different studies[1] since 1957
and because during the last 10 years reviews of those
studies have appeared in various journals and
monographs, it is perhaps appropriate at this juncture
to present a concise summary of the methodology and to
respond to various suggestions and reservations that
have been voiced concerning this method of isolating
Semitic sources/traditions behind Greek documents
written in the Koine period before A.D. 100.

The Procedure

1.   The 17 syntactical criteria were established
by an analysis of more than 4000 lines from 9
original Greek writers and more than 5700 lines
of 10 translated Hebrew and Aramaic writings of
the LXX.[2]

These are the control writings for Syntax
Criticism.

---

[1]"The Syntax of the Greek of Jeremiah. Part I: The Noun, Pronouns and
Prepositions in Their Case Constructions". Dissertation. Princeton Theological
Seminary, May 1957; cf. especially pages 6f, 20f, 80ff, 154ff, 312-316. "Some
Syntactical Criteria of Translation Greek", Vetus Testamentum, Vol. X, No. 3 (July
1960), pp. 295-310; "Syntactical Evidence of Aramaic Sources in Acts I-XV, New
Testament Studies, Vol. 10, No. 1 (October 1964), pp. 38-59; Syntactical Evidence of
Semitic Sources in Greek Documents, Septuagint and Cognate Studies 3 (Society of
Biblical Literature, 1974); "Syntactical Evidence of a Semitic Vorlage of the Testament
of Joseph" in Studies on the Testament of Joseph, ed. by G.W. Nickelsburg (Scholars
Press, 1976), pp. 105-123; "Syntax Criticism of the Testament of Abraham" in Studies on
the Testament of Abraham, ed. G.W. Nickelsburg (Scholars Press, 1976), pp. 95-120;
"Syntax Criticism of the LXX Additions to the Book of Esther", Journal of Biblical
Literature, Vol. 94 (1976), pp. 55-72; Syntax Criticism of the Synoptic Gospels (Edwin
Mellen Press, 1987).

[2]Cf. especially Syn Ev, pp. 5-48 and pp. 4-10 of SC Syn G.

2. The number of occurrences of each of these 17 criteria are then thrice counted[3] verse by verse throughout the document to be analyzed.

3. The percentages[4] of each of the criteria are then calculated a) for the document as a whole and b) for the smaller natural sub units (31 to 50 lines; 16 to 30 lines; 4 to 15 lines).

4. The net frequencies are then calculated for the document as a whole and for each sub-section;[5] and these are then presented graphically in comparison to the net frequencies of the control documents.[6]

5. Continued use of the methodology has suggested a further possible step in the evaluation of sections (16 to 30 lines and 4 to 15 lines) which fall into the area of overlap; and this has been employed from time to time throughout this present study.

   a) If the net frequencies of the entire document are clearly translation, then the

---

[3]The actual count of each criteria, both of the controls and of the documents being analyzed, are given in the various appendices of the above books. B. Wright's criticism that the actual counts have not been given, only applies to the initial study of prepositions made for my dissertation in 1957 and lost in the vandalization of our baggage in Madras, India in 1969 and thus could not be printed in the later publication (cf. B. Wright, "A Note on the Statistical Analysis of Septuagintal Syntax", Journal of Biblical Literature, Vol. 104 (1985), p. 111, note 5). Independent checks have confirmed the general accuracy of the counts (cf. e.g. E.C. Maloney's review in Catholic Biblical Quarterly, Vol. 51 (1989), p. 379; also Wright who, after noting a few [probably] typographical errors in the figures for the prepositions, writes: "For the most part, Martin's figures are accurate..." Op. cit., p. 111).

[4]For directions for counting and calculating percentages cf. Appendix 1 in SC Syn G, pp. 131-134 and Appendix 1 of Syn Ev, pp. 109f.

[5]For the method of calculation of net frequencies cf. Syn Ev, pp. 40-42 and SC Syn G, pp. 14f and 134f.

[6]Cf. e.g. Chart IA of this present study, p. 7.

pattern of distribution of smaller subsections is
compared to the patterns of such units in the
controls; and if their overall pattern conforms
to the pattern of such subsections of the
translation Greek controls, probably most of
these ambiguous subsections are also translation
Greek, particularly those whose net frequencies
are closest to the clear translation Greek area.
And b) vice versa--if the entire document has
original Greek net frequencies, if the overall
pattern of its subsections conforms to the
overall pattern of such subsections of the
original Greek controls, probably most of these
ambiguous subsections are also original Greek,
particularly those whose net frequencies are
closest to the clear original Greek area.

Responses to Various Suggestions and Reservations

1. ## The Criteria
    A number of the suggestions and reservations have
    concerned the 17 criteria chosen (which are a
    selection from a large number of syntactical
    features showing a difference between original
    Greek practice and translation Greek).[7]

    a. A number of reviewers have questioned
    the usefulness/validity of some or all of the
    first 8 criteria --the frequency of various
    prepositions in relation to the frequency of the

---

[7]Cf. the general comments in Syn Ev, pp. 1f and the pages of the dissertation
listed in note 1 of this appendix, as well as the final comment in the 1960 Vetus
Testamentum article, p. 310.

preposition en.[8]

Since en was used as a base for comparison (following Moulton here[9]), it has been suggested these are really only one criteria, not 8.[10] This is not quite the case, since the fluctuation of each preposition's occurrences is demonstrated to a degree. Also the same comparison base is used for both the original and the translation Greek controls. While it may be that in some cases a sharper distinction between the types of Greek could be obtained by using some other base of comparison (such as the number of occurrences per line, etc.), it should be noted that if these first 8 criteria are removed from the calculation of net frequencies, the gap (between the lowest net frequencies of the original Greek documents and the highest net frequencies of the translated documents as a whole as well as in their small sub units) is not significantly altered as the listing below shows:

---

[8]Cf. R. Sollamo, Renderings of Hebrew Semiprepositions in the Septuagent (1979), pp. 8-10; S. Farris, "On Discerning Semitic Sources in Luke 1-2" in Gospel Perspectives (1981), Vol. II, pp. 211f and The Hymns of Luke's Infancy Narratives (1985), pp. 57f. Also the reviews: R. Mowery in Critical Review of Books in Religion (1988), pp. 235-237; M. Reiser in Theologische Literaturzeitung, 113:7 (1988), cols. 516-518; also Syntax und Stil des Markusevangeliums (1984), pp. 27-31; Maloney, op. cit., pp. 379f.

[9]Cf. Martin, Dissertation, p. 166, note 1 (referring to Moulton, A Grammar of the New Testament, Vol. 1, p. 98).

[10]So Sollamo, op. cit., p. 9; but later qualified somewhat, note 7; then Farris, op. cit., pp. 211f; Mowrey, op. cit., pp. 235f.

Size of Unit	Criteria Used	
	1-17	Only 9-17[11]
Entire Document Lowest Original Gk. Net Frequency Highest Translation Gk. Net Frequency Gap between them	+9 -4 (+8 to -3) 12 spaces[12]	+7 -7 (+6 to -6) 13 spaces
31 to 50 Lines Lowest Original Gk. Net Frequency Highest Translation Gk. Net Frequency Gap between them	+6 +1 (+5 to +2) 4 spaces[13]	+3 -3 (+2 to -2) 5 spaces
16 to 30 Lines Lowest Original Gk. Net Frequency Highest Translation Gk. Net Frequency Area of Overlap	+3 +4 (+4, +3) 2 spaces[14]	0 +3 (0 to +3) 4 spaces
4 to 15 Lines Lowest Original Gk. Net Frequency Highest Translation Gk. Net Frequency Area of Overlap	0 +7 (0 to +7) 8 spaces[15]	+1 +6 (+1 to +6) 6 spaces

[11]Cf. the charts of Net Frequencies in Syn Ev, pp. 39, 55-85, 89-96 and in SC Syn G, pp. 11,12, 143-170.

[12]Charts IA and B, SC Syn G, pp. 16f.

[13]Charts IIA and B, ibid., pp. 19f.

[14]Charts IIIA and B, ibid., pp. 21f.

[15]Charts IVA and B, ibid., pp. 23f.

While Reiser[16] has called attention to some
problematic aspects of Syntax Criticism (and these are
addressed at various places in this appendix), he
bases his criticism of the method using only the first
8 criteria (the prepositions); whereas the method
requires the use of all 17 criteria.[17]   It was because
the prepositions by themselves often do not enable
positive demarcation between original and translation
Greek that other criteria were sought.   The
prepositions were found first and are remarkably
significant, but cannot be used by themselves to
evaluate a methodology which employs also 9 more
criteria and which draws conclusions on the basis of
all 17.

   b.   It has also been questioned whether those
criteria which occur infrequently in smaller sub units
should be retained as criteria.[18]   A glance at charts
on pages 11 and 12 of Syntax Criticism of the Synoptic
Gospels will show that in large units original Greek
will have occurrences of all criteria with the
exception of pros, and this could perhaps be dropped
as Reiser and Maloney have suggested.[19]   While
non-occurrence of a given criteria is not usually
taken as evidence for either original or translation

---

[16]Syntax und Stil, loc. cit.

[17]The documents he chose for comparison are not of the Koine period before the
second Christian Century, which is the period for which Syntax Criticism is claimed to
be valid--Hippocrates (V-VI BC); Passio Perpetua (late 2nd Christian century); Xenophon
of Ephesus (2nd Christian century)--cf. note 250 supra for the change which is
occurring in prepositional usage after the first Christian century.

[18]So Reiser, op. cit., p. 518; Maloney, op. cit., p. 379; Mowrey, op. cit., p.
236.

[19]Cf. note 18 supra.

Greek, it does, however, become significant in determining the net frequency figure for a document.[20]

c. The percentage figure used as the cut off point for distinguishing original Greek from translation Greek has also been questioned.[21]

As was noted already in Syntactical Evidence (p. 6) the line of demarcation could have been drawn either higher or lower on the graphs (pp. 8-37) in the clear area between original Greek and most of the translation Greek. The particular point chosen was selected in the first instance in connection with analyzing the totals for the control documents.

As the studies progressed, it was found that in the smaller sub units of the control texts a lower point should be adopted for demarcation in the case of the prepositions. Thus the 1960 and 1964 studies have different frequencies for prepositions than subsequent studies do as the chart below shows:

---

[20]Cf. Syntactical Evidence, p. 5.

[21]So Farris, "On Discerning Semitic Sources...", p. 203; also Mowery, op. cit., p. 235.

	1960,64 Studies	Subsequent Studies
dia		
with Gen.	.11	.06
all cases	.19	.18
eis	.79	.49
kata		
with Acc.	.24	.18
all cases	.27	.19
peri - all cases	.28	.27
pros - with Dat.	.025	.024
hupo - with Gen.	.13	.07

The evidence of the basic validity of these specific frequencies chosen as the demarcation for translation Greek becomes apparent in the net frequencies charts for the control documents, since these frequencies do in every case of texts of 31 lines or more in length clearly distinguish between the control original Greek and control translation Greek documents (cf. Charts IA,B and IIA,B in Syntax Criticism of the Synoptic Gospels, pp. 16-20) and do enable the distinguishing clearly of most of the smaller subsections of less than 31 lines (cf. Charts III A,B and IV A,B, pp. 21-24) of the control documents.

d. Farris suggests that some criteria should be weighted more than others and considers criteria 9-17

to be of more significance than 1-8.[22] Since,
however, different writers have different literary
habits, it does not seem very useful to try to weight
the criteria. It was hoped to find one single
criteria that always worked in even the smallest
units! Continued study has shown this is not likely;
but by using all 17 criteria it is possible often to
distinguish original Greek and translation Greek,
especially in larger units of text.

     e. Maloney has suggested that more criteria
could be added.[23] This is, of course, a continuing
goal, and there are indeed many syntactical features
which differ between original and translation Greek.[24]
Maloney notes 4 such:[25] verb-subject word order;
direct or indirect object pronouns immediately after
their verb; the frequency of third person pronouns in
the oblique cases and the frequency of ekeinos.
Detailed counting of these in the control documents
may substantiate that one or more of them could be
added to the present 17 criteria.

     In an earlier study[26] it was found that
subject-verb/verb-subject word order under certain
conditions may be useful in determining whether a
document was written originally in Greek or translated

---

[22]"On Discerning", pp. 212f.

[23]Op cit., p. 379f.

[24]Cf. again the references to paragraphs in Martin's Dissertation in note 1 of
this appendix for summaries of some that have been isolated in a study of Jeremiah.
Cf. also Vetus Testamentum article, pp. 309f. and the New Testament Studies article,
pp. 55-59.

[25]Op. cit., p. 379.

[26]Cf. the New Testament Studies article "Syntactical Evidence of Aramaic Sources
in Acts I-XV", pp. 55-59.

from a Semitic language, and whether the Semitic language was Hebrew or Aramaic. This will be discussed a bit more at the end of this appendix.

2. Evaluation of the Net Frequency Score in Smaller Units

Much of the uncertainty concerning the validity of Syntax Criticism has centered on its usefulness for units of 4 to 15 lines in length. This problem was addressed by an entire chapter in the initial study where texts were broken up into smaller sub-sections.[27] It needs to be emphasized here that in that study certainty of judgment that a document is translation Greek was claimed only

a. for texts of more than 50 lines in length showing net frequencies of -4[28] or lower
b. for texts of 31 to 50 lines showing net frequencies of +1[29] or lower
c. for texts of 16 to 30 lines showing net frequencies of +1 or lower[30]
d. for texts of 4 to 15 lines showing net frequencies of -1 or lower[31]

---

[27] Chapter II "Frequency Patterns in Small Units of Text" in Syntactical Evidence of Semitic Sources in Greek Documents, pp. 45-86.

[28] Cf. chart on p. 42.

[29] Cf. p. 107.

[30] Ibid.

[31] Ibid.

Probability[32] was claimed
    a. for units of 16 to 30 lines showing
        +2 to +4 net frequencies
    b. for units of 4 to 15 lines showing
        0 net frequencies

That study also showed that in such smaller units of 4 to 15 lines of known translation Greek an average of 37%[33] of translation Greek went undetected by using the net frequency figure of -1 or lower, depending on how literal or free the translation is and, perhaps also, whether the translator is translating Hebrew or Aramaic. Thus it is clear that the methodology of Syntax Criticism if used within the net frequency limits sketched above, is able to detect with certainty many of the translated sections in units of all sizes, but not able to detect all translation Greek in units of 4 to 15 and 16 to 30 lines. The above limitation does not invalidate the method even for smaller units of text; but demonstrates rather that while it is a very useful tool, it is not perfect. More than this has not been claimed in those studies.[34]

3. Other Explanations of the Clearly Semitic Nature of the Documents As Indicated by Syntax Criticism

---

[32]Ibid. since very few original units fall into these areas.

[33]Ibid., p. 52. The different documents ranged from 58% (Daniel-Aramaic-LXX translator) to 0% (2 Kings translator) undetected translation.

[34]Cf. also italicized statement in Syntactical Evidence of Semitic Sources in Greek Documents, p. 52.

Collins[35] and others[36] have suggested that there may be other explanations for the Semitic nature of the Greek than that the writer is translating Semitic sources. Collins suggests that the writers may be using "a poor quality Greek influenced by Semitic idiom"[37] and Reiser feels the entire methodology is invalid since no distinction has been made between different styles and genre.[38]

Both of these issues were addressed in the earlier studies, somewhat in <u>Syntactical Evidence of Semitic Sources in Greek Documents</u>[39] and more explicitly in <u>Syntax Criticism of the Synoptic Gospels</u>[40]

The reply to both of these issues is similar. If a writer's style fluctuates, in some sections being Semitic and in others not, particularly where the same genre is involved, it is difficult to see how in the one case it is the writer's natural Semitized vernacular which for some reason is not being followed in the other similar passage, or how the genre has

---

[35]Cf. his review in <u>The Catholic Biblical Quarterly</u>, Vol. 37 (1975), pp. 592f.

[36]So Reiser, <u>op. cit.</u>; Mowery, <u>op. cit.</u>; Farris, "On Discerning", pp. 213 and 215.

[37]<u>Op. cit.</u>, p. 593.

[38]"Aber leider zeigen seine Statistiken grundlegende methodische Mangel. So sollten bei einem syntaktisch-stilistischen Vergleich die Vergleichenen Texte wirklich vergleichbar sein, und zwar sowohl in Hinblick auf die Stilschicht, als auch in Hinblick auf die Gattung und Darstellungsart." <u>Op. cit.</u>, p. 518.

[39]<u>Re</u> Luke's natural style, cf. p. 87. Concerning the different genre, a careful reading of the data for the different parts of Acts 1:1-15:35 in the charts reveals that the same genre appears as original Greek and in a different place in the book as translation Greek.

[40]<u>Re</u> Semitized Greek vernacular of the writer cf. item 3, page 1 and the detailed discussion of that throughout the "Introduction". Concerning the various genre, cf. the detailed comparisons of genre in Acts and Mark, pp. 29-31.

influenced these criteria. A few examples must suffice[41]: Why is the style of the writer of Acts entirely original Greek in Acts 15:36-28:31 (whether it is narration, direct or indirect discourse, etc.) and sometimes original Greek and sometimes translation Greek in Acts 1:1-15:35? Why, for example, is Peter's arrest and trial in Acts 5:17-22 Semitic, but the similar story of Peter's arrest and trial in Acts 4:5-22 not? Why does Mark use Semitic Greek in the account of the Feeding of the 4000, but not use it in his account of the Feeding of the 5000? Why are some parables in Matthew translation Greek (e.g. the Workers in the Vineyard--20:1-16) and others not (e.g. Parable of the Pounds--25:14-30)? Why is one passion prediction in Mark clearly translation Greek (8:31-9:1) whereas the other 2 are not (Mk. 9:30-32 and Mk. 10:32-34)? And the list could be expanded.

Further, the control documents include Jewish writers writing original Greek whose acquaintance with Hebrew and Aramaic might be expected to skew the results toward translation Greek; yet in none of the cases has this occurred (Philo, Josephus, the author of Hebrews, the author of 2 Maccabees).[42]

4. Two Further Observations of Farris Should Be Remarked.

    a. It is interesting to note that he subjected the results of Syntax Criticism concerning Luke 1

---

[41]For details cf. Syntax Criticism of the Synoptic Gospels, pp. 29-31 and also the various charts throughout.

[42]Cf. Charts I, II, III, IV, in Syntax Criticism of the Synoptic Gospels, pp. 16-24.

and 2 to a statistical test and found that these
criteria did produce a statistically significant
difference between Luke 1 and 2 and the original
Greek controls.[43]

b. He also noted that if Paul's letters[44] are
analyzed by these 17 criteria, their net
frequencies are +2 and +3 for texts more than 50
lines in length, which falls in the center of the
gap between clear original Greek and clear
translation Greek. He correctly notes that "The
exact significance of this data may not
immediately be clear..."[45]

Because of the unclarity about the relative
balance between Paul's Semitic and Hellenistic
backgrounds, an analysis of the Pauline corpus has not
yet been carefully undertaken using the methodology of
Syntax Criticism. It should, however, be noted that
Bertholdt in his Einleitung claimed that 1
Thessalonians, for example, was translated from Paul's
Aramaic into Greek.[46]

There are indications in Paul's letters that he
was Aramaic speaking (cf. e.g. Philippians 3:5 "a
Hebrew of Hebrews"). Syntax Criticism studies to this
date have indicated that if a 1st Christian century or
earlier Koine Greek document of more than 50 lines of

---

[43]He found "that the results for Luke 1-2 were more extreme than 99% of the values
one might expect for original Greek." "On Discerning", p. 210.

[44]His sample was Romans 5 and Galatians 1:1-2:5 (50.5 lines and 56 lines
respectively). Ibid., p. 214.

[45]Ibid.

[46]J.H. Moulton, Introduction to the Literature of the New Testament (1914), p. 71.
I am indebted to Dr. E.A. Schick of Wartburg Theological Seminary for calling my
attention to this reference in a letter many years ago while I was in India.

text falls in the gap between original and translation
Greek areas, it is either because it contains some
smaller subsections which are original Greek and some
which are translated Greek--(cf. e.g. the data of
John's Gospel and James in the present study) or that
it is a very free translation (cf. the comments below
concerning 1 Esdras).

Can Greek Which Is a Translation of Hebrew Be Distinguished from Greek Which Is a Translation of Aramaic?

In "Syntactical Evidence of Aramaic Sources in
Acts I-XV" it was suggested that a study of
subject-verb order might make it possible not only to
distinguish translation Greek from original Greek but
also to distinguish translation of Hebrew from
translation of Aramaic.[47]

In connection with a study undertaken for a
meeting of the IOSCS[48] further evidence along this
line was found and it will be useful to present this
material here.

A number of studies over the years have noted
that in independent, main clauses, Greek which is a
translation of Hebrew has more initial verbs than

---

[47]Cf. pp. 55-59.

[48]"Syntax Criticism of Baruch" presented at the meeting of The International
Organization for Septuagint and Cognate Studies in Leuven, Belgium, August 1989.

texts which were written originally in Greek.[49]

Wieand has demonstrated that for such studies a distinction should be made between sentences in which an object is present and those which have no expressed object.[50] In the _tentative_ study which follows, this distinction will be observed wherever previous studies have made it also. An examination of the earlier studies in Howard, Rife, Wieand and Martin referred to above reveals that tentative ranges can be established for the various types of translation Greek and for original Greek. These are shown in the chart below. Next to these tentative ranges in that chart is the data for I Baruch and for that part of I Esdras for which there is no extant Massoretic text (3:1-5:6). As these data are compared to the ranges, tentative conclusions concerning these writings may be made.

---

[49]Cf. e.g. W.F. Howard "Semitisms in the New Testament" in his Appendix to Vol. II of J.H. Moulton _A Grammar of New Testament Greek_ (1920), pp. 416-419 and the earlier literature referred to there. Cf. also J.M. Rife, "The Mechanics of Translation Greek", _Journal of Biblical Literature_, Vol. LII (1933), pp. 249ff; D.J. Wieand, "Subject-Verb-Object Relationships in Independent Clauses in the Gospels and Acts", Ph.D. dissertation for Chicago University (1946); R.A. Martin, "Syntactical Evidence of Semitic Sources in Greek Documents", _New Testament Studies_, Vol. 10:1 (October 1964), pp. 55-59; E.C. Maloney, _Semitic Interference in Marcan Syntax_ (1981), pp. 51-53 and the works cited there. M. Reiser, _Syntax und Stil des Markusevangeliums_ (1984), pp. 46-96 disagrees, but cf. also the review by R.L. Mowery in _Journal of Biblical Literature_, Vol. 106 (1987), pp. 138f.

[50]_Ibid_. Other qualifications have been noted--imperatives need to be excluded, as well as verbs of saying. Howard, _op. cit._, pp. 417f; and Reiser would make additional distinctions, _ibid_.

Percentages of Preceeding Verbs When V,S,O and Only
V,S Are Present

Verb, Subject, Object Present

Greek Known to Be Translating Hebrew | Unknown Original

Rife	.44 - 1.00	
Wieand	.67	Baruch 1:1-3:8 .80
Martin	.46 -.63	Baruch 4:5-5:9 .67
I Esdras (Heb. MT)	.50	

Greek Known to Be Translating Aramaic

Rife	.14	
Martin	.14 -.33	
I Esdras (Aram. MT.)	.33	I Esdras(No MT) .25
		Baruch 3:9-4:4 .20
Original Greek		
Rife	.00 -.50	
Howard	.10 -.20	

Only Verb, Subject Present

Greek Known to Be Translating Hebrew

Wieand	.53	Baruch 1:1-3:8 .60
Martin	.52 -.82	
I Esdras (Heb MT)	.53	

Greek Known to Be Translating Aramaic

Martin	.28 -.47	Baruch 3:9-4:4 .50
I Esdras (Aram MT)	.44	Baruch 4:5-5:9 .50
		I Esdras (No MT) .50

Original Greek

Howard	.10 -.20
Martin	.00 -.23

The above chart suggests that in large amounts of
text Verb, Subject, Object order may distinguish Greek
which is a translation of Hebrew from 1) Greek which
is a translation of Aramaic and from 2) Original
Greek; with a clear dividing point of .60 (which would
leave some translation from Hebrew undetected).
Aramaic word order and Greek word order are similar in
this case.

Verb, Subject order may distinguish Greek which
is a translation of Hebrew from 1) Greek, which is a
translation of Aramaic and 2) both of these from
original Greek; with a dividing point of a) .50
between Hebrew and Aramaic and b) .25 between original
Greek and Greek which is a translation of a Semitic
language.

In the table below the above tentative
conclusions are applied to Baruch and related to the
results of Syntax Criticism of each section of Baruch:

Baruch	Net Freq. of 17 Criteria	Word Order	Tentative Conclusion
1:1-3:8	-10 (Clear Trans.)	VSO .80 (Heb.) VS .60 (Heb.)	Translation of Hebrew
3:9-4:4	-6 (Clear Trans.)	VS .50 (Aram.) VSO .20 (Aram. or Original)	Translation of Aramaic
4:5-5:9	+6 (Uncertain)	VSO .67 (Heb.) VS .50 (Aram)	Free Trans. of Hebrew

The tentative conclusion that the +6 net
frequencies of Baruch 4:5-5:9 are probably indicative
of free translation is based not only on the Word

Order data, but on the basis of a comparison with I
Esdras which is a very free translation of Ezra.

Section in I Esdras	Net Frequency	Word Order
Hebrew MT	+2 (Free Trans. of Hebrew)	VSO .50 (Heb.) VS .53 (Heb.)
Aramaic MT	+1 (Free Trans. of Aramaic)	VSO .33 (Aram.) VS .44 (Aram.)
No MT (3:1-5:6)	+5 (Uncertain)	VSO .25 VS .50
	Tentative Conclusion:	3:1-5:6 is free translation of Aramaic

The above tentative study is only meant to be
suggestive, in order to encourage further studies of
verb, subject word order to see if, indeed, this
syntactical feature is, as it appears, a useful tool
to help distinguish original Greek and translation
Greek in texts where it is not certain what the
original language was.

BIBLIOGRAPHY

Barnett, A.E. "James, Letter of" in IDB. (James).

Barrett, C.K. The Gospel According to St. John. 1960. (John).

Bauckham, R.J. Jude, 2 Peter in Word Biblical Commentary. 1983. (Jude; 2 Peter).

Beare, F.W. The Earliest Records. 1962. (Records).

_____. The First Epistle of Peter. 1961. (Peter).

_____. The Gospel According to Matthew. 1981. (Matthew).

Black, M. An Aramaic Approach to the Gospels and Acts. 1946.

Brooke, A.E. A Critical and Exegetical Commentary on the Johannine Epistles in The International Critical Commentary. 1957. (Epistles).

Brown, R.E. The Epistles of John in The Anchor Bible. 1982. (Epistles).

_____. The Gospel According to John in The Anchor Bible. 1966, 1970. (John 1; John 2).

Bultmann, R. The Gospel of John. 1971. (John).

_____. The History of the Synoptic Tradition. 1968. (History).

_____. The Johannine Epistles in Hermeneia. 1973. (Epistles).

Burney, C.F. The Aramaic Origin of the Fourth Gospel. 1922.

Buse, I. "St. John and the Markan Passion Narrative" in New Testament Studies. Vol. 4 (1957-58).

Caird, G.B. "John, the Epistles of" in IDB.

Dibelius, M. James in Hermeneia. 1976. (Dibelius-Greeven).

Dodd, C.H. The Johannine Epistles in The Moffatt New Testament Commentary. 1947. (Epistles).

Easton, B.S. "The Epistle of James" in IDB. (James).

184

Fitzmyer, J.A. The Gospel According to Luke in The Anchor Bible. 1981, 1985. (Luke 1; Luke 2).

Fortna, R. The Gospel of Signs. 1970.

Grant, F.C. The Earliest Gospel. 1943. (Earliest Gospel).

Haenchen, E. John in Hermeneia. 1984. (John 1; John 2).

Howard, W.F. The Fourth Gospel in Recent Criticism. 1955.

Interpreter's Dictionary of the Bible. (IDB).

Interpreter's Dictionary of the Bible. Supplement. (Supplement).

Kelly, J.N.D. A Commentary on the Epistles of Peter and of Jude in Black's New Testament Commentaries. 1969.

Knox, W.L. "The Epistle of St. James" in Journal of Theological Studies. Vol. XLVI (1945).

_____. The Sources of the Synoptic Gospels. (1953, 1957).

Koester, H. Introduction to the New Testament. Vol. 2. 1980. (Introduction).

Kümmel, W.G. Introduction to the New Testament. 1973. (Introduction).

Kysar, R. The Fourth Evangelist and His Gospel. 1975. (Fourth Evangelist).

_____. John in The Augsburg Commentary on the New Testament. 1986. (John).

Lindars, B. Behind the Fourth Gospel. 1971.

Martin, R.A. James in The Augsburg Commentary on the New Testament. 1982. (James).

_____. Syntax Criticism of the Synoptic Gospels. 1987. (SC Syn G).

_____. Syntactical Evidence of Semitic Sources in Greek Documents. 1974. (Syn Ev).

Mayor, J.B. The Epistle of James. 1966. (James).

Metzger, B.M. A Textual Commentary on the Greek New
     Testament. 1971.
Mitton, C.L. The Epistle of James. 1966. (James).
Moffatt, J. The General Epistles in The Moffatt New
     Testament Commentary. 1928. (James).
Reicke, B. The Epistles of James, Peter and Jude in
     The Anchor Bible. 1964. (James; Jude; Peter 1;
     Peter 2).
Ropes, J.H. A Critical and Exegetical Commentary on
     the Epistle of St. James in The International
     Critical Commentary. 1916. (James).
Sanders, J.N. "John, Gospel of" in IDB.
Smith, D.M. "John, Gospel of" in IDB Supplement.
Taylor, V. The Formation of the Gospel Tradition.
     1964. (Formation).
_____. The Gospel According to St. John.
_____. The Gospel According to St. Mark. 1966.
     (Mark).
_____. The Passion Narrative of St. Luke. 1972.
     (Passion).
Torrey, C.C. The Four Gospels. 1933.
_____. Our Translated Gospels. 1936.
Turner, N. Style in Moulton's New Testament Greek
     Grammar. 1976.
_____. Syntax in Moulton's New Testament Greek
     Grammar. 1963.
Ward, R.B. "James, Letter of" in IDB Supplement.
     (James).
Wilkens, W. "The Tradition History of the Resurrection
     of Jesus" in The Significance of the Message of
     the Resurrection for Faith in Jesus Christ
     (Studies in Biblical Theology, 2nd Series, No. 8).
     1968.

STUDIES IN THE BIBLE AND EARLY CHRISTIANITY